M000019606

The GMAT Cram Sheet

This Cram Sheet contains useful information about preparing for the GMAT. Be sure to read the book and take the practice tests before referring to this sheet. Review the information included on this Cram Sheet prior to entering the testing center, paying close attention to the areas where you feel you need the most review. Remember that the actual GMAT is a computer-based test, and it will adapt to your skill level. This Cram Sheet should not be used as a substitute for actual preparation; it is simply a review of important information presented in detail elsewhere in this book.

GENERAL TEST-TAKING STRATEGIES

1. Relax
   - ➤ Don't panic if you are having a hard time answering the questions. You do not have to answer all of the questions correctly to get a good score.
   - ➤ Take a few moments to relax if you get stressed during the test. When you get back to the test, you will feel better.

2. Be Aware of Time
   - ➤ Pace yourself. Budget enough time for each question so that you won't have to rush at the end of the section.
   - ➤ Because you cannot go back and change your answers, read each question carefully to determine exactly what is being asked. Taking the time to answer one question correctly is better than rushing and answering several questions incorrectly.
   - ➤ You have only a limited amount of time. Read and work actively through the test.
   - ➤ Stay focused. Ignore the things going on around you that you cannot control.

3. Guessing
   - ➤ You have to select an answer before you can move on, so making high-percentage guesses is important.
   - ➤ Eliminate answer choices that you know are wrong. The more you can eliminate, the better your chance of getting the question right.

4. Changing Your Mind
   - ➤ Do not second-guess yourself. Your first answer choice is more likely to be correct.
   - ➤ Change your answer only when you are sure it's wrong. Remember that you must select and confirm your answer before you are allowed to move on to the next question.

COMPUTER-BASED TEST-TAKING STRATEGIES

1. The Computer System

   Make sure that you practice with released and simulated exams before you take the actual GMAT.
   - ➤ Take advantage of the computer tutorial that is offered before you begin the actual test. Take as long as necessary so that you feel comfortable.
   - ➤ At any point during the test, you may review the instructions by clicking your mouse on the "HELP" icon.
   - ➤ Remember that any time spent reviewing instructions *after* you begin the test takes away from valuable testing time.
   - ➤ Be aware of scrollbars. Some images and text are too big to fit on your screen and require you to scroll down to view them.

2. Adaptive Questions
   - ➤ The questions for the Verbal and Quantitative sections are adaptive. The computer picks your question based on your response to the previous question and the specific test.

- ➤ Do not waste time trying to figure out whether you answered the previous question correctly or incorrectly. Just keep working through the test.

- ➤ The only way to move on to another question is to answer the question already on your screen. If you do not know how to answer, make your best educated guess and move on.

CRITICAL READING

GMAT Critical Reading includes Reading Comprehension passages and questions, Sentence Correction questions, Critical Reasoning questions, and Analytical Writing essay tasks. Following are specific strategies for each of the sections.

Reading Comprehension

GMAT Reading Comprehension questions require you to locate details within the text, make inferences regarding what is stated or implied in the text, determine the main idea, and analyze the author's viewpoint.

1. Read the questions carefully and make a mental note when the questions refer to specific lines or words. Do not try to memorize—just get an idea of what you should be looking for.

2. Answers to questions should be based on information in the passage *only*. Do not be worried if the topics discussed in the passages are unfamiliar. On the other hand, if you are familiar with the topic, do not let your prior knowledge interfere.

3. Read each passage for topic, scope, and purpose. Then skim for structure. Try to isolate one topic word or sentence for each paragraph. The details will still be there when you need them. Don't spend precious time trying to "learn" them.

4. Try to distinguish between which details are information and which details are the opinions of the author.

5. Do not stop on unfamiliar words the first time through. You may not need to know the meaning of a word to answer the questions. Remember that you will be rereading most of the passage as you work on the questions.

6. Try to predict an answer in your own words before looking at the answer choices. If an answer choice matches your predicted answer, it is most likely correct.

7. Paraphrase when you need to. Putting the question into your own words often makes it easier to answer.

Sentence Correction

GMAT Sentence Correction questions require you to make the sentence appropriate for standard written English.

1. The portion of the sentence that is underlined may need to be revised. When reading the sentence, pay attention to the underlined portion.

2. If the underlined portion seems correct within the sentence as it is, select answer choice A.

3. If the underlined portion does not seem correct, try to predict the correct answer. If an answer choice matches your predicted answer, it is most likely correct.

4. If your predicted answer does not match any of the answer choices, determine which of the selections is the clearest and most simple.

Critical Reasoning

GMAT Critical Reasoning questions test the reasoning skills involved in making and evaluating arguments and formulating or evaluating a plan of action.

1. Carefully read the statements or passage, paying particular attention to the evidence, conclusions, and any assumptions that are made.

2. Focus on the logic and reasoning of the argument, not your perspective on any of the factual statements.

3. Carefully read the question to determine exactly what is being asked.

4. Always look at *all* of the answer choices before you select the best answer.

Analytical Writing

The GMAT Analytical Writing section requires you to write essays based on the given prompts.

1. Analysis of an Issue

- ➤ You will have 30 minutes to complete this section. Use your time wisely.

- ➤ Discuss the issue from *any* perspective. Remember, there is no correct position—choose the position that you can most strongly support.

- ➤ No matter which position you take, make sure you have compelling reasons and examples to support it.

- ➤ Before you assert a position, try to show briefly that you grasp the complexities of the issue.

- ➤ Try not to leave any holes in your argument. Make sure you consider how someone might challenge or question your position.

- ➤ Do not worry about the number of examples included in your essay or length of your essay; just focus on the quality and cogency of your ideas.

EXAM CRAM™

GMAT

Steven W. Dulan
Advantage Education

que®
CERTIFICATION

Trademarks

All terms mentioned in this book that are known to be trademarks or service marks have been appropriately capitalized. Que Publishing cannot attest to the accuracy of this information. Use of a term in this book should not be regarded as affecting the validity of any trademark or service mark.

Warning and Disclaimer

Every effort has been made to make this book as complete and as accurate as possible, but no warranty or fitness is implied. The information provided is on an "as is" basis. The authors and the publisher shall have neither liability nor responsibility to any person or entity with respect to any loss or damages arising from the information contained in this book.

Bulk Sales

Que Publishing offers excellent discounts on this book when ordered in quantity for bulk purchases or special sales. For more information, please contact

U.S. Corporate and Government Sales
1-800-382-3419
corpsales@pearsontechgroup.com

For sales outside the U.S., please contact

International Sales
international@pearsoned.com

Publisher
Paul Boger

Executive Editor
Jeff Riley

Acquisitions Editor
Carol Ackerman

Development Editor
Steve Rowe

Managing Editor
Charlotte Clapp

Project Editor
Andy Beaster

Copy Editor
Nancy Albright

Indexer
Aaron Black

Proofreader
Lisa Wilson

Technical Editor
Michael Bellomo

Publishing Coordinator
Cindy Teeters

Interior Designer
Gary Adair

Cover Designer
Anne Jones

Page Layout
Toi Davis

About the Author

Steven W. Dulan, JD, has been involved with the GMAT preparation since 1989, when, as a former U.S. Army Infantry Sergeant and undergraduate student at Michigan State University, Steve became a GMAT instructor. He has been helping students prepare for success on the GMAT and other standardized exams ever since. Steve scored in the 99th percentile on every standardized test he has ever taken. After graduating from Michigan State, Steve attended The Thomas M. Cooley Law School on a full Honors Scholarship. While attending law school, Steve continued to teach standardized test prep classes (including ACT, SAT, PSAT, GRE, GMAT, and LSAT) an average of 30 hours each week and tutored some of his fellow law students in a variety of subjects and in essay exam writing techniques. Steve has also served as an instructor at Baker University, Cleary University, Lansing Community College, The Ohio State University-Real Estate Institute, and The Thomas M. Cooley Law School. Guest lecturer credits include Michigan State University, University of Michigan, Detroit College of Law, Marquette University, Texas Technical University, University of Miami, and Wright State University.

Thousands of students have benefited from Steve's instruction, coaching, and admissions consulting (and have entered the graduate programs of their choice). Steve's students have gained admission to some of the most prestigious institutions of higher learning in the world, and they have received numerous scholarships and fellowships of their own. Since 1997, Steve has served as the president of Advantage Education (www.study-smart.com), a company dedicated to providing effective and affordable test prep education in a variety of settings, including one-on-one tutoring via the Internet using its Personal Distance Learning^{SM} system. The information and techniques included in this book are the result of Steve's experiences with test preparation students at all levels over the years.

About the Technical Editor

Michael Bellomo holds an MBA from the University of California, Irvine, a Juris Doctor from the University of California, San Francisco, and a Black Belt certification in Six Sigma project management. He currently works with ARES Corporation, a project and risk management firm that works with the Department of Defense, NASA, and the Department of Energy. He has worked on projects relating to the International Space Station and been featured as the narrator for a multimedia presentation sent to Congress on the development of NASA's Orbital Space Plane.

Michael has written 15 books in various nonfiction fields, including technology, business operations, and graduate school prep.

Acknowledgments

I would like to acknowledge the contribution of the faculty and staff of Advantage Education. You are not only the smartest, but also the best. Special thanks to: Jennifer Kostamo, a quiet genius who almost always keeps her composure no matter how often she is rudely interrupted by me, and Pamela Chamberlain, our brilliant, versatile, and hard-working contributor/editor. Your extra effort helped to make this book a success.

Thanks to Carol Ackerman and Steve Rowe of Que Publishing for their help and insight throughout this project.

Most importantly, I would like to acknowledge the single biggest contributor to this work: Amy Dulan, my wife, colleague, co-author, editor, typist, employee, boss, and friend. None of this would have been possible without your hard work and dedication.

Contents at a Glance

Table of Contents

We Want to Hear from You!

As the reader of this book, *you* are our most important critic and commentator. We value your opinion and want to know what we're doing right, what we could do better, what areas you'd like to see us publish in, and any other words of wisdom you're willing to pass our way.

As an executive editor for Que Publishing, I welcome your comments. You can email or write me directly to let me know what you did or didn't like about this book—as well as what we can do to make our books better.

Please note that I cannot help you with technical problems related to the topic of this book. We do have a User Services group, however, where I will forward specific technical questions related to the book.

When you write, please be sure to include this book's title and author as well as your name, email address, and phone number. I will carefully review your comments and share them with the author and editors who worked on the book.

Email: feedback@quepublishing.com

Mail: Jeff Riley
            Executive Editor
            Que Publishing
            800 East 96th Street
            Indianapolis, IN 46240 USA

For more information about this book or another Que Certification title, visit our website at www.examcram.com. Type the ISBN (excluding hyphens) or the title of a book in the Search field to find the page you're looking for.

Introduction:
Getting Started

This book includes general information about the Graduate Management Admission Test (GMAT) and chapters with specific information on each of the test sections, as well as two simulated tests.

If you have enough time between now and your actual GMAT exam, (at least 3 weeks) you should work through this entire book. Some of the material is meant to be used as realistic practice material to get you ready for the whole experience of taking a GMAT exam.

As you work through the simulated tests, you should be aware that they are not actual exams. They are reasonably accurate simulations written by experienced experts. They contain basically the same mix of question types as a real GMAT. If you work through all the material provided, you can rest assured that there won't be any surprises on test day. Generally, students tend to score a little better on each successive practice test. But, GMAT exams are sensitive to individual conditions, such as fatigue and stress. Therefore, the time of day that you take your practice exams, your environment, and other things that might be going on in your life can have an impact on your scores. Don't get worried if you see some score fluctuation because of a bad day or because the practice test revealed weaknesses in your knowledge or skills. Simply use the information that you gather to help you improve.

In our experience, the students who see the largest increases in their scores are the ones who put in consistent effort over several weeks. Try to keep your frustration to a minimum if you are struggling. And, try to keep from becoming overconfident when everything is going your way.

What This Book Will Not Do

This book is not a substitute for regular textbooks or course work. It will not teach you everything you need to know about the subject matter tested on the GMAT. Although the GMAT is primarily considered a skills-based test, you will be required to have a basic understanding of certain mathematical concepts and standard written English. This book introduces you to some of those concepts, but it does not provide an in-depth review.

The focus of this book is on helping you maximize your GMAT score. Each chapter includes specific test-taking strategies, some content area review, and practice questions.

About the GMAT

The GMAT is offered only in English. It measures skills that are considered relevant for graduate study in business (MBA). It does not measure your knowledge of business procedures or law, or any specific area of content. It does not measure your value as a person. It does not predict your success in school, or in life.

The GMAT does a fairly good job of predicting how hard you will have to work to understand your MBA material. If you prepare for this test seriously now, you'll sharpen your comprehension, math, and reasoning skills, and you'll be able to focus on the relevant information in your course work more easily when you start business school.

The GMAT consists of multiple-choice and essay items. The multiple-choice questions are broken into Quantitative and Verbal sections.

The two essays (Analysis of an Issue and Analysis of an Argument) are grouped together as the Analytical Writing Assessment (AWA), which comes first and lasts for 1 hour (30 minutes for each essay).

The Quantitative Section comes second (you can take a break of up to 5 minutes between sections if you want to). It consists of 37 questions that you must answer in 75 minutes. The two different types of question are called Data Sufficiency and Problem Solving.

The Verbal Section consists of 41 questions and lasts up to 75 minutes. The questions come in three sections: Reading Comprehension, Critical Reasoning, and Sentence Correction.

The GMAT is a computer-adaptive test. Questions appear on your computer screen one at a time. You must answer each question before you can move forward to the next question. After you answer a question, you cannot change your answer. Within each set of multiple-choice questions, the items are selected by the computer software depending on your response to the previous question. The first question is a medium-difficulty question. If you get it correct, your next question will be more difficult and worth more points. If you get it wrong, your next question will be less difficult and worth fewer points. So, your GMAT score is arrived at through a complex formula that includes the number of questions that you answer correctly and the difficulty level of each question.

There are some questions in each set that are experimental and do not count toward your score. You will not be able to tell which ones they are, so you have to do your best on all questions as you work through your exam.

Registering for the GMAT

You must register in advance for the GMAT. How long in advance depends, in part, on your geographic location. You should register at least a few weeks before you want to take the test and allow at least a few weeks between your test and your application deadlines. Available dates and locations, as well as registration forms, are found online at www.mba.com.

Scoring the GMAT

Your overall GMAT scaled score will be between 200 and 800. The majority of GMAT-takers (about $\frac{2}{3}$) find themselves in the 400–600 range.

Verbal and Quantitative sections are scored from 0–60. Most test-takers score between 9 and 44 on Verbal and between 7 and 50 on Quantitative. These subscores are manipulated to arrive at the overall scaled score, which is the score that business schools use in making their admissions decisions.

The AWA is scored from 0 through 6 in .5 increments. The scorers are both human and computerized. The software used is very sophisticated and agrees with highly trained human graders around 90% of the time.

Your Quantitative and Verbal subscores, as well as your overall scaled score, are available immediately after you finish your GMAT. You will get an official score report by U.S. Mail about two weeks after your exam.

GMAT keeps your scores on file for 20 years. However, most MBA programs demand a score that is no more than 5 years old.

The Graduate Management Admission Council (GMAC), the folks who write and administer the GMAT, note that GMAT scores are not perfect and that they merely approximate your true performance potential based on one given day's work.

A Note on Scoring the Practice Tests

The practice tests in this book are created by experts to simulate the question types, difficulty level, and content areas that you will find on your real GMAT. However, as noted earlier, the actual GMAT is an adaptive test. GMAT exams are scored individually based on dynamic factors. Do not get overly concerned with your practice test scores; your goal should be to learn something from every practice experience and to get used to the format and types of questions on the GMAT.

Preparing for the GMAT

The Self-Assessment should be your first step. It will help you to focus on areas of strength and weakness in your knowledge base and skill set.

There is a detailed explanation for each of the practice questions in this book. You will probably not need to read each one of them. Sometimes, when you look back over your practice test answers, you can tell right away why you got a particular question wrong. We have heard many students call these errors "stupid mistakes." We suggest that you refer to these errors as "concentration errors." Everyone makes them from time to time, and you should not get upset or concerned when they occur. There is a good chance that your focus will be much better on the real test as long as you train yourself properly using this book. You should note the difference between those concentration errors and any questions that you get wrong because of a lack of understanding or holes in your knowledge base. If you have the time, it is probably worth reading the explanations for any of the questions that were difficult for you. Sometimes, students get questions correct but for the wrong reasons or because they simply guessed correctly. While you are practicing, you should mark any questions that you want to recheck and be sure to read the explanations for those questions.

Key Test-Taking Strategies

The following sections present important information that should help you approach the GMAT with confidence. Additional chapters in the book include strategies and techniques specific to each of the GMAT sections.

KSA

Cognitive psychologists, the ones who study learning and thinking, use the letters KSA to refer to the basic parts of human performance in all activities, ranging from academics to athletics, playing music to playing games. The letters stand for Knowledge, Skills, and Abilities. As mentioned previously, the GMAT measures certain predictable areas of knowledge, and it measures a specific set of skills. You probably already understand this since you are reading this book. In fact, thousands of students have successfully raised their GMAT scores through study and practice.

The human brain stores and retrieves factual knowledge a little differently from the way it acquires and executes skills. Knowledge can generally be learned quickly and is durable, even when you are under stress.

Skills, on the other hand, require repetition to be even near perfect. Psychologists use the term "perfectly internalized skills," which means that the skills are executed automatically, without any conscious thought.

You learn factual information by studying, and you acquire skills through practice. There is some overlap between these actions; you will learn while you practice, and vice versa. In fact, research shows that repetition is important for both information storage and skills acquisition.

There is a large difference between knowledge and skills, however: Knowing about a skill, or understanding how the skill should be executed, is not the same as actually having that skill. For instance, you might be told about a skill such as driving a car with a standard (stick-shift) transmission, playing the piano, or typing on a computer keyboard. You could have a great teacher, have wonderful learning tools, and pay attention very carefully. You might understand everything perfectly. But, the first few times that you actually attempt the skill, you will probably make some mistakes. In fact, you will probably experience some frustration because of the gap between your understanding of the skill and your actual ability to perform the skill.

Perfecting skills takes practice. You need repetition to create the pathways in your brain that control your skills. Therefore, you shouldn't be satisfied with simply reading this book and then saying to yourself, "I get it." You will not reach your full GMAT scoring potential unless you put in sufficient time practicing as well as understanding and learning.

Take shoelace tying for example. It is highly unlikely that you can remember the exact moment you tied your shoes this morning because, as an adult, you have perfectly internalized the skill of tying your shoelaces.

We hope that you will internalize the skills that you need on the GMAT so that you don't have to spend time and energy figuring out what to do during the exam. We are hoping that you will be well into each section while some of your less-prepared classmates are still reading the directions and trying to figure out exactly what they are supposed to be doing.

We suggest that you practice sufficiently so that you develop your test-taking skills, and, specifically, good GMAT-taking skills. While you practice, you should distinguish between practice that is meant to serve as a learning experience and practice that is meant to be a realistic simulation of your actual GMAT.

During practice that is meant for learning, it is okay to "cheat." You should feel free to disregard the time and just think about how the questions are put together; you can stop to look up information in textbooks or on the Internet, or look at the explanations in the back of the book. It is even okay to talk to others about what you are learning during your "learning practice."

You also need to do some simulated testing practice, where you time yourself carefully and try to control as many variables in your environment as you can. Some research shows that you will have an easier time executing your skills and remembering information when the environment that you are testing in is similar to the environment where you studied and practiced. It is important to note that you should not attempt any timed practice tests when you are mentally or physically exhausted. This will add unwanted stress to an already stressful situation.

Later in this book, we go into great detail about the facts that make up the "knowledge base" that is essential for GMAT success. First, let's explore the skills and strategies.

Manage Stress

In graduate school, stress arises from sources such as family expectations, fear of failure, heavy workload, competition, and difficult subjects. The GMAT tries to create similar stresses. The psychometricians (specialized psychologists who study the measurement of the mind), who contribute to the design of standardized tests, use artificial stressors to test how you will respond to the stress of college. In other words, they are actually trying to create a certain level of stress in you.

The main stressor is the time limit. The time limits are set on the GMAT so that most students cannot finish all the questions in the time allowed. You are required to answer one question before you can move on to the next question, so you might feel rushed to pick an answer. Use the specific strategies mentioned in Chapters 1 through 5 to help you select as many correct answers as possible in the time allowed.

Another stressor is the element of surprise that is present for most students. If you practice enough, there should be no surprises on test day.

Relax to Succeed

Probably the worst thing that can happen to a test-taker is to panic. Research shows that there are very predictable results when a person panics. To panic is to have a specific set of easily recognizable symptoms: sweating, shortness of breath, muscle tension, increased pulse rate, tunnel vision, nausea, light-headedness, and, in rare cases, even loss of consciousness.

These symptoms are the results of chemical changes in the brain brought on by some stimulus. The stimulus does not even have to be external. Therefore, we can panic ourselves just by thinking about certain things.

The stress chemical in your body called epinephrine, more commonly known as adrenalin, brings on these symptoms. Adrenalin changes the priorities in your brain activity. It moves blood and electrical energy away from some parts of the brain and to others. Specifically, it increases brain activity in the areas that control your body and reduces activity in the parts of your brain that are involved in complex thinking.

Therefore, panic makes a person stronger and faster—and also less able to perform the type of thinking that is important on a GMAT exam.

It is not a bad thing to have a small amount of adrenalin in your bloodstream because of a healthy amount of excitement about your exam. But, you should be careful not to panic before or during an exam.

You can control your adrenalin levels by minimizing the unknown factors in the GMAT testing process. The biggest stress-inducing questions are: "What do the GMAT writers expect?" "Am I ready?" "How will I do on test day?" If you spend time and energy studying and practicing under realistic conditions before your test day, you have a much better chance of controlling your adrenalin levels and handling the exam with no panic.

The goals of your preparation should be to learn about the test, acquire the knowledge and skills that are being measured by the test, and learn about yourself and how you respond to the different parts of the exam.

You should also consider which question types you will try on test day and which ones you will give an educated guess. You need to be familiar with the material that is tested on each section of your test. As you work through this book, make an assessment of the best use of your time and energy. Concentrate on the areas that will give you the highest score in the amount of time that you have until the exam. This will give you a feeling of confidence on test day even when you are facing very challenging questions.

Specific Relaxation Techniques

The following sections present various ways to help you be as relaxed and confident as possible on test day.

Be Prepared

The more prepared you feel, the less likely it is that you'll be stressed on test day. Study and practice consistently during the time between now and your test day. Be organized. Have your supplies and lucky testing clothes ready in advance. Make a practice trip to the test center before your test day.

Know Yourself

Get to know your strengths and weaknesses on the GMAT and the things that help you to relax. Some test-takers like to have a slightly anxious feeling to help them focus. Others folks do best when they are so relaxed that they are almost asleep. You will learn about yourself through practice.

Rest

The better rested you are, the better things seem. As you get fatigued, you are more likely to look on the dark side of things and worry more, which hurts your test scores.

Eat Right

Sugar is bad for stress and brain function in general. Consuming refined sugar creates biological stress that has an impact on your brain chemistry. Keep it to a minimum for several days before your test. If you are actually addicted to caffeine, (you can tell that you are if you get headaches when you skip a day) get your normal amount. Don't forget to eat regularly while you're preparing for the GMAT. It's not a good idea to skip meals simply because you are experiencing some additional stress. It is also important to eat something before you take the GMAT. An empty stomach might be distracting and uncomfortable on test day

Breathe

If you feel yourself tensing up, slow down and take deeper breaths. This will relax you and get more oxygen to your brain so that you can think more clearly.

Take Breaks

You cannot stay sharply focused on your GMAT for the whole time in the testing center. You are certainly going to have distracting thoughts, or times when you just can't process all the information. When this happens, close your eyes, clear your mind, and then start back on your test. This process should take only a minute or so. You could pray, meditate, or just visualize a place or person that helps you relax. Try thinking of something fun that you have planned to do after your GMAT.

Have a Plan of Attack

Know how you are going to work through each part of the exam. There is no time to create a plan of attack on test day. Practice enough that you internalize the skills you need to do your best on each section, and you won't have to stop to think about what to do next.

Be Aware of Time

You should time yourself on test day. You should time yourself on some of your practice exams. We suggest that you use an analog (dial face) watch. You can turn the hands on your watch back from noon to allow enough time for the section that you are working on. Remember, all that matters during the test is your test. All of life's other issues will have to be dealt with after your test is finished. You might find this attitude easier to attain if you lose track of what time it is in the "outside world."

What to Expect on Test Day

If you work through the material in this book and do some additional practice using the POWERPREP® software, you should be more than adequately prepared for the GMAT Test. Use the following tips to help the entire testing process go smoothly:

Do a Dry Run

Make sure that you know how long it will take to get to the testing center, where you will park, alternative routes, and so on. If you are testing in a place that is new to you, try to get into the building between now and test day so that you can absorb the sounds and smells, find out where the bathrooms and snack machines are, and so on.

Wake Up Early

You generally have to be at the testing center by 8:00 a.m. Set two alarms if you have to. Leave yourself plenty of time to get fully awake before you have to run out the door.

Dress for Success

Wear loose, comfortable clothes in layers so that you can adjust to the temperature. Remember your watch. There might not be a clock in your testing room.

Fuel Up

Eat something without too much sugar in it on the morning of your test. Get your normal dose of caffeine, if any. (Test day is not the time to "try coffee" for the first time!)

Bring Supplies

Bring your driver's license (or passport) and your admission ticket. If you need them, bring your glasses or contact lenses. You won't be able to eat or drink while the GMAT is in progress, but you can bring a snack for the break time.

Warm Up Your Brain

Read a newspaper or something similar, or review some practice material so that the GMAT isn't the first thing you read on test day.

Plan a Minivacation

Most students find it easier to concentrate on their exam preparation and on their GMAT if they have a plan for some fun right after the test. Plan something that you can look forward to as a reward for all the hard work and energy that you're putting in. Then, when it gets hard to concentrate, you can say, "If I do my work now, I'll have tons of fun right after the exam!"

The chapters in this book cover the specific sections on the GMAT. There are additional strategies and practice questions in each chapter. The full-length Practice Tests can be found directly following these content-area chapters. Plan to take one full-length test about 1 week prior to the actual GMAT. Read the explanations for the questions that you missed, and review the content-area chapters as necessary. Remember, practice as much as you can under realistic testing conditions to maximize your GMAT score.

A Final Note

Beginning in January 2006, the GMAT will be developed and delivered by a new vendor. Although the format of the test and the question types will not be affected, expect to see some of the following changes:

➤ An increase in the number of testing centers worldwide

➤ Increased security systems at the testing centers

➤ Several cosmetic changes to the computer-adaptive test, including different font and background colors and highlighted reading comprehension sections

➤ Delivery of the test exclusively via the computer-adaptive format, with no more paper-based tests given

Check out www.gmac.org for more detailed and up-to-date information regarding these and other projected changes.

Self-Assessment

This section assists you in evaluating your current readiness for the GMAT. Sample questions representing each section of the GMAT are included to help you pinpoint areas of strength and weakness in your knowledge base and your skill set. Take as much time as you need and make an honest effort to answer each question; then review the explanation that follows. Don't worry if you are unable to answer many or most of the questions at this point. The rest of the book contains information and resources to help you maximize your GMAT score.

Even if you already know that your strength is either verbal or math, attempt all of the questions in this section. Now is a good time to get familiar with the types of questions that will appear on the GMAT.

Analytical Writing

This section of the GMAT requires you to write two essays: the first essay will be the analysis of an issue, and the second essay will be an analysis of an argument. Your essays will be considered "first drafts," but should still be the best possible examples of the writing that you can produce under test conditions. We have included a sample essay prompt for each of the two required essays on the GMAT. Allow yourself 30 minutes to plan and write each essay. We suggest that you write essays based on these prompts and then refer to Chapter 1, "GMAT Analytical Writing Section," for a thorough discussion of GMAT essay writing techniques.

The GMAT Program has developed a pool of topics from which the test topics will be selected. This topic pool can be viewed at www.mba.com/mba/TaketheGMAT/Tools/AWATopics.htm. You should practice writing essays based on these topics. The practice should involve the use of a computer keyboard as opposed to simply writing out responses.

It is a good idea to find a writing coach with some knowledge of the GMAT to review your work and give you hints and suggestions. You can find one online at www.study-smart.com.

Issue Task

> "The only successful life is one based on unselfish service to others."

To what extent do you agree or disagree with this definition of a successful life? Support your position by using reasons and examples from your reading, your own experience, or your observation of others.

Argument Task

The following appeared as part of an advertisement for a new computer:

> The Bell 3000 has been adopted by 24% of the Fortune 500 companies. The average stock price of the Fortune 500 companies has improved by over 10% over the past six months. This shows that the Bell 3000 is the best choice for your business.

Discuss how well-reasoned you find this argument. In your discussion, be sure to analyze the line of reasoning and the use of evidence in the argument. For example, you may need to consider what questionable assumptions underlie the thinking and what alternative explanations may exist. Be sure to develop your response fully, using information from your own observations, experiences, or reading.

Verbal Assessment

This portion of the GMAT tests your ability to understand and use standard written English. It also assesses your critical thinking skills as well as your ability to reason effectively. The following sections demonstrate sample questions, similar to those that may appear on the GMAT.

Verbal Section—Reading Comprehension

Select the best answers to the questions that follow the passage.

When you visit a pub or a bar, the bartender might humorously ask, "What's your poison?" Although this expression has been accepted as a colloquial way of asking what type of alcoholic beverage is preferred, it is a fact that any alcohol in any amount is at least somewhat poisonous to the
5 human body. When the human body digests alcohol, *acetaldehyde* is the

first and, arguably, the most poisonous substance produced. *Acetaldehyde* is a carcinogen that is also found in common pollutants such as cigarette smoke and car exhaust. It is actually *acetaldehyde* and not the alcohol itself that is most damaging to the body. Most people believe that *congeners* are
10 responsible for the physical discomfort experienced after drinking alcohol. *Congeners* are additives and artificial ingredients that give drinks a specific flavor, color, or smell. *Congeners* are not the main culprits that make alcohol toxic, however. *Acetaldehyde* is partially responsible (along with simple dehydration) for the nausea, dizziness, and headaches that
15 some experience hours after drinking. This effect is commonly known as a "hangover." *Acetaldehyde* has also been linked with liver diseases, many types of cancer, and alcoholism. *Acetaldehyde* can alter the nucleotides that form DNA structures. When the delicate nucleotides are changed, mutations can occur. These mutations have been known to contribute to
20 several forms of cancer.

Most, if not all, of the biological and behavior effects of drinking alcohol can be attributed to *acetaldehyde*. Some scientists believe that alcoholism should even be renamed "acetaldehydism" because *acetaldehyde* contributes to alcohol addiction. Brain function can be disrupted by
25 *acetaldehyde* and this toxin can cause severe memory loss and impaired vision. A buildup of *acetaldehyde* can cause a person who drinks alcohol to become dangerously ill. If a large enough amount of *acetaldehyde* is present in the body, a person can actually die.

According to leading medical research, even moderate drinkers can
30 become victims of alcohol poisoning. The discomfort and pain experienced after drinking is the body's way of eliminating the poisons that were produced when the body metabolized the alcohol. The body requires time to cleanse itself and flush out the harmful toxins. Alcohol cannot be stored in the body and must be oxidized by enzymes in the liver.
35 Unfortunately, every human liver has a saturation point. When a human liver reaches its threshold, it can no longer convert the *acetaldehyde* into acetic acid. When this occurs, the *acetaldehyde* enters the bloodstream and can cause membrane damage, rapid heartbeat, headaches, and nausea.

Before extensive research on alcoholism was conducted, many scientists
40 believed that everyone's liver metabolized alcohol identically. However, new research suggests that in addition to its negative effects on the body, *acetaldehyde* may also be a large factor in causing addiction. It has been shown that alcoholics convert *acetaldehyde* at twice the normal rate. Therefore, the conversion of *acetaldehyde* into acetic acid is much slower
45 in alcoholics. This process leads to impaired mitochondria function and

causes a decrease in the production of endorphins (the brain chemicals that are responsible for good moods and happiness). Alcoholics need alcohol to help them produce chemicals to replace their natural endorphins.

So, the next time someone asks you to "name your poison," give some 50 thought to the chemical processes that you are initiating in your body.

1. The primary purpose of the passage is to

- (A) educate the general public about how the human liver functions
- (B) challenge the notion that alcohol is not harmful to the human body
- (C) suggest ways that people can combat the effects of alcohol with medication
- (D) identify some harmful effects of alcohol and clarify what makes alcohol harmful
- (E) summarize two theories about alcohol abuse and treatment

2. According to the author, *acetaldehyde* differs from acetic acid in that *acetaldehyde*

- (A) is the byproduct that occurs after acetic acid is converted by the liver
- (B) production can be reduced significantly and effectively by prescription medications
- (C) is a byproduct of the human liver after alcohol is consumed
- (D) is less of a factor in causing alcoholism and brain damage in humans
- (E) is the first substance created as the body metabolizes alcohol

3. The author's assertion that *acetaldehyde* can be converted into acetic acids suggests that

- (A) acetic acid is harmless to the human body and does not cause liver damage
- (B) not all *acetaldehyde* enters the bloodstream in a normally functioning body
- (C) some livers are able to process alcohol without the help of acetic acids
- (D) acetic acid is also responsible for causing headaches, nausea, and impaired vision
- (E) acetic acid plays a role in forming alcohol addictions by killing endorphins

4. It can be inferred from the passage that if a person's liver does not become saturated,

- (A) a person will be less likely to experience alcohol-induced membrane damage, headaches, and nausea
- (B) *acetaldehyde* will not be created when the alcohol is processed by the liver
- (C) a person is not likely to feel the effects of the alcohol he or she has consumed
- (D) the person has not consumed a poisonous amount of alcohol
- (E) that person likely consumed drugs that combat the production of *acetaldehyde*

5. According to the passage, all of the following can cause or contribute to alcohol addiction EXCEPT

- (A) creating *acetaldehyde* faster than normal
- (B) a slower than normal conversion of *acetaldehyde* into acetic acid
- (C) a loss of endorphins caused by drinking alcohol
- (D) taking drugs that increase the amount of *acetaldehyde* in the body
- (E) impaired mitochondria function

Verbal Section—Reading Comprehension: Answer Key and Explanations

1. The best answer is D. The primary purpose of the passage is to introduce and identify some of the harmful effects of drinking alcohol, and to clarify what actually makes alcohol harmful. The passage indicates that it is not *congeners* or the alcohol itself that cause most of the negative effects that occur after drinking alcohol, but that most of the danger lies in the conversion of alcohol to *acetaldehyde*. The passage also details how alcohol is processed in the body and what effects *acetaldehyde* can have on the body. Answer choice A is too specific. Although the passage discusses the function of the liver in the body, the primary purpose of the passage is not to educate the public on the function of the human liver. Answer choice B is incorrect because although the passage indicates that alcohol can be harmful to the body, the notion that alcohol is *not* harmful to the body is not presented in the passage. Answer choices C and E are beyond the scope of the passage; there is no real discussion of medication or treatment.

2. The best answer is E. The passage states, "When the human body digests alcohol, *acetaldehyde* is the first and, arguably, the most poisonous substance produced." Answer choice A is incorrect because the passage states that acetic acids are produced when the liver processes *acetaldehyde*, not the other way around. Answer choice B is incorrect because it is beyond the scope of the passage; there is no real discussion of medications. Answer choice C is incorrect because the passage indicates that both substances are byproducts of the human liver. Answer choice D is incorrect because, according to the passage, *acetaldehyde* contributes greatly to alcohol addiction and brain damage.

3. **The best answer is B.** The liver is apparently able to process a certain amount of *acetaldehyde*. It is only when the liver reaches its saturation point that *acetaldehyde* enters the bloodstream. Answer choices A, D, and E are incorrect because the passage does not specify exactly what acetic acids are or what affect they have on the body. Answer choice C is not supported by information in the passage.

4. **The best answer is A.** The passage states, "Unfortunately, every liver has a saturation point. When a liver reaches its threshold, it can no longer convert the *acetaldehyde* into acetic acid. When this occurs, the *acetaldehyde* enters the bloodstream and can cause membrane damage, rapid heartbeat, headaches, and nausea." Therefore, it can be inferred that a person is less likely to experience these symptoms if the liver does not become saturated and *acetaldehyde* does not enter the bloodstream. Answer choice B is incorrect because the passage indicates that *acetaldehyde* is produced when any amount of alcohol is processed by the liver. Answer choice C is incorrect because the passage states that simple dehydration accounts for at least some of the physical effects of drinking alcohol. Answer choice D may have appeared to be correct. However, the passage specifically states that any amount of alcohol is poisonous to the body. Therefore, even small amounts of alcohol will poison the body to some degree. Answer choice E is beyond the scope of the passage; there is no real discussion of drugs or medication.

5. **The best answer is D.** The passage does not include information regarding drugs that increase the amount of *acetaldehyde* in the body. All of the other answer choices are mentioned in the passage as contributing to an addiction to alcohol.

Verbal Section—Critical Reasoning

Select the best answer from the choices given.

1. Even though computer memory chips produced using a new manufacturing method will cost significantly more than memory chips that
are currently available, the new chips should still be cost effective for
adoption by the government of the State of Michiana. Not only will
the new chips increase productivity by reducing processing time for
computers, but they are virtually impervious to heat buildup, thereby
reducing the likelihood that they will ever need to be replaced.

Which of the following issues must be studied in order to evaluate
the argument presented above?

(A) The cost per kilowatt hour that the government of Michiana pays for
electricity.

(B) The amount of money spent on developing the new manufacturing
method.

(C) The average monthly savings that can be realized by reducing the
processing time in Michiana's computers.

(D) The average percentage of the new chips that are rejected by quality
control supervisors before the chips leave the factory.

(E) The amount of savings per unit that the manufacturers of the new
chips can expect to realize in the future as production volume
increases.

2. The average life expectancy of a resident of the United States is 74
years. Children born in Alaska live an average of 78 years, and those
born in Texas live an average of 70 years. Therefore, if a newly mar-
ried couple in Texas were to move to Alaska to begin their family,
their children could be expected to live longer than if the family had
remained in Texas.

Which of the following, if true, would most seriously weaken the
conclusion drawn in the passage?

(A) Actuaries, statisticians who work for insurance companies, do not
believe that moving to Alaska will add significantly to the average
Texan's life expectancy.

(B) The governor of Texas has falsely accused statisticians of falsifying
their results for political reasons.

(C) The longevity of Alaska's current population is mostly due to genetic
factors.

(D) Twenty-five percent of all Texans should expect to live longer than 78
years.

(E) Most areas of Alaska have water pollution levels far below the national
average for the entire United States.

3. Which of the following statements, if true, would most significantly strengthen the conclusion drawn in the passage?

    (A) As population density increases in Alaska, average life expectancy figures are expected to decline.

    (B) Environmental factors that tend to support longer lives are numerous in Alaska but far less abundant in Texas.

    (C) Twenty-eight percent of all Texans who move to Alaska live longer than 78 years.

    (D) Over the last 15 years, the average life expectancy has risen at a higher rate for Texans than for Alaskans.

    (E) Scientific surveys reveal that the average life expectancy of Alaskans who move to Texas is approximately equal to that of Alaskans who stay in Alaska.

4. A new policy has been proposed in Congress that would prevent government officials above a certain rank from serving as lobbyists for at least 4 years after they leave government service. One official who would be covered by the new rule concluded, however, that such a restriction would be unfortunate because it would prevent such officials from making a living for 4 years.

The official's conclusion logically depends on which of the following assumptions?

    (A) Laws should never restrict the actions of former government officials.

    (B) Lobbyists are usually people who have served as high-level government officials.

    (C) Low-level government officials who leave government service are able to make a living only as lobbyists.

    (D) High-level government officials who leave government service are capable of making a living only as lobbyists.

    (E) High-level government officials who leave government service are currently allowed to act as lobbyists for only 4 years.

5. Which of the following best completes the passage below?

In a recent survey of high school students, three-fifths admitted to being at least a little dishonest. The survey may underestimate the percentage of high school students who are dishonest because _____.

- (A) some dishonest students taking the survey may have claimed on the survey to be honest
- (B) some usually honest students taking the survey may have claimed on the survey to be dishonest
- (C) some students who claimed on the survey to be at least a little dishonest may be very dishonest
- (D) some students who claimed on the survey to be dishonest may have been answering honestly
- (E) some people who are not high school students are probably at least somewhat dishonest

Verbal Section—Critical Reasoning: Answer Key and Explanations

1. **The best answer is C.** The argument is focused on the State government and indicates that the new chips will be cost effective. The only answer choices that would provide any new information about Michiana's costs are A and C. Since the argument does not discuss any electricity savings, answer choice A is not relevant. The remaining answer choices deal with the costs to the manufacturer, rather than with the costs to Michiana.

2. **The best answer is C.** In order to conclude that the couple should move to Alaska to raise their family, the argument uses data on longevity. If the longevity is due to genetics, there is nothing special about Alaska that is keeping people alive longer. Because the couple's genetics are already determined, moving to Alaska would not be supported by the data presented.

3. **The best answer is B.** The couple would increase the likelihood of lengthening their children's lives by moving to Alaska if there is something different about Alaska. Remember that strengthening an argument is not the same as proving it. Any choice that tends to support the conclusion of the argument is correct for a "strengthening" question.

4. **The best answer is D.** The argument states that the high-ranking officials would be prohibited from serving as lobbyists. It does not say that they would be prohibited from any other type of employment. So, when the concerned official concludes that the officials would not be able to

make a living for the 4-year period, he or she must be assuming that they are not capable of doing other work.

5. **The best answer is A.** In order for the survey to underestimate the proportion of high school students who are dishonest, at least some of the dishonest students must have claimed to be honest. Answer choice E may have appeared to be correct because it is an undeniably true statement. However, the question is very specific in asking for a statement that would explain a possible flaw in the research that was conducted on high school students. Therefore, answer choice E is irrelevant and incorrect.

Verbal Section—Sentence Correction

Select the answer choice that creates the most effective sentence.

1. The local downtown shops <u>are suffering due to a decrease in available parking</u> because of summer road construction.
   - (A) are suffering due to a decrease in available parking
   - (B) are suffering a parking decrease due to availability
   - (C) are suffering, from a decrease in the availability of parking spaces to the general public
   - (D) have suffered recently, decreasing parking,
   - (E) have recently suffered decreased parking availability

2. Teachers at this high school, <u>one who</u> holds a Ph.D., are known for encouraging students to look at college as preparation for graduate school.
   - (A) one who
   - (B) one of them who
   - (C) and one of them who
   - (D) one of whom
   - (E) one of which

3. Although the Royalist Party entered this election season with far more endorsements than <u>they had in their previous campaigns</u>, it had endorsements from only two well-known entertainers.
   - (A) they had in their previous campaigns
   - (B) their previous campaigns had had
   - (C) they had for any precious campaign
   - (D) in their previous campaigns
   - (E) for any previous campaign

4. Although the term "nimrod" is popularly applied to an especially foolish or hapless character, in mythology <u>it is someone who is</u> a skilled hunter and outdoorsman.

    (A) it is someone who is

    (B) it is a person

    (C) they are people who are

    (D) it refers to someone who is

    (E) it is in reference to people

5. The company did not pay annual bonuses to some managers because it believed that <u>to do it rewards</u> them for cutting essential staff.

    (A) to do it rewards

    (B) doing so would reward

    (C) to do this would reward

    (D) doing it rewards

    (E) to do it would reward

Verbal Section—Sentence Correction: Answer Key and Explanations

1. **The best answer is A.** As it is written, this sentence clearly expresses the intended idea: that the summer construction has reduced the number of available parking spaces, thereby hurting local downtown shops. Answer choices B, C, D, and E are awkward and wordy, and do not effectively convey the main idea of the sentence.

2. **The best answer is D.** The plural subject "teachers," must be followed by an appositive that specifically identifies one of the teachers. The phrase "one of whom" correctly indicates that only one of the group of teachers has a Ph.D. Answer choice A is incorrect because the singular pronoun "who" cannot refer to the plural subject "teachers." Answer choices B and C are not grammatically correct because they include two subjects ("one of them" and "who"). Answer choice E is incorrect because "which" is a relative pronoun that refers to objects or things, not to people.

3. **The best answer is E.** The word "than" is followed by a clause referring to the singular subject "Party;" therefore, the clause should contain the singular pronoun "it," not the plural pronoun "they." Answer choices A, B, C, and D are incorrect because each contains a form of the plural pronoun "they."

4. **The best answer is D.** To maintain parallel construction within this sentence, it is necessary to include the verb phrase "refers to." Answer choices A and B are incorrect because the pronoun "it" has an unclear antecedent. Answer choice C includes the plural pronoun "they," so it is incorrect. Likewise, answer choice E includes the plural noun "people," which is incorrect.

5. **The best answer is B.** Answer choice B appropriately uses the adverb "so" to refer back to the verb "pay." Answer choices A, C, D and E incorrectly use the pronouns "it" or "this" to refer back to the verb.

 You should now have a good idea of the types of questions found on the different Verbal sections of the GMAT. If this is your weak area, refer specifically to the chapters in the book that focus on strengthening your verbal skills.

Quantitative Assessment

This portion of the GMAT measures your ability to apply mathematical concepts effectively, as well as your ability to analyze and solve quantitative problems. The following are sample questions, similar to those that may appear on the GMAT:

Problem Solving

Solve each problem and select the best answer from the choices given.

1. Of the following, which is <u>least</u>?

   (A) $\dfrac{1}{0.3}$

   (B) $(0.3)^2$

   (C) 0.03

   (D) $\dfrac{0.3}{3}$

   (E) 0.3

2. If $3a + 4b = -8$ and $5a + 20 = 0$, what is the value of b?

   (A) -2
   (B) 0
   (C) 1
   (D) 5
   (E) 8

3. The contents of a certain drawer consist of 14 ties and 16 shirts. How many shirts must be removed from the drawer so that 70% of the articles of clothing in the drawer will be ties?

    (A) 3

    (B) 6

    (C) 10

    (D) 17

    (E) 26

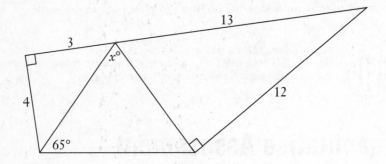

4. In the figure above, what is the value of x?

    (A) 50

    (B) 55

    (C) 65

    (D) 70

    (E) 75

5. What is the 216th digit to the right of the decimal point in the repeating decimal $0.\overline{15329}$?

    (A) 9

    (B) 5

    (C) 3

    (D) 2

    (E) 1

Quantitative Section—Problem Solving: Answer Key and Explanations

1. **The correct answer is B.** To solve this problem you should recognize that whenever you divide a whole number by a fraction, the quotient will be larger than the dividend. Therefore, $\frac{1}{0.3}$ will be greater than 1, so you can eliminate answer choice A. Also, if you square a decimal, the product will be smaller than the original number. Therefore, $(0.3)^2$ is less than 0.3, so you can eliminate answer choice E. Perform the operations in each of the remaining answer choices, as follows:

   ➤ Answer choice B: $(0.3)^2 = 0.09$

   ➤ Answer choice C can now be eliminated, because 0.03 is greater than 0.09.

   ➤ Answer choice D: $\frac{0.3}{3} = 0.1$, which is also greater than 0.09.

2. **The correct answer is C.** The first step in determining the value of b is to calculate the value of a, as follows:

   ➤ $5a + 20 =$

   ➤ $5a = -20$

   ➤ $a = -4$

   Now, substitute -4 for a in the first equation and solve for b:

   ➤ $3(-4) + 4b = -8$

   ➤ $-12 + 4b = -8$

   ➤ $4b = 4$

   ➤ $b = 1$

   You could also substitute the values given in the answer choices for b in the first equation to solve for a, and then substitute that value into the second equation, as follows:

   ➤ Answer choice A: $3a + 4(-2) = -8$

       ➤ $3a + (-8) = -8$

       ➤ $3a = 0$, so $a = 0$

       ➤ $5(0) + 20$ does not equal 0; eliminate answer choice A.

➤Answer choice B: $3a + 4(0) = -8$

> $3a + 0 = -8$

> $3a = -8$, so $a = -\dfrac{8}{3}$

> $5(-\dfrac{8}{3}) + 20$ does not equal 0; eliminate answer choice B.

➤Answer choice C: $3a + 4(1) = -8$

> $3a + 4 = -8$

> $3a = -12$, so $a = -4$

> $5(-4) + 20 = 0$; answer choice C is correct.

3. **The correct answer is C**. There are a total of 30 articles of clothing in the drawer ($14 + 16 = 30$). If x shirts must be removed from the drawer, leaving $30 - x$ articles of clothing, the 14 ties would constitute 70% of $30 - x$. Set up a proportion and calculate this value as follows:

> 14 is to $30 - x$ as 70% is to 100%

> $14 \div (30 - x) = .70$

> $14 = .70(30 - x)$

> $14 = 25.9 - .7x$

> $-7 = -.7x$

> $10 = x$

If you calculated 70% of the total number of items in the drawer and rounded up, you would get answer choice E.

4. **The correct answer is A**. The easiest way to solve this problem is to first recognize that a triangle with sides 3 and 4 will have a hypotenuse of 5, and that a triangle with a hypotenuse of 13 and one side of 12 will have a third side of 5. Therefore, the middle triangle is an isosceles triangle, with two sides equal to 5. The angles opposite the equal sides will be congruent, which means that the middle triangle has interior angles equal to 65°, 65°, and x°. Since the sum of the angles must be 180°, x must be equal to $180° - 2(65°)$, or 50°.

You could also use the Pythagorean theorem, which says that $a^2 + b^2 = c^2$, where c is the hypotenuse, to calculate the lengths of the sides of the triangles as follows:

➤ First triangle: $3^2 + 4^2 = c^2$

   ➤ $9 + 16 = c^2$

   ➤ $25 = c^2$

   ➤ $5 = c$

➤ Second triangle: $a^2 + 12^2 = 13^2$

   ➤ $a^2 + 144 = 169$

   ➤ $a^2 = 25$

   ➤ $a = 5$

Again, you see that two of the sides of the middle triangle are equivalent, which means that the angles opposite those sides are equivalent, or congruent. Therefore, angle x must be equal to $180 - 2(65)$, or 50.

5. **The correct answer is E**. To solve this problem, notice that the fifth and final term of the repeating decimal is 9. This means that every digit to the right of the decimal point that is a multiple of 5 will also be 9. Because 215 is a multiple of 5, you know that the 215th digit will be 9. Therefore, the 216th digit must be 1 (remember that the decimal repeats). If you mistakenly thought that the 216th digit would be the same as the 6th digit, you may have selected either answer choice A (if you counted 0 as a repeating digit) or E (if you did not count 0 as a repeating digit).

Data Sufficiency

Select the best answer based on the following criteria:

➤ A if Statement (1) ALONE is sufficient, but Statement (2) alone is NOT sufficient.

➤ B if Statement (2) ALONE is sufficient, but Statement (1) alone is NOT sufficient.

➤ C if BOTH Statements TOGETHER are sufficient, but NEITHER Statement ALONE is sufficient.

➤ D if EACH Statement ALONE is sufficient.

➤ E if Statements (1) and (2) TOGETHER are NOT sufficient.

1. How many miles long is the route from Long Lake to Grand Bay?
   (1) It will take 1 hour less time to travel the entire distance at an average of 45 miles per hour than at an average rate of 40 miles per hour.
   (2) It will take 9 hours to travel the first half of the total distance at an average rate of 20 miles per hour.

2. If n and m are positive integers, what is the value of n?
   (1) $n = 4.758m$
   (2) $m = 3.753$

3. Brian and Monica each received a salary increase. Which one received the greater dollar increase in his or her salary?
   (1) Brian's salary increased 4%.
   (2) Monica's salary increased 2.5%.

4. Lauren can drive from her school to the mall by one of two possible routes. If she must also return by one of these routes, what is the distance of the shorter route?
   (1) When Lauren drives from her school to the mall by the shorter route and returns by the longer route, she drives a total of 22 miles.
   (2) When Lauren drives both ways, from her school to the mall and back, by the longer route she drives a total of 26 miles.

5. A tie and a pair of cufflinks cost a total of $46.88. How much does a pair of cufflinks cost?
   (1) The tie costs twice as much as the cufflinks.
   (2) The tie costs $39.78

Quantitative Section—Data Sufficiency: Answer Key and Explanations

1. **The correct answer is D.** The standard formula needed for this problem is rate × time = distance ($rt = d$). From statement (1) it can be determined that $d = 40t$ and $d = 45(t - 1)$ when t is the time it takes to travel the entire distance at 40 miles per hour. These equations can be solved simultaneously to first find the value of t and then the value of d. Statement (1) alone is sufficient to solve the problem. However, statement (2) alone is also sufficient because the statement can be expressed as $\frac{d}{2} = 20(9)$. This can be solved for d.

2. **The correct answer is C.** From statement (1) you know that n is the product of 4.758 multiplied by m. Statement (2) tells you that $m = 3.753$. Therefore, you need both statements (1) and (2) to solve the problem and neither statement is sufficient alone.

3. **The correct answer is E.** Both statements (1) and (2) give a percent increase without indicating any information about the other person's salary. Because you do not know what the beginning salaries were for either Brian or Monica, you cannot tell which person received the greater dollar increase. Therefore, statements (1) and (2) together are not sufficient and neither statement is sufficient alone.

4. **The correct answer is C.** Statement (1) alone is not sufficient because there are many pairs of numbers that, when added together, equal 22. Therefore, you do not know the distance of either the short route or the long route. From statement (2), it is possible to determine the distance of the longer route, but not the shorter route. Statement (2) alone is insufficient and it takes statements (1) and (2) together to determine the distance of the shorter route ($22 - 13 = 9$).

5. **The correct answer is A.** From statement (1) it can be determined that the total cost of the tie and cufflinks is three times the cost of the cufflinks alone. The cufflinks cost only $\frac{1}{3}$ of the total price of the tie and cufflinks together. Therefore, statement (1) alone is sufficient. Statement (2) alone is also sufficient because you know that the cost of the cufflinks is the difference between the total cost and the cost of the tie.

 You should now have a good idea of the types of questions found on the different Quantitative, or Math, sections of the GMAT. If this is your weak area, refer specifically to the chapters in the book that focus on strengthening your quantitative skills.

Now that you've assessed your readiness for GMAT, you can begin to work on the remaining sections of the book. Focus first on the areas in which you need the most improvement, and apply the strategies and techniques provided. The old adage "practice makes perfect" really holds true here, so be sure to try all of the practice questions included in the chapters, as well as the two full-length practice tests at the end of the book.

GMAT Analytical Writing Section

The Analytical Writing portion of the GMAT is purely a skills test. This means that you are not tested on any knowledge whatsoever. Instead, you are given an opportunity to demonstrate your ability to reason clearly and write coherently and concisely.

There are two separate tasks within this section: "Analysis of an Issue," (the Issue task) and "Analysis of an Argument," (the Argument task.) You are allowed 30 minutes for each task, including reading and prewriting.

The Issue task requires you to write a short essay supporting your position on a given issue. Although you cannot be sure what the issue will be in advance, we give you some examples later in this chapter so that you can get an idea of the type of issue that is likely to appear.

On the Argument task, you are given one argument, which you must respond to in the time allowed. On this task, you are expected to respond to an argument and discuss how well its evidence supports its conclusion. Essentially, you must critique the argument in detail as opposed to creating your own argument as you must on the Issue task.

The computer-adaptive GMAT allows you to cut and paste text, as well as to undo or delete text. However, it does not allow you to manipulate the font in any way, and it does not include a spell-check function. Be sure to use the tutorial before you begin to type your essay and use the "help" feature throughout the essay section as needed.

Each essay is scored on a scale of 0–6 by two carefully trained people (usually a college faculty member) using a *rubric* or scoring guide. The process contains a number of safeguards to ensure fairness. For instance, the essays are randomly assigned to the readers, who have no way of learning the identity of the writer. Two readers grade each essay. The scores of the two readers are then averaged. If the two scores given to a single essay differ by more than one point, a third—senior—reader is called in to assign the final grade.

The essays are scored holistically, which means that a reader evaluates the whole essay and simply assigns a single number grade to the essay. Although many factors may enter into the reader's decision, the most important factors are critical thinking (logic) and analytical writing (also logic). Logic is far more important than mechanics such as spelling and grammar. However, we suggest that you not take any chances with mechanics. If you aren't absolutely certain how to use a semicolon properly, just replace it with a period and a capital letter. (By the way, that is exactly how you will know that you have used it correctly: If you can replace your semicolon with a period and a capital letter, you have two independent clauses that are closely related and have, therefore, used the semicolon correctly.)

Essays that receive the following scores exhibit one or more of the characteristics listed:

➤ **0:** Response does not address the assigned task, is in a foreign language, is indecipherable, or contains no text (not attempted).

➤ **.5–1: Fundamentally deficient.** The essay is extremely confusing and/or mostly irrelevant. There is little or no development of ideas. Contains severe and pervasive errors. Does not present a logical analysis of the argument.

➤ **1.5–2: Seriously weak.** Contains frequent problems in sentence structure and/or use of language. Errors obscure meaning. Lacks analysis or development of ideas.

➤ **2.5–3: Shows some competence.** Contains little analysis or development of ideas. Limited organization with flawed control or numerous sentence structure and/or language errors. Essay is vague and lacks clarity.

➤ **3.5–4: Competent.** Main ideas are supported with relevant evidence and examples. Shows adequate organization and is reasonably clear. Argument is identified and important features are analyzed. There is adequate control of sentences and language but may include some errors that reduce overall clarity.

➤ **4.5–5: Generally thoughtful analysis of complex ideas.** Sound reasons and well-chosen examples support conclusions. Well organized and focused. Uses sentences of varying length and complexity. Any errors are minor and do not affect the meaning of the essay.

➤ **5.5–6: Insightful, in-depth analysis of complex ideas.** Compelling logic and very persuasive examples. Essay is well organized and focused and displays skill in structuring sentences; vocabulary is precise and relevant. If there are any errors, they do not affect the logic or meaning of the essay.

Now that you have an idea of what the graders are looking for, let's look at the specifics of the tasks.

Issue Task

The topics presented are usually of general public interest. You are expected to think clearly and critically about them and then create a thoughtful, well-reasoned essay supporting your position. There is never a "correct" answer. Your task is simply to write a good essay from whatever perspective you choose.

Read the topic carefully, and remember that the time starts running from the moment that the issues are revealed to you on the computer screen. You will be given some scratch paper. It might be helpful to make a few notes about the pluses and minuses of various sides to the issue. You will definitely earn points if, in your essay, you reveal an ability to anticipate counter arguments to your position and deal with them effectively.

There are many possible responses to any issue prompt. You might agree or disagree in part, or in whole. You may attack the underlying assumptions in the statement that is given. You may decide to discuss the fact that the statement you are writing about has only limited applicability in certain situations. You should certainly use at least one example to support your position. You may choose to use more than one example, and that is fine as long as the examples you select are relevant and you stay focused on your main idea.

The issues are carefully chosen so that they aren't biased toward any one college major or profession. However, luck is a bit of a factor on this section of the GMAT. If you happen to be presented with an issue that you know something about, you will probably feel more comfortable in writing about it. However, be careful to respond to the issue presented. Don't answer a question that wasn't asked just because you happen to know something about the subject matter.

Sample Essay Prompt: Analysis of an Issue

Directions: Analyze the issue presented and explain your views on the issue. Consider various perspectives while effectively developing your own position. Take a few minutes to think about the issue and plan a response. Organize and fully develop your ideas; be sure to leave time to evaluate your response and revise as necessary.

> "Executive compensation is something that benefits the public in proportion to the amount of the compensation. Although some commentators worry that money spent on executive compensation may be excessive and wasteful, the benefits to executive morale, the company, and the public good far outweigh any supposed negatives from a high level of compensation."

With which do you agree more—the statement in support of high executive compensation, or that against it? Support your position by using reasons and examples from your reading, your own experience, or your observation of others.

➤ *The following essay received a score of 6 because it is well organized and focused, uses the language effectively, and provides an insightful in-depth analysis of a complex issue*:

> While massive executive compensation may be a habit in business circles, it is a harmful one in many ways. A more equitable division of a company's resources would help not only the average worker, who could be paid more, but also the company as a whole, not to mention the good of the entire public.

> True, there may be a minimum salary floor below which executive morale, and ego, will be impacted negatively. If a long-time, savvy executive who had done a spectacular job, received only twice as much pay as

a newly hired bottom-rung manual worker, that would be an unlikely scenario for producing high executive morale or loyalty.

However, Japan offers an example of executive compensation which is generous without being out-of-bounds. Many studies have shown that Japan is an extremely economically productive country, at the same time that Japanese companies routinely pay their leaders far less than American companies do, in proportion to the salaries of common workers. (e.g., a Japanese company might pay the top executive 15 times what a common worker makes, while an American company might pay its top executive 100 times what a common worker makes.) Therefore, one can limit executive compensation without harming the company, or the economy.

In addition, the signal sent to the public by outrageous bonuses or salaries for the "upper corporate crust" can be highly negative: merely recall the Enron scandal and similar business disasters. While the sorts of bloated over-compensation in these cases may surely have boosted the morale of the executives in question, it may also have hurt or bankrupted the companies, damaged public confidence in the American economy, and even put some of the executives in question into disgrace or even prison. A "poison pill" of sorts for those leaders, when one thinks about it.

One does not need to be a social progressive or reformer to see how an emphasis on paying workers fairly rather than stuffing the bank accounts of their managers and CEO's can be of help to workers, companies, and societies. The workers obviously profit more. (And may be able to support their own companies, cf. Henry Ford noting that paying a man a whole $5 a day would lead to more Ford workers purchasing Model Ts.) The companies will tend to work better with happier workers. And the public good will correspondingly profit.

The truly savvy executive, then, will not demand an overly large slice of the pie. Large, perhaps, but not enough to "kill the golden goose" and damage his company, thus placing his own job in jeopardy. And this concern for equity and stability may "far outweigh," even for the executive's own long-term good, the urge for the biggest salary in town.

➤ *The following essay received a score of 4 because, although the ideas were supported with relevant examples, the essay lacks focus and includes errors that reduce its overall clarity*:

This issue presents a dilemma: how much pay is too much for a business executive? There may be no exact formula, and there should probably be some balance between high executive compensation and low, or moderate, executive compensation. This essay will argue it should lean toward higher compensation, but still appreciate a need for balancing.

In our free enterprise system, there is no slave labor. Therefore, workers need an incentive to work. If a company is asking Joe Executive to handle a whole company, with hundreds of managers, and thousands of workers, that is a substantial responsibility. So, as an incentive, pay of millions of dollars may be necessary. Maybe tens of millions, for a really gigantic corporation leader.

This could even help make the company look good to the public, by the way. The media and business magazines will pick up that the company can afford to pay huge salaries, so the company will look dynamic and successful.

On the other hand, what if a lazy chief executive gets paid millions of dollars, plus stock options, and doesn't work hard enough to really earn it? This would make the company look foolish and silly.

Also, what if paying too much money to the top honcho forces the corporation to pay too little to the workers? This could lower worker morale. So the company would be hurt.

So, on the whole, some kind of fair split has to be enacted by the board of directors. The leaders must receive a very large salary, to keep up their morale, so they can help the company. (And companies that do an excellent job, help the "public good" and the economy, as well.) But there must be enough money left to pay the lower-class workers, and perform all the company's functions. Companies keeping this "fair split" of compensation between managers and employees will do well in business.

➤ *The following essay received a score of 2 because it seriously lacks any development of the stimulus, and contains frequent errors that either distract from or obscure the author's intended meaning:*

It is clear that paying executives more will make them do a better job. A high up leader who is paid like a common worker at McDonalds will not have a reason to do a very good job, so all the big companies pay their top execs real good.

There is no use in complaining about it. "Big pay for big wheels" has been the practice for hundreds of years, it is not ever going to stop. People may as well get used to things the way they are, which helps business stability too.

One day I intend to be a top executive leader. I can't imagine doing lots of work unless I get paid really well. So if that's the way most people think, let it be an established business practice.

Argument Task

Read the prompt in the Argument task even more carefully than you read the prompt in the Issue task. You are being asked to critique an argument, not to present your own views on the subject. You should look for any potential flaws in the structure of the argument. This means that you must examine the relationship between the evidence that is stated, any assumptions (unstated evidence) that are made, and the conclusion of the argument. You should also give some thought to the implications of the argument. That is, what will probably follow if the conclusion of the argument is accepted at face value?

Pay special attention to the structural signal words that indicate *evidence* (since, because, and so on), *conclusion* (therefore, thus, and so on), *contrast* (but, however, on the other hand, and so on), and *continuation* (similarly, next, and so on). We usually glide over these terms as we read. However, in this case, you are analyzing and critiquing the *structure*. So, you need to pay careful attention to the building blocks of the argument; these signals are the signposts that point out the function of each sentence within the argument.

Sample Essay Prompt: Analysis of an Argument

Directions: Write a critique of the argument presented. Discuss how well reasoned you find this argument and clearly analyze the use of evidence. Take a few minutes to identify and evaluate the argument before you begin to write your response. Organize and fully develop your ideas; be sure to leave time to evaluate your response and revise as necessary.

> The following appeared as part of an article in a business newspaper:
>
> "The minimum wage is a bad idea. It hurts employment, since employers could hire more people if they didn't have to pay workers as much. Thus, not only the non-hired workers, but the whole economy, is hurt."

Discuss how well-reasoned you find this argument. In your discussion, be sure to analyze the line of reasoning and the use of evidence in the argument. For example, you may need to consider what questionable assumptions underlie the thinking and what alternative explanations may exist. Be sure to develop your response fully, using information from your own observations, experiences, or reading.

➤ *The following essay received a score of 6 because it correctly identifies and supports the argument, and contains compelling logic and persuasive examples. Any errors are minor and do not affect the logic of the essay:*

Although at first, there seems to be some substantial truth to the argument, there is still much weakness and lack of definition.

Starting with the opening pronouncement, "The minimum wage is a bad idea," we see that the argument as a whole may not be terribly durable. For one, "bad idea" is not only highly general, it is emotional. Even "imprudent" or "impractical" would be more dry and forensic than just a straight-out "bad idea," which reeks of the emotionally manipulative.

Now as for the later claims: it is true that in many cases, employers might be able to employ a larger group of workers if the employees were all being paid less than a minimum wage floor might demand. However, this is not an ironclad rule. What if, for example, an employer pays a minimum wage that motivates workers very well, so that the company is able to expand rapidly and hire many new workers? Admittedly, the company might not have been able to hire as many workers at first, because of the required minimum wage; but over time, it may be able to hire a higher total number of workers, as our just-mentioned "rapid expansion" scenario reveals to us. Therefore, the argument that minimum wage will hurt hiring of workers, is hardly ironclad at all, although it has some small logical force to take note of.

We may be able to take for granted in most cases, that hiring of workers will help employment, since "hiring" and "employment" are nearly synonymous; then again, issues like worker retention, worker health, etc., may be addressed through the prism of minimum wage. That is, if a higher wage helps workers stay on longer with the same company and also show up to work more often, due to improved health care, that too is an "employment" issue; therefore, "hiring" is not the only factor germane to "employment."

And as for "the economy," while economies profit from employing many people (as a rule), the argument does not address issues such as inflation, which may occur in an "overheated" economy that does not have a sufficient reserve pool of unemployed workers. Nor does the argument address the fact that poorly paid workers may not themselves be able to contribute much to the economy in the way of either purchases or savings. Therefore, this argument too is weak and incomplete, like the previous argument that the minimum wage will hurt the hiring of workers.

If the argument were more fully fleshed out and qualified, with some of the issues and examples just given, it could be made far stronger. Unfortunately, as is, it is a "minimal" and inconclusive argument against the minimum wage.

➤ *The following essay received a score of 4 because it shows an adequate grasp of the argument and is reasonably clear. However, it includes some errors in logic and construction that reduce its overall clarity*:

This is a solid argument for various reasons. There is a general statement at first, "The minimum wage is a bad idea", which could put off those who like to do detailed analysis. However, the argument as a whole makes sense, despite some generality in the first sentence of the argument.

Admittedly, there is an assumption in the second sentence, that employers could hire a larger number of workers if there were no minimum wage. However, that is a logical assumption. If employer A has 6 dollars, and has to pay a minimum wage of 2 dollars, she can only hire 3 workers at most ($3 \times 2 = 6$), whereas she could hire 6 if she could pay only 1 dollar. There is also the assumption that employment will be hurt if employers can't hire more people. But that is practically ipso facto, since that is pretty much the definition of hurting employment, that is, not being able to increase the work force. So the assumption makes sense.

As for the whole economy: it also seems natural that if fewer people are working, then fewer products will be made. So, the argument that if less people are hired, because of minimum wage, the economy will suffer, is a sensible argument.

The components of the presented argument add up, in almost a mathematical way. So, minimum wage is truly a "bad idea," as the logic of the argument's different parts show.

➤ *The following essay received a score of 2 because it lacks analysis of the argument, is vague, and contains pervasive structural and grammatical errors*:

The minimal wage keeps people out of poverty so it is good for the whole economy. So, the argument is wrong. Even if some workers are not hired, that is to bad for them. A few workers do not equal the whole economy, though.

Workers need resource to survive. If they were paid just 10 cents a day, they could not live. If no workers were living, there would be no economy. That is another logical reason for minimum wage.

Maybe maximum wage would help too. Keeping down the maximum wage, might let more money go to pay the minimum wagers. So the government can set mandatory rules and help the economies in America.

Strategies for Writing Well

As noted earlier, humans acquire skills through practice. Because the Analytical Writing section is a test of your writing skills, you should practice writing under test-like conditions in order to score better. Specifically, you should practice the type of writing that is rewarded by the scoring rubric. The best way to make sure that you are on track is to have someone with experience in this area, someone you trust (such as a tutor), give you specific feedback on your practice essays. You can gain something by reading your own essays and comparing them to a rubric. Writers tend to develop blind spots when it comes to areas that need improvement in their own essays. It is always a good idea to get a fresh set of eyes to review your work. It does not take long for an experienced grader to give feedback that can be immensely valuable.

If you critique your own essays, put them away for a week or so and then take them out for another spin. You might find errors and lapses in logic that were not evident to you as you were writing the essay.

Make sure that you understand the issue or argument that is presented before you begin writing. Remember that you will receive a score of 0 if your response is off the topic.

Your essay should start with a clear statement of your position on the issue. There should be no doubt in the reader's mind about which side you are on from the beginning of your essay. For the argument task, clearly identify important features of the argument. Use the scratch paper that is provided to outline the structure of your essay. Your outline does not have to include complete sentences. It does have to include the ideas that you will put into your final draft. You need to be sure that you have a clear picture of where you are going and how you will get there before you start to type your answer.

Too often, GMAT test-takers make broad, general statements in their essays without giving any specific support. Make sure that you provide clear, simple examples of the general statements that you make, and that your evaluations are logical and well supported. In your response to the argument task, be sure to include a cause and effect relationship between your evidence and your conclusion.

The practice tests included later in this book contain additional essay prompts. Use these as well as the prompts that can be found in the GMAT topic pool (www.mba.com/mba/TaketheGMAT/Tools/AWATopics.htm) to write as much as possible between now and test day.

Putting It to Practice

Now that you've got a good feel for how to approach the different writing assignments found on the GMAT, try some sample writing prompts in the "Exam Prep Questions" section. Because grading the essay is subjective, we've chosen not to include any "graded" essays here. Your best bet is to have someone you trust, such as your personal tutor, read your essays and give you an honest critique. If you plan on grading your own essays, review the grading criteria and be as honest as possible regarding the structure, development, organization, technique, and appropriateness of your writing. Focus on your weak areas and continue to practice in order to improve your writing skills.

Exam Prep Questions

Issue Task

Directions: Analyze the issue presented and explain your views on the issue. Consider various perspectives while effectively developing your own position. Take a few minutes to think about the issue and plan a response. Organize and fully develop your ideas; be sure to leave time to evaluate your response and revise as necessary.

> "In order to force companies to improve their practices and products, society should rely primarily on government action—such as strict regulation and inspections—rather than on consumer action—such as refusal to buy products or private law suits."

To what extent do you agree or disagree with this opinion? Support your position by using reasons and examples from your own reading, your own experience, or your observation of others.

Argument Task

Directions: Write a critique of the argument presented. Discuss how well reasoned you find this argument and clearly analyze the use of evidence. Take a few minutes to identify and evaluate the argument before you begin to write your response. Organize and fully develop your ideas; be sure to leave time to evaluate your response and revise as necessary.

"In the first 2 years that Plissken has served as mayor of the city of Russell, the tax rate and the unemployment rate have both increased. Under Carpenter, who served as mayor for the preceding 4 years, the tax rate and the unemployment rate both decreased. Clearly, the residents of Russell would best be served if they voted Plissken out of office and reelected Carpenter."

Discuss how well-reasoned you find this argument. In your discussion, be sure to analyze the line of reasoning and the use of evidence in the argument. For example, you may need to consider what questionable assumptions underlie the thinking and what alternative explanations may exist. Be sure to develop your response fully, using information from your own observations, experiences, or reading.

GMAT Verbal Section:
Sentence Correction

Terms You Need to Know

- ✓ Active voice
- ✓ Adverbial clause
- ✓ Ambiguous pronoun
- ✓ Collective noun
- ✓ Context
- ✓ Dependent pronoun
- ✓ Gerund
- ✓ Idiom
- ✓ Main clause
- ✓ Misplaced modifier
- ✓ Parallel construction
- ✓ Parenthetical phrase
- ✓ Participle
- ✓ Passive voice
- ✓ Redundancy
- ✓ Relative clause
- ✓ Relevance
- ✓ Rhetorical skill
- ✓ Subject-verb agreement
- ✓ Verb tense

Concepts You Need to Master

- ✓ Altering sentence structure to make the meaning more clear
- ✓ Identifying common grammatical errors
- ✓ Identifying errors in usage, style, and sentence construction
- ✓ Predicting answer choices
- ✓ Quickly eliminating incorrect answer choices
- ✓ Using words and phrases in context

The GMAT Sentence Correction section is designed to measure your understanding of the conventions of standard written English. Each question requires you to use your knowledge of grammar, usage and style, and sentence construction to identify an ineffective sentence and determine which answer choice creates the most accurate, clear, and effective sentence. Questions in this section consist of a sentence that is either completely or partially underlined, followed by five answer choices. Each answer choice phrases the underlined portion in a different way, except for answer choice A, which repeats the original phrasing. If you think that the original version is best, select answer choice A.

General Strategies

You can usually trust your impulses when answering many of the questions on the GMAT Sentence Correction section. In other words, if a sentence sounds right to you, it probably is. You should recognize when and how to apply basic rules of grammar, even if you don't recall what the specific rule is. You can tap into the part of your brain that controls speech and hearing as you read the sentences to yourself, "silently/aloud." This technique is called *subvocalization*, and it triggers the part of your brain that "knows" how English is supposed to sound. Remember, the GMAT Sentence Correction section does NOT require you to state a specific rule, only to apply it correctly.

In addition to being grammatically correct, an effective sentence must clearly convey an idea or relationship. The GMAT tests your ability to recognize and improve ineffective expression by eliminating awkward, wordy, or poorly structured phrases that obscure or confuse the intended meaning of a sentence.

Follow these strategies to select the best answers on the Sentence Correction section of the GMAT:

➤ The portion of the sentence that is underlined may need to be revised. When reading the sentence, pay attention to the underlined portion. If the underlined portion makes the sentence awkward or contains errors in standard written English, it needs to be revised.

➤ If the underlined portion seems correct within the sentence as it is, mark (A) on your answer sheet. The test is designed to assess your ability to improve sentences, which also includes recognizing when a sentence is best as it is written.

➤ If the underlined portion does not seem correct, try to predict the correct answer. If an answer choice matches your predicted answer, it is most likely correct.

➤ If your predicted answer does not match any of the answer choices, determine which of the selections is the clearest and simplest. Read the sentence again, replacing the underlined portion with the answer choices in order from B–E (remember that answer choice A will always be a repeat of the original underlined portion).

➤ Subvocalize to allow your brain to "hear" the sentence with each of the answer choices inserted. Your brain may automatically make the necessary improvement or recognize the best version of the sentence.

➤ Look for common problems, such as redundancy, misplaced modifiers, faulty parallelism, ambiguous pronouns, and disagreement between the subject and the verb. Be sure that the answer choice you select does not contain any of these errors.

Read the Entire Sentence

The first step in determining the best answer is to read the *entire* sentence carefully, not just the underlined portion. Try to pick up on the general idea that is being conveyed. Understanding the general meaning or relationship of the sentence helps you select an answer that is logically and stylistically consistent with the rest of the sentence.

Most readers have a natural tendency to correct errors subconsciously while reading, so read the underlined portion carefully when working through these questions.

Examine the Underlined Portion

After you understand what the sentence is trying to say, focus on the underlined portion. This part of the sentence indicates exactly which skill(s) are being tested. Before you look at any of the answer choices, evaluate the underlined portion for specific errors. Determine the rule or rules that have been violated and what you might change to make the sentence better.

Look for Common Grammar Errors

GMAT Sentence Correction questions require you to consider many different grammar rules. The following sections include some of the more common types of grammar rules tested on the GMAT. Remember that more difficult questions might consist of several different errors that need to be corrected.

Basic Grammar Review

The GMAT Sentence Correction section tests many conventions of standard written English. The following is a quick overview of the most common types of errors that appear on the test. This is by no means a comprehensive discussion. Rather, this information is provided to refresh your memory regarding key grammar rules that definitely are tested.

 The GMAT Sentence Correction section does not test spelling or capitalization. In addition, punctuation is not directly tested, but you are required to be familiar with basic punctuation rules in order to answer some questions.

Subject/Verb Agreement

A well-constructed sentence contains a subject and a verb and expresses a complete thought. The *subject* is who or what the sentence is about. The *verb* tells you either what the subject is doing or what is being done to the subject. The subject and verb must agree; that is, they must share the same person, number, voice, and tense. Some complex sentences on the GMAT might try to conceal the subject, making proper subject-verb agreement more of a challenge. *Voice* defines whether the subject performs the action of the verb or receives the action of the verb. The *active* voice is usually the preferred mode of writing.

Your best strategy for questions with misleading subject-verb agreement is to determine the correct subject immediately. Eliminate parenthetical phrases and other extraneous information. Try to isolate the subject and verb in question.

We have included some examples of sentences in which the subject and verb do not agree, followed by corrected versions of each sentence:

➤ **Incorrect**: Jill, along with her sisters, *have* graduated from college.

   The singular subject *Jill* requires the singular verb *has*. The noun contained within the prepositional phrase (sisters) is not part of the subject.

➤ **Correct**: *Jill*, along with her sisters, *has* graduated from college.

➤ **Incorrect**: Either the students or the teacher *are* at fault.

If subjects are joined by *or* or *nor*, the verb should agree with the closer subject, which, in this case, is the singular subject *teacher*. (Also, remember that you should use *either* with *or* and *neither* with *nor*.)

➤ **Correct**: Either the students or the *teacher is* at fault.

Misplaced Modifiers

A sentence should contain at least one main clause. A complex sentence may contain more than one main clause, as well as one or more relative clauses. Relative clauses follow the nouns that they modify. In order to maintain clarity within a sentence, it is important to place a relative clause near the object that it modifies. A *modifier* is a word, phrase, or clause that modifies, or changes, the meaning of another word or part of the sentence. Often, a modifier helps explain or describe who, when, where, why, how, and to what extent. Misplaced modifiers can inadvertently change the meaning of the sentence. We have included some examples of sentences that contain misplaced modifiers, followed by revised versions of each sentence:

➤ **Misplaced Modifier**: Running blindly through the woods, the flashlight was of no use to me.

The sentence as it is written implies that the flashlight was running blindly through the woods, which does not make sense.

➤ **Revised Sentence**: The flashlight was of no use to me as I ran blindly through the woods.

➤ **Misplaced Modifier**: The book includes tips for protecting yourself against identity theft from the Federal Trade Commission.

The way it is written, the sentence implies that the Federal Trade Commission steals identities. The modifying phrase "from the Federal Trade Commission" is more logical following the subject "tips."

➤ **Revised Sentence**: The book includes tips from the Federal Trade Commission for protecting yourself against identity theft.

Your best strategy for questions with misplaced modifiers is to place the noun or pronoun being modified directly after the modifying word, phrase, or clause. Make sure that the sentence is clear in that you know exactly "who" is doing "what," "how" something happens, and so on.

Parallel Construction

Parallel construction, or *parallelism*, allows a writer to show order and clarity in a sentence or a paragraph by putting grammatical elements that have the same function in the same form. Parallelism creates a recognizable pattern within a sentence and adds unity, force, clarity, and balance to writing. All words, phrases, and clauses used in parallel construction must share the same grammatical form. We have included some examples of sentences that include faulty parallelism, followed by revised versions of each sentence:

➤ **Faulty Parallelism**: Ava wanted three things out of college: *to get* a good education, *to mak*e good friends, and *experiencing* life.

In this sentence, the verb forms do not match. The first two verb forms include infinitives (*to get* and *to make*), and the third verbal is a participle.

➤ **Revised Sentence**: Ava wanted three things out of college: *to get* a good education, *to make* good friends, and *to experience* life.

➤ **Faulty Parallelism**: The distance from Los Angeles to Detroit is greater than Detroit to Windsor, Canada.

In this sentence, two unlike things are being compared: "distance" and "location."

➤ **Revised Sentence**: The distance from Los Angeles to Detroit is greater than the distance from Detroit to Windsor, Canada.

A common error on the GMAT involves weak parallel comparisons that are difficult to identify at first glance. When evaluating sentences and answer choices where two or more elements are being compared, make sure that there is an explicit, parallel relationship.

Noun/Pronoun Agreement

The English language contains two forms of nouns: *proper nouns*, which name a specific person, place, or object, and *common nouns*, which name a nonspecific person, place, or object. Proper nouns begin with an uppercase letter, and common nouns do not. *Pronouns* take the place of either a proper or a common noun. Be sure to maintain consistency in pronoun person and number. It is not grammatically correct to use the plural pronoun "their" to represent neutral gender. Instead, use "his" or "her," whichever is appropriate. This is an example of a major difference between standard written English and the English that we ordinarily use when speaking. For instance, it is commonly accepted to say "Tell the student to bring their score report to the tutoring session" when we are unsure of the gender of the student. However, this is not correct for standard written English. Remember the following rules:

➤ **Singular pronouns must refer to singular nouns**. Singular pronouns include his, her, it, its, one, each, either, neither, someone, anyone, everyone, something, anything, everything, somebody, anybody, and everybody.

➤ **Plural pronouns must refer to plural nouns**. Plural pronouns include they, their, them, both, few, others, many, several, we, us, and our.

Your best strategy for questions with misleading pronouns is to determine exactly which noun the pronouns refer to in the sentence. Try to isolate the pronoun(s) and noun and see whether the two agree. Consider the following examples:

➤ **Misleading Pronoun**: Despite the controversy surrounding the candidates, the committee made *their* decision very quickly.

In this sentence, the plural pronoun *their* incorrectly refers to the singular noun *committee*. To correct this sentence, replace *their* with *its*.

➤ **Misleading Pronoun**: *Several* of the group elected to return home following the decision.

In this sentence, the plural pronoun *several* refers to the singular noun *group*. To correct this sentence, add the plural noun *members* after the plural pronoun *several*.

In addition, a pronoun should be placed so that it clearly refers to a specific noun. If it does not, it is known as an *ambiguous pronoun*:

➤ **Ambiguous Pronoun**: Jeff and Chadwick left rehearsal early to get *his* guitar repaired.

In this sentence, it is unclear whose guitar is getting repaired.

➤ **Revised Sentence**: Jeff and Chadwick left rehearsal early to get *Chadwick's* guitar repaired.

➤ **Ambiguous Pronoun**: Some foods are dangerous for your pets, so *they* should be placed out of reach.

In this sentence, it is unclear what should be placed out of reach: the potentially dangerous foods or your pets.

➤ **Revised Sentence**: Some foods are dangerous for your pets; *these foods* should be placed out of reach.

Verb Tense

Verb tenses provide the reader with information about when the action took place and whether the action has been completed. Verbs often change form or use helping words such as will, have, and are to indicate shifts in tense. You should be familiar with the basic categories of verb tense in Table 2.1.

Table 2.1 Basic Categories of Verb Tense		
Verb Tense	**Description**	**Example**
Present	Current action or condition	They exercise twice a week.
Simple past	Completed action or condition	He dressed in a suit for work last week.
Future	Action or condition that will (or will not) occur in the future	She will go to the dentist tomorrow.
Present perfect	Action or condition that began in the past and leads up to the present	He has played the violin since 1985.
Past perfect	Action or condition that took place in the past before another event	The movie had started before I arrived.
Progressive	An action or condition in progress (any of the above tenses can be progressive)	They are studying for the exam.

In most sentences, all the verbs must be in the same tense; however, more complicated sentences include several different events that occur at different times. In these types of sentences, the verb tense indicates the order in which each event occurs.

Your best strategy for a question with incorrect verb tense is to establish the meaning and context of the sentence and then use your knowledge of verb tense to determine when an event occurred or which tense should be used. Consider the following examples:

➤ **Incorrect Verb Tense**: Last week, I *have received* credit for the term paper that I submitted to my professor.

This sentence incorrectly uses the present perfect tense *have received* to describe an action that took place in the past. To correct the sentence, remove the helping verb *have*.

➤ **Incorrect Verb Tense**: Mandy changed her major again; now she *studied* chemistry.

This sentence incorrectly uses the past tense verb *studied* to describe an action that is currently ongoing. The action is better described using the progressive verb, *is studying*.

Participles and Gerunds

A *participle* is a verb form that functions as an adjective. Present tense participles end in "ing." When you see a word that ends in "ing" decide whether it is being used as a verb or as an adjective. Other words ending in "ing" could be verbs acting as nouns. These are called *gerunds*. Some sentences may contain a participle or a gerund without a verb; these are incomplete sentences, and should be corrected.

➤ **Incomplete Sentence**: Yesterday, the *winning* float in the parade.

The sentence as it is written is incomplete; the word *winning* is a participle, and is being used as an adjective to describe the float. The sentence should be revised so that the *winning float* either performs an action, or has an action performed upon it.

➤ **Revised Sentence**: Yesterday, the *winning float* in the parade *was displayed* on campus.

➤ **Incomplete Sentence**: The *releasing* of personal information by many school districts to third parties.

The sentence as it is written is incomplete; the word *releasing* is being used as a noun in this sentence. The sentence should be revised so that the subject, *many school districts*, is actually performing an action.

➤ **Revised Sentence**: Many school districts *prohibit the releasing* of personal information to third parties.

Your best strategy for correcting errors involving participles and gerunds is to make sure that the sentence includes an actual verb and that some action is indicated.

Idiom

Idiom refers to the common or everyday usage of a word or phrase. Idiom is part of standard written English and must be considered when making corrections to or improving sentences on the GMAT. The following is a short list of common idiomatic phrases as they might be used in a sentence:

Correct	Incorrect
Please *look up* that word in the dictionary.	Please *look on* that word in the dictionary.
My sister *listens to* many types of music.	My sister *listens with* many types of music.
That is a very *eye-catching* bracelet.	That is a very *eyeball-catching* bracelet.
The figurine should be placed *on top of* the cake.	The figurine should be placed *at top of* the cake.
He is often *singled out from* a crowd.	He is often *singled out with* a crowd.
I captured a caterpillar that *turned into* a butterfly.	I captured a caterpillar that *turned out of* a butterfly.
I sat *across from* my best friend on the bus today.	I sat *across with* my best friend on the bus today.

Rhetoric

Rhetoric refers to the effective and persuasive use of language. Rhetorical skills, then, refer to your ability to make choices about the effectiveness and clarity of a word, phrase, sentence, or paragraph. The GMAT Sentence Correction section tests your rhetorical skills by asking you to improve sentences. Good writing involves effective word choice as well as clear and unambiguous expression. The best-written sentences will be relevant based on the context of the paragraph, will avoid redundancy, and will clearly and simply express the intended idea.

Although there are thousands of different word usage errors that could appear on the GMAT, the test repeatedly includes commonly misused words such as:

➤ **fewer/less**—*fewer* should be used when an actual count can be made; *less* should be used when referring to quantity.

➤ **number/amount**—*number* should be used when the items can be counted; *amount* should be used to denote quantity.

➤ **among/between**—*among* should be used when three or more persons or objects are involved; *between* should be used when only two persons or objects are involved.

➤ **if/whether**—*if* should be used when referring to a future possibility; *whether* should be used when listing alternatives.

➤ **like/such as**—*like* should be used to indicate similarity; *such as* should be used to indicate an example.

The test requires you to determine which word should be used in a particular sentence, so it is important for you to be familiar with the proper usage.

> ➤ Avoid weak or ambiguous expressions that fail to express an idea clearly. An effective sentence should clearly express a single idea or several well-connected ideas.
>
> ➤ For the most part, avoid answer choices that use the passive voice.
>
> ➤ Pay attention to the meanings of the words used in a sentence. Effective sentences should use words that have appropriate and reasonable meanings.
>
> ➤ Avoid answer choices that have overly wordy or redundant construction. An effective sentence should use only words that are necessary and essential to the meaning.
>
> ➤ Avoid awkward phrases and overly complicated or complex sentence constructions.

Selecting an Answer

Before you look at the answer choices, try to predict an answer on your own. If your phrase or phrases match one of the answer choices, it is most likely correct. Remember that experts create incorrect answers to distract you. If you predict an answer, you are less likely to get caught up on these confusing incorrect answers.

Do not read answer choices alone. Instead, read each answer choice along with the entire sentence, eliminating incorrect answers as you go. If the sentence becomes unclear, wordy, or awkward after you insert an answer choice, eliminate it. A correct answer choice never has a grammatical error, so eliminate any answer choices that contain obvious errors.

After you think you have selected the correct answer, ask yourself if the completed sentence "sounds" correct. Ensure that the sentence is free of grammatical errors and effectively combines words into phrases that express a logical idea.

If you are having trouble identifying specific errors, but know that something is incorrect, try to narrow your choices by focusing on the elements of the underlined portion that vary from one choice to the next. You may be able to eliminate more answer choices this way.

Finally, make sure that you always consider all the choices before you confirm your answer, even if your predicted answer is among the choices. The difference between the best answer and the second best answer is sometimes very subtle.

Putting It to Practice

Now that you've got a good feel for how to approach the sentence completion questions found on the GMAT, try these sample questions. Be sure to read the explanations to help you gain a better understanding of why the correct answer is correct.

Exam Prep Questions

Directions: The Sentence Correction questions contain a sentence that is either partially or completely underlined. Following the sentence are five answer choices, each giving you a different way to phrase the underlined portion of the sentence. Answer choice A repeats the original sentence; choose answer choice A if you do not want to change the underlined portion. The remaining answer choices are different.

Your answer choices will depend on the standards of written English, especially sentence construction, grammar, and word choice. The questions test your ability to express an idea clearly, simply, and correctly, without being awkward or redundant, while obeying all grammar rules.

1. Most news stories, whether in print, broadcast on television, or posted on the web, are created by individuals responsible for a series of different tasks such as <u>sorting through press releases and to determine which are newsworthy</u>, deciding which facts to use, preparing the actual story, and creating an appropriate headline.
   - (A) sorting through press releases and to determine which are newsworthy
   - (B) to sort through press releases determining which are newsworthy
   - (C) to sort through and determine which press releases are newsworthy
   - (D) to sort through press releases and determine which are newsworthy
   - (E) sorting through press releases and determining which are newsworthy

2. A recent study hypothesizes that after many years, an adult may still exhibit the symptoms of posttraumatic stress disorder from an event <u>taking place when children</u>.
   - (A) taking place when children
   - (B) occurring when children
   - (C) that occurred when a child
   - (D) that occurred when they were children
   - (E) that has occurred as each was a child

3. <u>Basing it on simulated historical data and recently collected information</u>, scientists have accurately predicted the time and magnitude of the next earthquake that, if occurs, will destroy most of the San Francisco Bay Area.

   (A) Basing it on simulated historical data and recently collected information

   (B) Based on simulated historical data and recently collected information

   (C) With simulated historical data and recently collected information as the basis

   (D) Using simulated historical data and recently collected information

   (E) They used simulated historical data as a basis and used recently collected information

4. Development on the fragile, constantly changing ecosystems of barrier islands not only reduces natural protection from storms, thereby increasing the risk of property damage, <u>and also destroys</u> the habitat of many forms of wildlife.

   (A) and also destroys

   (B) and also is destroying

   (C) as well as destroying

   (D) but also destroy

   (E) but also destroys

5. The escalating <u>rate for tuition is keeping many students from attending college</u>; some blame the school administrators for poor allocation of funds, but the administrators themselves blame the lack of state and private funding.

   (A) rate for tuition is keeping many students from attending college

   (B) rate in tuition is rising and keeps many students from attending college

   (C) rate on tuition has risen to keep many students from attending college

   (D) tuition rates is keeping many students from attending college

   (E) tuition rate is rising and many students are kept from attending college

6. Each of the achievements awarded with a Nobel Prize in 1901—Chemistry, Literature, Medicine, Peace, and Physics—<u>was given to people that</u>, in that field, produced outstanding work or conferred great inventions on mankind.

   (A) was given to people that

   (B) was given to a person who

   (C) were given to a person that

   (D) were given to people who

   (E) were each given to people who

7. The first major financial decision for most young people starting their careers <u>are if they should purchase a home or condominium, or continue renting</u> a living space.

    (A) are if they should purchase a home or condominium, or continue renting

    (B) are whether to purchase homes or condominiums or continue renting

    (C) are between purchasing homes or condominiums or continuing to rent

    (D) is if they should be purchasing a home, condominium, or renting

    (E) is whether to purchase a home or condominium or to continue renting

8. Of all the possible threats to the survival of small businesses, the possibility of being involved in a contrived lawsuit <u>is probably the more greater concern</u> of most business owners who offer products and services.

    (A) is probably the more greater concern of

    (B) is maybe the greater concern for

    (C) is probably the greatest concern of

    (D) are the greatest of concerns for

    (E) are probably the greater concerns of

9. Although some environmentalists believe that voluntary support of energy-efficient appliances will be easy to acquire, others believe that consumers will support energy efficiency <u>only if it would be required by the law</u>.

    (A) only if it would be required by the law

    (B) only if the law requires it

    (C) if only it was required by the law

    (D) if only it is required by the law

    (E) if it was required only by the law

10. One advantage of whole grains over refined grains, in addition to well-known nutritional benefits, <u>is that the necessary milling operations, and hence the costs, are fewer</u> because the bran and germ are left on the grain, rather than taken off during milling.

    (A) is that the necessary milling operations, and hence the costs, are fewer

    (B) is that the necessary milling operations, and hence the costs is less

    (C) are that the necessary milling operations, and hence the costs, are less

    (D) are the necessary milling operations and the costs, both fewer than

    (E) are the necessary milling operations, and costs, hence both less

11. The Truth in Lending Act assures compliance with a variety of statutory provisions regarding credit transactions; specifically, the act <u>requires that a creditor disclose information about the finance charges they will assign to their accountholders</u>.

(A) requires that a creditor disclose information about the finance charges they will assign to their accountholders

(B) requires that a creditor disclose information about the finance charges they will assigns to its accountholders

(C) requires that a creditor disclose information about the finance charges it will assign to its accountholders

(D) require that a creditor disclose information about the assignment of their finance charges to its accountholders

(E) require creditor disclosure information on the assignment of its finance charges to their accountholders

12. Heart disease, the leading cause of death for both men and women in the United States, <u>believed to be</u> caused by several different factors.

(A) believed to be

(B) is believed to be

(C) some believe it to be

(D) some believe it is

(E) it is believed that it is

13. Franz Josef Gall, one of the pioneering phrenologists, was the first to consider the brain <u>to be an organ of mental function and to identify what regions</u> are responsible for different mental functions.

(A) to be an organ of mental function and to identify what regions

(B) an organ of mental function and to identify which regions

(C) as being an organ of mental function and to identify what regions

(D) as if it was an organ of mental function and identified what regions

(E) organs of mental function and identifying which regions

14. Geoffrey Chaucer is credited <u>as having</u> introduced vernacular English literature—most famously with the Canterbury Tales.

(A) as having

(B) as being that who

(C) with having

(D) for having been the one that

(E) having been the one who

15. From 1861 on, the separate states of Italy were officially united under one king; however, there was a definite contrast <u>between those who lived in the more wealthy, industrialized north with those who lived in the more poor, rural south</u>.

    (A) between those who lived in the more wealthy, industrialized north with those who lived in the more poor, rural south

    (B) between those living in the wealthier, industrialized north or those living in the poorer, rural south

    (C) between those who lived in the more wealthy, industrialized north and those who lived in the more poor, rural south

    (D) among those who lived in the more wealthy, industrialized north and those who live in the more poor, rural south

    (E) among those who lived in the more wealthy, industrialized north with those who live in the more poor, rural south

16. Since 1950, when the transition from animal-powered devices to mechanically powered equipment was complete, the number of acres farmers can efficiently and systematically farm <u>have grown, but the acres of land available have decreased</u>.

    (A) have grown, but the acres of land available have decreased

    (B) have grown, and the acres of land available has decreased

    (C) have grown, but the acres of land available is decreasing

    (D) has grown, but the acres of land available have decreased

    (E) has grown, but the acres of land available is decreasing

17. A recent publication estimated that, over the working lives of adults in a household, the average income for a household of two college graduates is $1.8 million more than <u>a household where there are two high school graduates</u>.

    (A) a household where there are two high school graduates

    (B) of a household where both are high school graduates

    (C) a household in which two are high school graduates

    (D) those households with two high school graduates

    (E) that for a household of two high school graduates

18. In the late 1400s, the <u>discovery of the New World, development of European interest in Africa, and India, and the emergence of opportunities to generate great wealth suddenly begins to transform</u> the traditional ways of life.

    (A) discovery of the New World, the development of European interest in Africa, and India, and the emergence of opportunities to generate great wealth suddenly begins to transform

    (B) discovery of the New World, development of European interest in Africa, India, and the emergence of opportunities, to generate great wealth, suddenly transforming

    (C) discovery, the New World, the development of European, interest in Africa and India, emergence of opportunities to generate great wealth, and suddenly began to transforms

    (D) discovery for the New World, development for European interest in Africa and India, and the emergence for opportunities to generate great wealth was suddenly transforming

    (E) discovery of the New World, the development of European interest in Africa and India, and the emergence of opportunities to generate great wealth suddenly began to transform

19. Doctors claim that patients typically either <u>ignore the symptoms of anemia and mistake the symptoms as those of other conditions</u>.

    (A) ignore the symptoms of anemia and mistake the symptoms as those of other conditions

    (B) ignores the symptoms for anemia or will mistake these for other conditions

    (C) ignore the symptoms of anemia or mistake the symptoms for those of other conditions

    (D) ignore the symptoms for anemia or mistake it for symptoms of other conditions

    (E) ignore the symptoms of anemia and mistake the symptoms for those of other conditions

20. In 1908, Henry Ford, one of the pioneering automotive engineers, transformed personal transportation by introducing the Model T, <u>creating a vehicle that was easy to operate, maintain, and handle</u> on rough roads.

    (A) creating a vehicle that was easy to operate, maintain, and handle

    (B) creating a vehicle more easier to operate, maintain, and handle

    (C) and creates a vehicle easy to operate, maintain, and handle

    (D) and created a vehicle, easy to operate, maintain, and handle

    (E) and he created the easier to operate, maintain, and handle

Answers to Exam Prep Questions

1. **The best answer is E.** The verb phrases listed in the sentence must be parallel in form. The remaining verb phrases "deciding," "preparing," and "creating" are expressed in the present participial form; they end in "ing." Therefore, the verb phrases in the underlined portion must be "sorting" and "determining." Answer choice E is the only selection that is parallel to the rest of the sentence. The remaining answer choices fail to maintain parallelism.

2. **The best answer is D.** This sentence requires that all verbs and nouns refer to the plural noun "men and women." Answer choice D correctly uses the phrase "they were" and the plural noun "children" to refer to "men and women." Answer choices A, C, and E incorrectly use the singular noun "child" to refer to the plural noun "men and women." Answer choice B uses the plural noun "children," but it is awkward.

3. **The best answer is D.** Answer choice D most clearly and concisely describes how the scientists worked. Answer choice A is incorrect because it is unclear as to what "it" refers. Answer choice B suggests that the "scientists" were "based on simulated historical data," which is nonsensical. Answer choices C and E would create wordy, awkward sentences.

4. **The best answer is E.** The use of the phrase "not only" requires the correlating conjunction "but also." Answer choice E uses the correct conjunction and uses the singular verb "destroys" to refer to the singular subject "development." Although answer choice D correctly uses the conjunction "but also," it incorrectly uses the plural verb "destroy." Answer choices A, B, and C are incorrect because they fail to use the correct conjunction.

5. **The best answer is A.** The sentence is best as written. "For" is an appropriate preposition to follow "rate," and the progressive verb "keeping" is appropriate to describe an ongoing action. In answer choices B, C, and E, it is redundant to state that an "escalating rate" is also "rising," "has risen," or "is rising." In answer choice D, the plural subject "rates" does not agree with the singular verb "is."

6. **The best answer is B.** The singular subject "each" requires the singular verb "was." Answer choice B correctly uses the singular verb "was" and the pronoun "who" to introduce a clause that refers to "people." As it is written, the sentence correctly uses the singular verb

"was," but it uses "that" to introduce a clause that refers to "people." Answer choices C, D, and E incorrectly use the plural verb "were."

7. **The best answer is E.** The subject of the sentence is a single "decision." Therefore, the plural verb "are" should be replaced with the singular verb "is." Answer choice E correctly uses the singular verb "is" and appropriately introduces the alternatives, to purchase or to rent, with "whether." Answer choices A, B, and C incorrectly use the plural verb "were." Answer choice D correctly uses the singular verb "is," but uses "if" instead of "whether."

8. **The best answer is C.** The singular noun "lawsuit" requires the use of the singular verb "is," not the plural verb "are." In addition, the sentence is comparing a "lawsuit," or one concern of small business owners, to several other concerns of small business owners. This type of comparison requires the superlative "greatest," rather than the comparative "greater." Answer choice C correctly uses the superlative "greatest" and the singular verb "is." Answer choices A and B use the comparative "greater," and answer choices D and E use the plural verb "are."

9. **The best answer is B.** This sentence describes a condition and its result; something "will" happen in the future only if something else happens right now. In other words, "consumers will support" "only if the law requires it." The only answer choice that follows this form is answer choice B. The remaining answer choices use incorrect verb tense or are awkward and unclear.

10. **The best answer is A.** The sentence is best as written. The singular subject of the sentence, "one advantage," requires the use of the singular verb "is." In addition, the plural noun "operations" requires the use of the plural verb "are." Answer choice B correctly uses the singular verb "is," but also incorrectly uses the singular verb "is" following "operations." Answer choices C, D, and E incorrectly use the plural verb "are."

11. **The best answer is C.** The singular noun "creditor" requires the use of singular pronouns. Answer choice C correctly uses the pronouns "it" and "its" to refer to the "creditor." In answer choices A, B, and D, the plural pronouns "their" and "they" incorrectly refer to the singular noun "creditor." Although answer choice E uses singular pronouns, the construction of the sentence is awkward.

12. **The best answer is B.** As it is written, the underlined portion creates a sentence fragment. To be correct, the verb "is" must be used to connect "heart disease" and the phrase "caused by several different

factors." Answer choice B correctly uses the verb "is" to make this connection. The remaining answer choices do not complete the sentence.

13. **The best answer is B**. The verb "consider" does not require the use of "to be," "as being," or "as if." Therefore, answer choices A, C, and D are incorrect. Answer choice B is correct because it eliminates any unnecessary phrases. In addition, the verb phrase "to identify" is parallel with "to consider." Answer choice E is incorrect because "identifying" is not parallel with "to consider."

14. **The best answer is C**. It is idiomatic to "credit" someone "with having" done something, rather than "as having" done something. Therefore, answer choice C is the best answer.

15. **The best answer is C**. The use of the preposition "between" requires the conjunction "and," rather than the conjunction "with." Answer choice C corrects this error without changing the rest of the sentence.

16. **The best answer is D**. The singular subject of the sentence, "number," requires the use of the singular verb "has," not the plural verb "have." Therefore, answer choices A, B, and C are incorrect. Answer choice D corrects this error without changing the rest of the sentence. Answer choice E correctly uses the singular verb "has," but it incorrectly uses the singular, progressive verb phrase "is decreasing."

17. **The best answer is E**. As it is written, the sentence compares the "average income" of one household to another "household," which does not make sense. Answer choice E correctly uses the singular pronoun "that" to refer to "income," thus establishing a logical comparison. The remaining answer choices fail to create a clear and logical comparison between the income of one household and the income of another household.

18. **The best answer is E**. As it is written, it is unclear where the elements listed in the underlined portion are separated. In addition, the phrase "in the late 1400s" indicates that the sentence refers to an event that occurred in the past, which makes the correct verb phrase "began to," not "begins to." Answer choice E is the only selection that clearly separates the elements of the list with a comma, maintains parallel construction of the elements in the list, and uses the correct verb tense.

19. **The best answer is C**. This sentence requires the use of the conjunction "or," not "and," to complete the *either...or* construction. In addition, it is idiomatic to "mistake" something "for those" of another

thing, rather than "as those" of another thing. Answer choice C is the only selection that correctly uses the *either ...or* construction and the correct idiomatic phrase.

20. **The best answer is A.** The sentence is best as written. In answer choice A, it is clear that the "creating of the Model T" made possible the "introducing a vehicle." In addition, the construction of the phrase that follows is clear and concise. Answer choice B uses the redundant phrase "more easier," and answer choices C, D, and E fail to clearly convey that one event caused another.

GMAT Verbal Section: Critical Reasoning

Terms You Need to Know

✓ Argument
✓ Assumption
✓ Conclusion
✓ Context
✓ Critical reasoning
✓ Discrepancy
✓ Hypothesis
✓ Inference
✓ Paradox
✓ Phenomenon
✓ Premise
✓ Relevance

Concepts You Need to Master

✓ Applying the scientific method
✓ Chain of reasoning
✓ Drawing conclusions/inferences based on information presented
✓ Identifying evidence and conclusion
✓ Identifying unwarranted assumptions
✓ Paraphrasing given material
✓ Recognizing errors in logic

The GMAT Critical Reasoning questions are meant to test your understanding of arguments and their components. An argument is a conclusion supported by evidence. Each Critical Reasoning question on the GMAT is based on a stimulus argument. (Sometimes there are two questions in a row that are based on a single argument.) The questions reward those who can recognize well-constructed arguments or spot flaws in arguments.

 These questions are not knowledge questions. So, take all "facts" at face value and do not answer any questions based on whatever prior knowledge of the subject matter that you may have.

Argument

There are really only two parts to an argument: *evidence* and *conclusion*. A mere statement alone is neither evidence nor conclusion. For example, consider the following statement:

Steve wears glasses.

This statement, without anything more, is simply a statement. We don't know whether it is factual. We don't know whether the author of the statement is going to reason from this proposition toward a further conclusion, or whether this is the ultimate conclusion that the author is trying to support. We need context to determine whether this statement is evidence or conclusion, as follows:

Steve wears glasses.

People who wear glasses are smart.

Therefore, Steve is smart.

In the example, the original statement, "Steve wears glasses," is used as evidence. Note that we are not absolutely sure of the *truth* of the conclusion because we are not absolutely sure of the truth or falsity of the statement that people who wear glasses are smart. On the other hand, the *validity* of the argument is unassailable. An argument is valid when its conclusion is well supported by the evidence presented.

Alternatively, the original statement may be *supported by evidence* rather than *used as evidence*, as shown in the following example:

Steve is nearsighted.

People who are nearsighted wear glasses.

Therefore, Steve wears glasses.

Again, we are not 100% sure of the truth of the conclusion because at least one piece of evidence is questionable. As we are all aware, not all nearsighted people wear glasses. Some wear contacts; some have surgery. (Some drive very slowly in front of me on the freeway.) However, the argument is valid. And, it illustrates that the original statement, "Steve wears glasses," is neither evidence nor conclusion on its own, and can be either evidence or conclusion, given the proper context.

Note that both of the arguments include two pieces of evidence. This is a minimum for a properly constructed argument. If you try to create an argument with only one piece of evidence, you leave holes, called *assumptions*. For example

Socrates is a man.

Therefore, Socrates is mortal.

This one has been around for thousands of years. It includes an assumption.

Logicians define assumptions as *suppressed premises* because they call a piece of evidence a *premise*.

The assumption, or unstated evidence, is that all men are mortal. (In Socrates' case, this was proven beyond doubt by a hemlock cocktail.) So, the complete argument looks like this:

Socrates is a man.

Men are mortal.

Therefore, Socrates is mortal.

We are able to derive the statement "Men are mortal," because it is the only statement that provides a connection between the unlike terms in the original, incomplete argument. Because Socrates appears in both the first piece of evidence and the conclusion, linked to two different words "man" and "mortal," we need a statement linking those two terms.

So, assumptions are important to understanding arguments, in that assumptions are simply unstated evidence.

We all make many assumptions every day. Some are *safe* or *warranted* assumptions. Others are a bit shaky. For instance, I can usually safely assume that other drivers on the road are going to stick to the convention of driving on the right side of the road. However, it is less safe to assume that a co-worker has the same political beliefs that I do or even likes the same sports teams.

Language

There are certain words that tend to trip up some test-takers. Here are the practical issues that surround the most common culprits:

➤ **Some**: This word literally means "at least one." If you read sentences so that you hear "at least one," you'll have an easier time following arguments. For example:

Some oak trees in the forest are taller than the tallest maple trees.

Becomes:

At least one oak tree in the forest is taller than the tallest maple tree.

➤ **Or**: To a logician, there are two kinds of "or": *inclusive* and *exclusive*. An *exclusive or* means A or B *but not both*. An *inclusive or* means A or B *or both*. On the GMAT, *or* is always inclusive. For example:

"Steve is taking Katie *or* Kara along to the library" means that Steve is taking either Katie or Kara, or both, to the library.

On the GMAT, an *exclusive or* will have the words "but not both" added. This is actually quite rare.

➤ **Phenomenon**: The word *phenomenon* (plural: *phenomena*) often gives test-takers pause. It simply means "thing." All you have to do is substitute "thing" for "phenomenon" in any sentence and you have not altered the meaning at all. For example

Researchers have observed many unusual *phenomena* at the crash site.

Becomes:

Researchers have seen many unusual *things* at the crash site.

Note that we also paraphrased "observed" to "seen." It is a good idea to simplify the language of the arguments and question stems as much as you can without changing the meaning or structure.

Question Types

The GMAT tests your understanding of arguments with several question formats, including: Conclusion (Inference), Assumption, Weakening/Strengthening, Evaluation, Flaw, Paradox, and Parallel Structure.

Conclusion (Inference)

An *inference* is simply a type of conclusion. Although the GMAT often asks conclusion questions that require you to choose the answer that is a summary of the argument, the test makers may take you in unexpected directions and ask you to select a correct answer choice that is based on only some of the information provided. In either case, the validity of the argument is the important factor that leads you to only one answer choice.

Here is a *conclusion* question similar to those found on the GMAT:

➤ Increases in funding for police patrols often lower the rate of crimes of opportunity such as petty theft and vandalism by providing visual deterrence in high-crime neighborhoods. Levels of funding for police patrols in some communities are increased when federal matching grants are made available.

   Which of the following can be correctly inferred from the statements above?
   (A) Areas with little vandalism can never benefit from visual deterrence.
   (B) Communities that do not increase their police patrols are at higher risk for crimes of opportunity late at night.
   (C) Visual deterrence is the most effective means of controlling petty theft.
   (D) Federal matching grants for police patrols lower the rate of crimes of opportunity in some communities.
   (E) Only federal matching grants are necessary to reduce crime in most neighborhoods.

The correct answer, D, is a summary of the information provided; it is the logical end of a chain of reasoning started in the stimulus argument. A logical map of the chain might look something like this:

Increased funding ➜ Increased visual deterrence ➜ Lower crime

The last statement could be mapped as follows:

Federal grants ➜ Increased patrol funds

Answer choice D makes the chain complete by correctly stating that federal grants can lead to lower crime in some communities. Now the logical chain appears thus:

Federal grants ➜ Increased funding ➜ Increased visual deterrence ➜ Lower crime

The other answer choices may not be correctly inferred because they go beyond the scope of the argument. They may be objectively, factually correct, or they may be statements that you would tend to agree with. However, you are limited to the argument presented when choosing a correct answer.

Following are some other question stems that the GMAT uses to indicate conclusion/inference questions:

➤ If the above statements are true, which of the following must be true?

➤ Which of the following conclusions is best supported by the statements above?

➤ The statements above, if true, best support which of the following conclusions?

➤ The author is arguing that

➤ Which of the following conclusions can most properly be drawn from the information above?

Never say "never." Incorrect choices on Critical Reasoning questions often contain categorical language. *Categorical language* is language that is absolute, such as: never, always, all, none, only, and so on. Although it is possible that these words might appear in a correct choice, you should avoid them unless you are certain of the correct answer.

Assumption

As mentioned earlier, an assumption is a piece of evidence that is not stated. It is something that the author of the argument is taking for granted when reasoning from the stated argument to the stated conclusion.

Here is an assumption question similar to those found on the GMAT:

➤ Traditionally, decision making by doctors that is carefully, deductively reasoned has been considered preferable to intuitive decision making. However, a recent study found that senior surgeons used intuition significantly more than did most residents or mid-level doctors. This confirms the alternative view that intuition is actually more effective than careful, methodical reasoning.

The conclusion above is based on which of the following assumptions?

(A) Methodical, step-by-step reasoning is inappropriate for making many real-life medical decisions.

(B) Senior surgeons have the ability to use either intuitive reasoning or deductive, methodical reasoning in making decisions.

(C) The decisions that are made by mid-level and entry-level doctors can be made as easily by using methodical reasoning as by using intuitive reasoning.

(D) Senior surgeons use intuitive reasoning in making the majority of their decisions.

(E) Senior surgeons are more effective at decision making than are mid-level doctors.

The correct answer, E, provides a missing link in the author's reasoning by making a connection from the evidence: that intuition is used more by senior surgeons than other, less-experienced doctors, and the conclusion: that, therefore, intuition is more effective. None of the other choices helps bridge this gap in the chain of reasoning. Although some of the other statements may be true, they are not responsive to the question. In fact, they mostly focus on irrelevant factors such as appropriateness, ease of application, ability, or whether the doctors in question use the technique in a majority of their decisions.

Following are some other question stems that GMAT uses to indicate assumption questions:

➤ The official's conclusion logically depends on which of the following assumptions?

➤ The conclusion above would be more reasonably drawn if which of the following were inserted into the argument as an additional premise?

➤ The argument above assumes that

➤ The conclusion drawn in the first sentence depends on which of the following assumptions?

➤ The conclusion of the above argument cannot be true unless which of the following is true?

 Most of the wrong answer choices on the GMAT Critical Reasoning Section are wrong because they are irrelevant. The GMAT is set up to reward test-takers who have the ability to sort out relevant information from irrelevant information.

Weakening/Strengthening

The GMAT also includes questions that ask you to *weaken* or *strengthen* an argument. Most of the time, you are expected to choose the answer that either attacks or supports an assumption inherent in the argument. It is much less likely that you will find a correct answer that directly contradicts evidence that is stated in the argument. Our suggested technique is the same for both weakening and strengthening questions: First, identify the stated conclusion. Then, identify the stated evidence. Next, look for missing links that must be completed in order to create a strong chain of reasoning. If you are looking for the choice that weakens the argument, you need an answer choice that makes that assumption *less* likely to be true. Conversely, if you are trying to strengthen the argument, you need a choice that makes the assumption *more* likely to be true. The correct choice will not always completely disprove the conclusion or make it certain. There is a bit of subtlety required to get a maximum score on these questions.

Weakening

The following is an example of a weakening question:

➤ A drug that is very effective in treating some forms of cancer can, at present, be obtained only from the bark of the raynhu, a tree that is quite rare in the wild. It takes the bark of approximately 5,000 trees to make one pound of the drug. It follows, then, that continued production of the drug must inevitably lead to the raynhu's extinction.

> Which of the following, if true, most seriously weakens the above conclusion?
>
> (A) The drug made from raynhu bark is dispensed to doctors from a central authority.
>
> (B) The drug made from the raynhu bark is expensive to produce.
>
> (C) The leaves of the raynhu are used in a large number of medical products.
>
> (D) The raynhu can be propagated from cuttings and cultivated by farmers.
>
> (E) The raynhu generally grows in largely inaccessible places.

The correct answer, D, provides an alternate source of the raynhu bark. Even though the tree is rare in the wild, the argument is silent on the availability of cultivated trees. The author of the argument must be assuming that there are no raynhu trees other than those in the wild, in order to make the leap from the stated evidence to the conclusion that the raynhu is headed for extinction. So, to correctly weaken the argument, the test makers require you to attack an important assumption. The other answer choices all contain information that is irrelevant. Note that the correct choice does not make the conclusion of the argument impossible. In fact, it is possible that there may be domesticated raynhu trees and the species could still become extinct. Answer choice D is correct because it makes the conclusion about extinction less likely to be true.

Here are some other question stems that the GMAT uses to indicate weakening questions:

➤ Which of the following, if true, would most seriously undermine the conclusion drawn in the passage?

➤ Which of the following, if true, is the most appropriate reason for residents *not* to participate in the program?

➤ Which of the following, if true, would cast the most doubt on the accuracy of the group's contention?

➤ Which of the following, if it were discovered, would be pertinent evidence against the speculation above?

➤ Each of the following, if true, weakens the conclusion above EXCEPT

Strengthening

The following is an example of a strengthening question:

➤ Three years after the Hydraulic Falls Dam was built, none of the six fish species native to the area was still reproducing adequately in the river below the dam. Because the dam reduced the average temperature range of the water from approximately 40° to approximately 10°, biologists have hypothesized that sharp increases in water temperature must be involved in signaling the affected species to begin their reproduction activities.

Which of the following statements, if true, would most strengthen the scientists' hypothesis?

(A) The native fish species were still able to reproduce in nearby streams where the annual temperature range remains approximately 40°.

(B) Before the dam was built, the river annually overflowed its banks, creating temporary backwaters that were used as breeding areas for the local fish population.

(C) The lowest temperature ever recorded in the river prior to dam construction was 30°; whereas the lowest recorded river temperature after construction was completed has been 40°.

(D) Nonnative fish species, introduced after the dam was completed, have begun competing with the native species for food.

(E) Five of the species of fish native to the dam area are not known to be native to any other river.

The correct answer, A, most strengthens the conclusion that the scientists reached. It does so by showing that there is a control group. In other words, a similar population, not subjected to the same change as the population near the dam, did not experience the same type of result. This type of thinking is often referred to as the *scientific method*. It is often tested on the GMAT on problems that do not always involve scientific material. It is relevant to any time when there is a cause-effect relationship. Remember all that you learned about control groups and isolating variables. It will help you reason your way through this type of question.

Note that this question also adheres to the principal stated previously; you will usually attack or support assumptions when weakening or strengthening arguments. In this case, you are rewarded for choosing the answer that supports the assumption that the scientists must be making, which is, "If the dam had not altered the annual temperature variation in the river, the fish would be reproducing as they had before." In other words, they must be assuming that *nothing else* caused the lack of reproduction.

As with the weakening question above, the answer to this strengthening question does not *prove* the scientists' conclusion once and for all. It does make it *more likely* that the conclusion is correct.

Here are some question stems that GMAT uses to indicate strengthening question stems:

➤ Which of the following, if true, would most significantly strengthen the conclusion drawn by the researchers?

➤ Which of the following, if true, could proponents of the plan above most appropriately cite as a piece of evidence for the soundness of their plan?

➤ Which of the following, if true, would most support the claims above?

➤ Which of the following, if true, would most strongly support the position above?

➤ Which of the following, if true, most strongly supports the hypothesis?

Evaluation

Some GMAT Critical Reasoning questions ask you to *evaluate* an argument. These questions are closely related to assumption, weakening, and strengthening questions. The correct answer identifies a question that must be answered or information that must be gathered to determine how strong the stimulus argument is. The information will be related to an assumption that the author is making. For example:

➤ Although dentures produced through a new computer-aided design process will cost more than twice as much as ordinary dentures, they should still be cost effective. Not only will fitting time and X-ray expense be reduced, but the new dentures should fit better, diminishing the need for frequent refitting visits to the dentist's office.

Which of the following must be studied in order to evaluate the argument presented above?

(A) The amount of time a patient spends in the fitting process versus the amount of money spent on X-rays

(B) The amount by which the cost of producing dentures has declined with the introduction of the new technique for producing them

(C) The degree to which the use of the new dentures is likely to reduce the need for refitting visits when compared to the use of ordinary dentures

(D) The degree to which the new dentures are more carefully manufactured than are ordinary dentures

(E) The amount by which the new dentures will drop in cost as the production procedures become standardized and applicable on a larger scale

The correct answer, C, highlights an assumption in the stimulus argument. It shows that the author must be assuming that the reduction in refitting with the new dentures compared to ordinary dentures is significant in order to conclude that that difference will help offset an initial outlay that is twice as much. In other words, if you answer the question posed by answer choice C with "not much," the argument is weakened. If you answer it with "a tremendous amount," the argument is strengthened. The other answer choices are all irrelevant because no matter what the answers are, there is no impact on the relationship between the evidence presented in the stimulus argument and its conclusion.

Here are some other question stems that GMAT uses to indicate evaluation questions:

➤ Which of the following investigations is most likely to yield significant information that would help to evaluate the researcher's hypothesis?

➤ To evaluate the argument above, it would be most useful to compare X and Y with regard to which of the following characteristics?

Flaw

Another type of question that you will encounter asks you to *identify a flaw* in the stimulus argument. The question tells you that there is a problem with the logic of the argument. You just have to choose the answer that describes the flaw. Consider the following example:

➤ Some observers have taken the position that the recently elected judge is biased against men in divorce cases that involve child custody. But the statistics reveal that in 40% of such cases, the recently elected judge awards custody to the fathers. Most other judges award custody to fathers in only 20%–30% of their cases. This record demonstrates that the recently elected judge has not discriminated against men in cases of child custody.

The argument above is flawed in that it ignores the possibility that

(A) A large number of the recently elected judge's cases involve child custody disputes.

(B) Many judges find objectivity in child custody cases to be difficult to achieve.

(C) The recently elected judge is prejudiced against men in divorce cases that do not involve child custody issues.

(D) The majority of the child custody cases that have reached the recently elected judge's court have been appealed from a lower court.

(E) The evidence shows that men should have won custody in more than 40% of the recently elected judge's cases involving divorcing fathers.

The correct answer, E, points out a flaw in the argument. Specifically, it points out that the author of the argument was comparing the recently elected judge to other judges, not to the evidence presented in the recently elected judge's cases. In other words, the author of the argument made an unwarranted assumption that the recently elected judge did not rule against many men in custody battles where the evidence clearly favored the men. As with strengthening and weakening questions, the correct answer in flaw questions often involves unwarranted assumptions.

Here are some other question stems that GMAT uses to indicate a flaw question:

➤ The manufacturer's response is flawed as a refutation of the consumer advocate's argument because it

➤ Which of the following points to the most serious logical flaw in the author's argument?

➤ The argument is flawed in that it ignores the possibility that

➤ Which of the following indicates a flaw in the reasoning above?

Make sure that you answer the question that is being asked. Often there is something obvious about an argument that occurs to you as you read it, but the question is asking about something else entirely.

Paradox

Some GMAT questions ask you to resolve a *paradox*, which is an apparent contradiction or discrepancy. In other words, there are two facts that are both true, and yet they appear to be in direct conflict with one another. For example:

➤ Town Y is populated almost exclusively by retired people and has almost no families with small children. Yet Town Y is home to a thriving business specializing in the rental of furniture for infants and small children.

> Which of the following, if true, best reconciles the seeming discrepancy described above?
>
> (A) The business specializing in the rental of children's furniture buys its furniture from distributors outside of Town Y.
>
> (B) The few children who do reside in Town Y all know each other and often stay over night at each other's houses.
>
> (C) Many residents of Town Y who move frequently prefer to rent their furniture rather than buy it outright.
>
> (D) Many residents of Town Y must provide for the needs of visiting grandchildren several weeks a year.
>
> (E) Children's furniture available for rental is of the same quality as that available for purchase.

The correct answer, D, explains why a town of mostly retired residents might need to rent children's furniture. The other answer choices all contain irrelevant information. This further illustrates the fact that, on all question types, if you eliminate the irrelevant choices, the remaining choice will most likely be correct.

Here are some other question stems that GMAT uses to indicate paradox questions:

➤ Which of the following, if true, best reconciles the seeming discrepancy described above?

➤ Which of the following, if true, would best explain the opposition of X to the proposed law?

➤ Which of the following, if true, best explains the discrepancy above?

➤ Which of the following, if true, most helps to resolve the apparent paradox?

➤ Which of the following, if true, most helps to resolve the paradox outlined above?

 Paraphrasing is a very important technique. We've found that our students can usually identify the credited response, even on questions that they answered incorrectly, if we paraphrase the argument and the question stem for them. The process of simplifying the language reveals that the actual ideas that are dressed up in complicated sentence structure and elevated vocabulary are usually fairly straightforward.

Parallel Structure

The last type of Critical Reasoning question that we'll cover is the *parallel structure* question. In this type of question, you must choose the answer that has the same structure as the stimulus argument. In other words, you have to find the argument that is analogous to the given argument in that it includes the same relationship between the evidence presented and the conclusion. For example:

➤ It is true that it is against international law to provide aid to certain countries that are building nuclear programs. But, if Russian companies do not provide aid, companies in other countries will.

Which of the following is most like the argument above in its logical structure?

(A) It is true that it is against United States policy to negotiate with kidnappers. But if the United States wants to prevent loss of life, it must negotiate in some cases.

(B) It is true that it is illegal to sell diamonds that originate in certain countries. But there is a long tradition in Russia of stockpiling diamonds.

(C) It is true that it is illegal for an attorney to participate in a transaction in which there is an apparent conflict of interest. But, if the facts are examined carefully, it will clearly be seen that there is no actual conflict of interest in the defendant's case.

(D) It is true that it is against the law to steal cars. But someone else certainly would have stolen that car if the defendant had not done so first.

(E) It is true that company policy forbids managers from making personal loans to employees without advance clearance from at least one vice president. But there have been many managers who have disobeyed this policy.

The correct answer, D, has the same structure as the stimulus argument. If you just replace "aid to developing nuclear powers" with "car theft," and "Russian companies" with the "defendant," it is essentially the same argument. Sometimes the parallel structure is easier to see if you use symbols to represent the terms of the argument: It is true that X is illegal. But, if Y doesn't do it, others will. Granted, the stimulus argument is in the future tense and the credited answer is in the past tense. However, it certainly is *most* like the stimulus.

Note that the answer choices that deal with the United States and Russia are not credited. This is a common characteristic of the parallel structure questions. The answer choices that contain the same or similar terms as the stimulus argument are rarely correct.

Here are some other question stems that GMAT might use to indicate parallel structure questions:

➤ Which of the following arguments proceeds in the same way as the above argument?

➤ Which of the following conclusions is supported in the same way as the above conclusion?

➤ Which argument below contains the same flaw as the argument above?

➤ Which of the following has the most similar structure to the argument above?

➤ Each of the following is similar in structure to the above EXCEPT

A Note on Question Format

In addition to the straightforward multiple-choice format shown in the examples above, there are some additional formats that you may encounter on the GMAT. The logical relationships tested will be the same ones listed above. However, the question stems may vary slightly. The most common variations are *completion*, and *EXCEPT*.

A *completion* question can be a conclusion, assumption, or any other of the question types previously mentioned. It simply includes a blank that must be filled in by the correct answer choice.

For example:

➤ Which of the following best completes the passage below?

In a survey of high school students, three-fifths admitted to being at least somewhat dishonest. However, the survey may underestimate the proportion of students who are dishonest, because _____.

(A) some dishonest students taking the survey might have claimed to be honest on the survey

(B) some generally honest students taking the survey might have claimed on the survey to be dishonest

(C) some students who claimed on the survey to be at least a little dishonest may be very dishonest

(D) some students who claimed on the survey to be dishonest may have been answering honestly

(E) some people who are not high school students are probably at least somewhat dishonest

The correct answer, A, properly completes the passage because it provides a missing piece of evidence. So, this is actually just an assumption question with a bit of a format twist.

Similarly, an *EXCEPT* question will generally be one of the types discussed previously. However, the question stem will force you to use the process of elimination because you have to find the one choice that does not weaken, strengthen, and so on, the argument. For example:

➤ The beer industry is still very profitable and the projections are that it will remain so. In the United States this year, the total amount of beer sold by breweries has increased, even though the number of adults who drink beer has decreased.

Each of the following, if true, could explain the simultaneous increase in beer sales and decrease in the number of adults who drink beer EXCEPT:

(A) During this year, the number of women who have begun to drink beer is greater than the number of men who have quit drinking beer.

(B) The number of underage people who have begun to drink beer is greater than the number of adults who have quit drinking beer during the same period.

(C) During this year, the number of nondrinkers who have begun to drink beer is greater than the number of people who have quit drinking beer.

(D) The people who have continued to drink beer consume more beer per person than they have in the past.

(E) More of the beer made in the United States this year was exported to other countries than was the case last year.

The correct answer, A, is actually an irrelevant fact. In this case, the test makers framed the question in such a way that you are forced to choose the answer that has no bearing on the argument. Because the statistics refer to the number of adults who drink beer, without regard to sex, the fact that there has been a shift in the balance between male beer drinkers and female beer drinkers has no effect on the apparent conflict. Each of the other statements would help to explain the discrepancy. This question is just a paradox question with a formatting twist.

Putting It to Practice

Now that you've got a good feel for how to approach the critical reasoning questions found on the GMAT, try these sample questions. Be sure to read the explanations to help you gain a better understanding of why the correct answer is correct.

Exam Prep Questions

Directions: Read the question and any accompanying information, and then select the best answer choice from those given.

1. The less frequently employees leave the office for a restaurant lunch each week, the fewer sick days they take. Even employees who reduce their number of restaurant lunches by only one per week take less sick time than those who eat lunch at restaurants every day. Therefore, if companies started to offer on-site cafeterias, the absentee rate in those companies would decrease significantly.

   Which of the following, if true, most seriously weakens the argument above?

   (A) Employees who eat in cafeterias sometimes make personal phone calls upon returning to their work areas.

   (B) Employees who are frequently absent are the least likely to eat in a company cafeteria.

   (C) Employees who eat in company cafeterias usually eat more healthy meals at home.

   (D) Employees who eat in company cafeterias use their working time no more productively than those who eat restaurant meals.

   (E) Employees who eat in company cafeterias tend to take more frequent breaks in the morning and afternoon than those who eat their lunch in restaurants.

2. Many people argue that alcohol advertising plays a crucial role in causing teenagers to start or continue drinking. In Finland, however, where there has been a ban on alcohol advertising since 1977, drinking is at least as prevalent among teenagers as it is in countries that do not ban such advertising.

Which of the following draws the most reliable conclusion from the information above?

(A) Alcohol advertising cannot be the only factor that affects the prevalence of drinking among teenagers.

(B) Advertising does not play a role in causing teenagers to start or continue drinking.

(C) Banning alcohol advertising does not reduce the consumption of alcohol.

(D) More teenagers drink if they are not exposed to alcohol advertising than if they are.

(E) Most teenagers who drank alcohol in 1977 did not stop when the ban on alcohol advertising was implemented.

3. A company's two divisions performed with remarkable consistency over the past 4 years; the heavy equipment division has accounted for approximately 25% of dollar sales and 45% of profits, and the consumer products division accounts for the balance.

Which of the following can be properly inferred regarding the past 4 years from the statement above?

(A) Total dollar sales for each of the company's divisions has remained roughly constant.

(B) The heavy equipment division has faced stiffer competition in its markets than has the consumer products division.

(C) The consumer products division has realized lower profits per dollar of sales than has the heavy equipment division.

(D) The product mix offered by each of the company's divisions has remained unchanged.

(E) Highly profitable products accounted for a higher percentage of the consumer products division's sales than those of the heavy equipment division.

4. The local board of education found that, because the current chemistry curriculum has little direct relevance to the real world, chemistry classes attract few high school students. So to attract students to chemistry classes, the school board proposed a curriculum that emphasizes principles of chemistry involved in producing and testing foam insulation.

Which of the following, if true, provides the strongest reason to expect that the proposed curriculum will be successful in attracting students?

(A) In the real world the production and testing of foam insulation is of major importance in the building trades.

(B) The number of students interested in chemistry today is much lower than the number of students interested in chemistry 50 years ago.

(C) Equipment that a large producer of foam insulation has donated to the school could be used in the proposed curriculum.

(D) Knowledge of chemistry is becoming increasingly important in understanding the technology used in the real world.

(E) Several fundamental principles of chemistry are involved in producing and testing foam insulation.

5. When five semi-trucks owned by Trustworthy Trucking crashed in the same week, Trustworthy Trucking ordered five new trucks from the same manufacturer. This decision surprised many in the trucking industry; ordinarily, when a product is involved in accidents, users become reluctant to buy that product.

Which of the following, if true, provides the best indication that Trustworthy Trucking's decision was logically well supported?

(A) Although during the previous year only one truck built by the same manufacturer crashed, competing manufacturers had a perfect safety record.

(B) The trucks owned by Trustworthy Trucking crashed due to driver error; but because of the excellent quality of the trucks there were no injuries.

(C) The federal government issued new guidelines for trucking companies in order to standardize safety requirements governing inspections.

(D) Consumer advocates pressured two major trucking companies into purchasing safer trucks so that the public would be safer on the highways.

(E) Many employees of the company that manufactured the trucks owned by Trustworthy Trucking had to be replaced because they found jobs with the competition.

6. Which of the following best completes the passage below?

Students gain prestige when they attend an Ivy League college. They want to be associated with something important and special. Allowing students with poor test scores to attend Ivy League colleges should not be encouraged because _____.

   (A) Ivy League students currently represent a shrinking portion of the population of all college students

   (B) continued enrollment at Ivy League colleges depends directly on the maintenance of an aura of exclusivity

   (C) Ivy League students are concerned with the quality of education as well as the cost of tuition

   (D) admitting students with poor test scores will allow Ivy League colleges to reduce the number of scholarships awarded to all students

   (E) maintaining exclusivity is not necessarily a primary goal of Ivy League colleges

Questions 7–8 are based on the following:

Manufacturers R and S each have the same number of employees who work the same number of hours per week. According to records maintained by each manufacturer, the employees of Manufacturer R had more job-related accidents last month than did the employees of Manufacturer S. Therefore, employees of Manufacturer S are less likely to have job-related accidents than are employees of Manufacturer R.

7. Which of the following, if true, would most strengthen the conclusion above?

   (A) Manufacturer R provides more types of health-care benefits than does Manufacturer S.

   (B) Manufacturer R paid more for new job-related medical claims than did Manufacturer S.

   (C) Manufacturer R holds more safety inspections than does Manufacturer S.

   (D) Manufacturer S maintains more accurate records than does Manufacturer R.

   (E) Manufacturer R makes products that are more hazardous for employees to produce than does Manufacturer S.

8. Which of the following, if true, would most weaken the conclusion above?

   (A) The employees of Manufacturer R lost more time at work due to job-related accidents than did the employees of Manufacturer S.

   (B) Manufacturer S considered more types of accidents to be job-related than did Manufacturer R.

   (C) The employees of Manufacturer R were sick more often than were the employees of Manufacturer S.

   (D) The majority of job-related accidents at Manufacturer R involved a single machine.

   (E) Several employees of Manufacturer R each had more than one job-related accident.

9. The bionic prosthetic limb industry argues that because new prosthetics will not be developed unless high development costs can be recouped in later sales, the current 10 years of protection provided by patents should be extended in the case of newly developed prosthetics. However, in other industries, new product development continues despite high development costs, a fact that indicates that the extension is unnecessary.

Which of the following, if true, most strongly supports the bionic prosthetic limb industry's argument against the challenge made above?

   (A) No industry other than the bionic prosthetic limb industry has asked for an extension of the 10-year limit on patent protection.

   (B) An existing patent for a prosthetic limb does not legally prevent bionic prosthetic limb companies from marketing alternative prosthetics, provided that they are sufficiently dissimilar to the patented prosthetic limb.

   (C) Much recent industrial innovation has occurred in products for which patent protection is often very ineffective.

   (D) Clinical testing of new prosthetic limbs, which occurs after the patent is granted and before the new limb can be marketed, often now takes as long as 5 years to complete.

   (E) There are several industries in which the ratio of research and development costs to revenues is higher than it is in the prosthetic limb industry.

10. In the past, most bus companies minimized bus weight to minimize fuel costs. The safest bus seats were heavy, and bus companies equipped their buses with few of these seats. Last year the seat that sold best to bus companies was the safest one—a clear indication that bus companies are assigning a higher priority to safety than to minimizing fuel costs.

Which of the following, if true, most seriously weakens the argument above?

(A) The best-selling bus seat two years ago was not the safest seat on the market.

(B) No bus company has announced that it would be making safe seating a higher priority this year.

(C) The price of fuel was higher this year than it had been in most of the years when the safest bus seat sold poorly.

(D) Due to increases in the cost of materials, all bus seats were more expensive to manufacture last year than in any previous year.

(E) Because of technological innovations, the safest bus seat on the market last year weighed significantly less than most other bus seats on the market.

Answers to Exam Prep Questions

1. **The best answer is B.** Offering on-site cafeterias might not produce significantly lowered absentee rates if employees who are frequently absent do not eat in on-site cafeterias. Answer choices A and E indicate that offering on-site cafeterias would have undesirable consequences, and answer choice D suggests that on-site cafeterias would fail to produce an added benefit, but none of these choices has any bearing on absenteeism. Answer choice C is irrelevant because it deals with eating meals at home.

2. **The best answer is A.** If alcohol advertising were the only factor affecting whether teenagers started or continued to drink, there would be a difference between the number of teenagers who drink in Finland and the number of teenagers who drink in other countries. Because there is no difference, alcohol advertising cannot be the only factor affecting the prevalence of drinking among teenagers. The remaining answer choices make some claim about the effects of alcohol advertising or the banning of such advertising, but no information about the effects of banning alcohol advertising, if any, is presented in the passage.

3. **The best answer is C.** Based on information given, the heavy equipment division made 45% of the profits on 25% of the dollar sales $(\frac{45}{25})$, and the consumer products division made 55% of the profits on 75% of the dollar sales $(\frac{55}{75})$. Thus, the consumer products division made a lower profit per dollar of sales. There is no information provided about total sales or competition, so answer choices A and B are incorrect. Likewise, neither the product mix nor the breakdown between highly profitable versus not highly profitable products is given, so answer choices D and E are incorrect.

4. **The best answer is A.** In order for the proposed curriculum change to attract students to chemistry classes, producing and testing foam insulation must be directly relevant to the real world. Answer choice A provides the best evidence for this. The remaining answer choices do not indicate why the new curriculum would be attractive to students.

5. **The best answer is B.** Trustworthy Trucking's decision would be most logically sound if the cause of the crashes was something other than deficiencies in the trucks, particularly if there is evidence that

the trucks provided protection against injuries. The remaining answer choices either suggest that Trustworthy Trucking's decision was illogical or they do not provide a reason for Trustworthy Trucking's decision.

6. **The best answer is B**. The paragraph calls for an explanation for why allowing students with poor test scores to attend Ivy League colleges would be a bad idea. Answer choice B, which suggests that enrollment in Ivy League colleges depends on those colleges remaining special, provides such an explanation. Admitting students with poor test scores would likely lead to a reduction in the prestige associated with Ivy League colleges. The remaining answer choices are not supported by the context of, or the assumptions made in, the paragraph.

7. **The best answer is E**. The fact that Manufacturer R makes products that are more hazardous to produce might account for its higher incidence of job-related accidents. Therefore, this statement would support, or strengthen, the conclusion reached in the question. Health care benefits, paying for job-related medical claims, and accurate recordkeeping are irrelevant to a discussion of job-related accidents in this context, so answer choices A, B, and D are incorrect. If Manufacturer R held more safety inspections, the conclusion might actually be weakened, so answer choice C is incorrect.

8. **The best answer is B**. The information used to support the conclusion comes from the manufacturers own records. Because, however, answer choice B indicates that, as compared with Manufacturer R, Manufacturer S overstates the number of job-related accidents, answer choice B weakens the conclusion drawn. Answer choice A is a consequence that might be expected from the information given; it does not weaken the conclusion, so answer choice A is incorrect. Answer choice C contains irrelevant information, and answer choices D and E support the conclusion drawn.

9. **The best answer is D**. The bionic prosthetic limb industry's argument is best supported by an explanation of why the patent period sufficient for other industries is not sufficient for the prosthetic limb industry. Answer choice D indicates that clinical testing currently takes up half of the protection period and supports the argument for extending the protection period. None of the other answer choices offer a justifiable reason for extending the protection period.

10. **The best answer is E.** Because the safest seats were the lightest seats last year, buying them could actually be part of a strategy to minimize fuel costs, rather than an indication that bus companies are assigning a higher priority to safety. Answer choice A simply confirms that safety measures have improved. Answer choice B does not weaken the argument regarding a shift in priorities. Answer choices C and D do not effectively address the current seat-safety issue, so those choices are incorrect.

4

GMAT Verbal Section: Reading Comprehension

Terms You Need to Know

✓ Assumption
✓ Extrapolation
✓ Imply
✓ Inference
✓ Vocabulary in context

Concepts You Need to Master

✓ Comparing and contrasting information presented in one or more reading passages
✓ Determining the meaning of words using context
✓ Drawing conclusions based on information presented in the reading passage
✓ Locating important details within a reading passage
✓ Using introductory and transitional phrases to select appropriate word or words

The GMAT Reading Comprehension questions are designed to measure your ability to read, understand, and analyze a written passage. Correctly answering a question requires you to recognize both what is stated and what is implied within the passage and to establish the relationships and ideas expressed in the passage.

Reading Comprehension questions appear in the Verbal section of the GMAT. Each passage discusses subjects in the areas of humanities, social sciences, and the biological or physical sciences. Typically, there are several passages approximately 350 words in length on the computer-adaptive GMAT. Each passage is followed by two to five questions, each with five answer choices. You should select the best possible answer for each question.

 The Verbal section of the GMAT contains other types of questions along with the Reading Comprehension questions. A passage and its questions can appear in any order within the section and do not necessarily appear near other Reading Comprehension passages.

General Strategies

Probably the biggest mistake that you could make is to read any exam passages as though you are studying for a college exam. The "open-book" aspect of the passage-based Reading Comprehension sections means that you should read in a way that helps your brain work through the information efficiently. You should *not* read slowly and carefully as though you have to remember the information for a long period of time. You should read loosely and dwell only on information that you are sure is important because you need it to answer a question. This type of reading should be very goal-oriented. If the information you are looking at does not help answer a question, you should not linger over it. The best scores on this section are usually earned by students who have two key skills: *paraphrasing* and *skimming*. These skills are discussed in more detail later. The following are the general strategies you should master for the GMAT Reading Comprehension section:

➤ Determining the main idea

➤ Skimming

➤ Reading and answering the questions

➤ Using the process of elimination

➤ Handling assumptions and inferences

Determining the Main Idea

The main idea of any piece of writing is the primary point that the author is trying to convey. Typically, the main idea is expressed within the first paragraph of the passage. The main idea has three components:

➤ Topic (What?)

➤ Scope (What about it?)

➤ Purpose (Why did the author write this?)

If you can answer these three questions, you understand the main idea. Consider the following scenarios:

1. The world's tropical rainforests are being decimated at an alarming rate. Each day, thousands of acres of trees are destroyed in both developing and industrial countries. Nearly half of the world's species of plants and animals will be eliminated or severely threatened over the next 25 years due to this rapid deforestation. Clearly it is imperative that something be done to curtail this rampant destruction of the tropical rainforests.

2. Tropical rainforests are crucial to the health and welfare of the planet. Experts indicate that over 20% of the world's oxygen is produced by the Amazon rainforest alone. In addition, more than half of the world's estimated 10 million species of plants, animals, and insects live in the tropical rainforests. These plants and animals of the rainforest provide us with food, fuel wood, shelter, jobs, and medicines. Indigenous humans also inhabit the tropical rainforests.

The *topic* of both passages is tropical rainforests. However, the *scope* of each passage is very different. The first passage discusses destruction of the tropical rainforests, whereas the second passage introduces the diversity of the rainforests and indicates why the rainforests are important. The *purpose* of each passage is similar, but the tone of the second passage is more informational than that of the first passage.

 As you read for the main idea, and particularly the author's purpose, avoid arguing with the author. If you disagree with any viewpoints expressed in a passage, do not let your personal opinions interfere with your selection of answer choices.

Too often, students confuse the topic with the main idea. The topic of a passage only answers the question "What?" If you notice only the topic, you are missing some very important information.

The introductory paragraph often indicates the topic or topics being discussed, the author's point of view, and exactly what the author is trying to prove. So, read a little more slowly at the beginning until you get a grip on the three components of the main idea, and then you can shift to the next higher gear and skim the rest of the passage.

The Reading Comprehension section is not meant to test your knowledge about a particular subject. You should answer questions based on the information presented in the passage only, not on any prior knowledge that you may have of the subject. You may be asked to draw a conclusion (inference), but you should do so based only on what the writer's words actually state or imply.

Skimming

The goal with skimming is to get a general understanding of the structure of the passage. This is key so that you can find pertinent facts when you refer to the passage as you answer questions.

You should also pay close attention to paragraph breaks. While reading through paragraphs follow these tips to help you gather information more effectively:

➤ Try to determine the subtopic for each paragraph quickly.

➤ Focus on the general content of each paragraph.

➤ Determine the purpose of each paragraph.

Note that the first sentence is not always the topic sentence. So, don't believe those who say that you can read the first and last sentence of each paragraph and skip the rest of the sentences completely. You are better off skimming over all of the words even if you end up forgetting most of what you read almost immediately.

Remember that the idea while skimming is to not waste time. Keep moving through the material. When you come to a word or phrase that is unfamiliar, don't use context clues; just read past it. There is always time to come back if you need to, but there is strong chance that you won't need to figure out exactly what that one word or phrase means in order to answer the bulk of the questions that accompany the passage. If you waste some of your precious time, you'll never get it back. With perseverance and practice, you will start to get comfortable with a less-than-perfect understanding of the passage.

Reading and Answering the Questions

Following these tips as you read and answer the questions in the Reading Comprehension section.

➤ Before you read the questions and answers, take a moment to summarize mentally the main idea and the structure of the passage.

➤ Read the question and make sure that you understand it, paraphrasing if you need to. Use the structure of the passage to lead you to the correct answer. Go back to the part of the passage that relates to the question, and that part will probably contain the answer to your question.

➤ Some of the questions on the GMAT ask you to draw conclusions based on the information that you read. However, even these questions should be answered based on the information in the passage. There are always some strong hints, or evidence, that will lead you to an answer.

➤ Some of the questions contain references to specific lines of the passage. The trick for these question types is to read a little before and a little after the specific line that is mentioned. Remember that you must answer the questions based on the context of the passage, so be sure that you fully understand what that context is. As a minimum, read the entire sentence that contains the line that is referenced.

➤ Some of the questions might not tell you where to look for the answer, or they might question the passage as a whole. In situations like this, think about what you globally learned about the passage while you were skimming it. Note the subtopics for the paragraphs and let them guide you to the part of the passage that contains the information that you are looking for.

After you find the information in the passage that provides the correct answer, try to answer the question in your mind. Do this before you look at the answer choices. Remember that four of the five answer choices are incorrect. Not only are they incorrect, but they were written by experts to confuse you. They are less likely to confuse you if you have a clear idea of an answer before you read the answer choices. Try to predict an answer for the question, and then skim the choices presented and look for your answer. You may have to be a little flexible to recognize it. Your answer may be there dressed up in different words. If you can recognize a paraphrase of your predicted answer, mark it.

It is possible for an answer choice to be both true *and* wrong. The answer that you choose must respond correctly to the question being asked. Simply being true is not enough to make an answer correct. The best answer is always supported by details, inference, or tone.

Using the Process of Elimination

Elimination is the process that most test-takers use for all the questions that they answer. The process of elimination is a good tool. It just shouldn't be the only tool in your box. It is reliable, but slow. It is useful to you as a back-up strategy for the questions where you cannot predict an answer or when you find that your prediction is not listed as a choice.

It can be hard to break the habit of always applying the process of elimination. It is likely that you have developed this habit because past exams have given you too much time to answer questions. The GMAT time constraints are too limiting; you cannot use the process of elimination on most questions and still have time to answer all the questions. Although the process of elimination is a good tool to have in your repertoire, it is worth repeating that it should be used as a backup tool.

If you find that you need to use the process of elimination, be sure to eliminate any answer choices that are clearly incorrect—including answer choices that are outside the scope of the passage, which are very common in this section. For example, an answer choice might be too specific or too general or might have no relation to the content of the passage or the question being asked.

Finally, be careful always to consider all the choices before you confirm your answer, even if your predicted answer is among the choices. The difference between the best answer and the second best answer is sometimes very subtle.

Handling Assumptions and Inferences

You must know the difference between information stated directly in the passage and assumptions and inferences. The reading passages contain factual information about which you may be asked. They also include information about which you will be asked to make an inference.

An *inference* is a conclusion based on what is stated in the passage. You can infer something about a person, place, or thing by reasoning through the descriptive language contained in the reading passage. In other words, the author's language *implies* that something is probably true. Consider the following:

Due to rising energy costs and the increasing level of global competition, today's farmers must employ energy-efficient, high-yield farming techniques.

What can be inferred about farmers of the past from the above statement?

The statement includes information about the effects of *rising* energy costs and the *increasing* level of global competition on today's farmers. A reasonable inference, or conclusion, that can be drawn is that farmers of the past did not have to be as concerned about energy-efficient, high-yield farming techniques as today's farmers must be, because both energy costs and global competition were lower. The information necessary to reach this conclusion is implied in the passage.

An *assumption*, on the other hand, is unstated evidence. It is the missing link in an author's argument. The following is a classic example of a conclusion based on stated evidence and unstated evidence (assumption):

Socrates is a man.

Therefore, Socrates is mortal.

Because you are given that Socrates is a man, the conclusion that Socrates is mortal *must* be based on the assumption that men are mortal.

Socrates is a man.	(Stated evidence)
Men are mortal.	(Unstated evidence)
Therefore, Socrates is mortal.	(Conclusion)

Some of the evidence is not stated, but the final conclusion leads you to the existence of that missing evidence, or assumption.

Common Question Types

The following subsections discuss the types of questions you are likely to encounter on the GMAT Reading Comprehension section. Specific approaches to each question type are also included. You will begin to recognize the different question types as you work through the sample questions and practice exams. The main question types include:

➤ Main idea/primary purpose

➤ Specific detail

➤ Purpose of detail

➤ Conclusion/inference

➤ Extrapolation

➤ Structure

➤ Weakening

➤ Except

Main Idea/Primary Purpose

These types of questions may ask about the main idea of the whole passage or of a specific paragraph. They also ask about the author's point of view or perspective and the intended audience. These questions may also ask you to determine the best title for the passage.

Strategy: Answer these questions according to your understanding of the three components of the main idea, that are mentioned previously (topic, scope, and purpose). It is also worth noting that the incorrect choices are usually either too broad or too narrow. You should eliminate the answer choices that focus on a specific part of the passage and also eliminate the answer choices that are too general and could describe other passages besides the one on which you are working.

Specific Detail

These questions can be as basic as asking you about some fact that is easily found in the passage. Some questions even provide specific line references or text from the passage. Questions that begin "According to the author" or "According to the passage" might be specific detail questions.

Strategy: When you skim the passage, make sure that you establish the structure of the passage and the purpose of each paragraph. If you have a clear idea of how the passage is organized, you should be able to refer quickly to the portion of the passage that contains the answer. Otherwise, use the line or paragraph references in the questions, if they are given. Sometimes the answer choices are paraphrased, so don't just select the answers that contain words that appear in the passage. Make sure that the choice you select is responsive to the question being asked.

Purpose of Detail

These question types ask you to determine the author's purpose in mentioning certain details, as well as how details contained within the passage might support the main idea. Questions that begin "The author mentions...probably in order to" are most likely purpose of detail questions.

Strategy: Making a connection between the supporting details and the main idea of the passage helps you answer these questions correctly. Think of the details as the building blocks of the author's thesis. This should provide you with some insight into why the author included these details in the passage. Refer specifically to any line references given in the questions.

Conclusion/Inference

These question types require you to put together information in the passage and use it as evidence for a conclusion. You have to find language in the passage that leads you to arrive at the inference that the question demands. Questions that begin "According to the author" or "It can be inferred from the passage" might require you to locate clues or evidence that lead you to the answer.

Strategy: Understanding the main idea of the passage or paragraph, and particularly the author's tone, is key for these types of questions. Although you have to do a bit of thinking for these questions, you should be able to find very strong evidence for your answers. If you find yourself creating a long chain of reasoning and including information from outside the passage, stop and reconsider your selection.

Extrapolation

These types of questions ask you to go beyond the passage itself and find answers that are *probably* true based on what you know from the passage. They can be based on the author's tone or on detailed information in the passage. You are often required to reason by analogy or to discern relationships between a situation presented in the passage and other situations that might parallel those in the passage. These questions might begin with "The author anticipates" or "Which of the following best exemplifies...as it is presented in the passage."

Strategy: You need to be sensitive to any clues about the author's tone or attitude and any clues about how the characters in the passage feel. Eliminate any choices that are outside the scope of the passage. As with the inference questions, the GMAT rewards short, strong connections between the passage and the correct answers.

Structure

This type of question might ask you to describe the structure of the passage or how a particular detail or paragraph functions within the passage as a whole. Questions that begin "The last paragraph performs which function" or "Which of the following describes the organization of the passage" are structure questions.

Strategy: You need to recognize the author's purpose in writing the passage and determine how the author develops the main thesis or argument. If the passage is purely informational, for example, the author might simply make a statement followed by some supporting details. On the other hand, the author might offer comparisons between two different theories in order to persuade the reader that one theory is better. Pay attention to both the language and the connotation.

Weakening

These questions require you to select the answer choice that weakens the author's argument. Weakening does not necessarily mean to disprove completely; it merely means to make the conclusion of the argument somewhat less likely. These questions take the form of "Which of the following, if true, would most weaken the author's argument in lines."

Strategy: The best approach to answering these questions correctly is to first make sure that you understand the author's argument or main point. To weaken the author's argument, you should usually attack the author's assumptions (unstated evidence). In some cases, the correct answer actually contradicts a statement made in the passage.

Except

This type of question is often phrased as follows: "The author probably believes all of the following "EXCEPT," or "All of the following are listed in the passage as examples of biodiversity EXCEPT."

Strategy: The best answer in these instances includes information that is *not* directly stated in the passage or *cannot* be inferred from information stated in the passage.

Putting It to Practice

The following section is a simulated GMAT Reading Comprehension passage. Read the directions carefully before you begin to answer the questions. After you select an answer, circle it in the book. Make guesses as necessary. Remember that on the actual computer-adaptive exam, you are required to select an answer before you can move on to the next question. Be sure to read the explanations to help you gain a better understanding of why the correct answer is correct.

Exam Prep Questions

Directions: Each Reading Comprehension question is based on the content of the accompanying passage. Read the passage and choose the best answer from each of the questions that follow. The correct answers refer to information that is stated or implied in the passage:

Although oil and gasoline remain important energy sources, it is natural gas that currently supplies around 25% of America's energy needs. A recent study shows that natural gas use was roughly 22 trillion cubic feet (TCF) annually. Natural gas demand is increasing at phenomenal rates
5 because of its ability to create cleaner fuel for electrical power. Experts predict that annual demand is likely to increase to almost 32 TCF in less than a decade. At a consumption rate of 32 TCF per year, the United States would have only about a five-year supply of natural gas. Known natural gas reserves in North America are quickly becoming exhausted. In
10 the past 30 years, known supplies have dwindled from almost 300 TCF to around 150 TCF.

It is no wonder that natural gas has become a controversial and critical topic of discussion among politicians, business leaders, and consumers. It is apparent that the United States will need to increase imports of natural
15 gas drastically to relieve shortages. One way that economists believe this can be done is by importing liquid natural gas. Experts predict that liquid natural gas imports will increase by almost 500% in a few short years. Currently, the country imports very little liquid natural gas. The process of transporting liquid natural gas is complicated and expensive. This is the
20 most obvious reason why America has been reluctant to choose liquid natural gas over other energy sources. Converting natural gas into liquid natural gas involves cooling natural gas as it is collected to –260° Fahrenheit. This transforms the gas into a liquid. This liquid is then injected into a specially designed vessel for transport. When the liquid
25 natural gas reaches its destination, the liquid is reheated into its original

gaseous state and flowed into a pipeline. Even though new technology has considerably decreased transportation costs for liquid natural gas, it is still often uneconomical. This is especially true for nations with other energy sources.

30 It is a common misconception that there are abundant sources of natural gas. Although liquid natural gas imports continue to increase, the public demand for natural gas increases at an even higher rate. Even though the United State has several facilities that can process liquid natural gas, these facilities are consistently unable to obtain enough liquid 35 natural gas to operate at their fullest capacity. Even when liquid natural gas is obtainable, there is a fear that low natural gas prices in the United States will make liquid natural gas uneconomical. Most business leaders and politicians are reluctant to create new facilities to process liquid natural gas because they are expensive and risky. This limits the capacity to 40 process liquid natural gas even if it becomes more readily available.

The United States also faces competition from Asia in securing liquid natural gas. Competition for liquid natural gas will most likely become even more ferocious as other large countries such as Japan and China become more desperate for fuel sources. Some of the more daring politi-45 cians and business leaders believe that building new liquid natural gas facilities will help companies and consumers take advantage of future increased liquid natural gas imports. Currently, Canada is the largest liquid natural gas supplier for the United States. However, liquid natural gas imports from Canada will decrease considerably in the next decade as 50 Canadian consumption increases and supplies of natural gas dwindle. Therefore, consumers and business leaders should not rely on liquid natural gas to solve America's energy crisis, and consumers should continue to expect high prices as demand grows and supplies decline.

1. The primary purpose of the passage is to

    (A) discuss the benefits of using natural gas over oil or gasoline to produce energy

    (B) educate the public about how natural gas is converted to liquid natural gas

    (C) suggest that there are better ways to convert natural gas into liquid natural gas other than heating and cooling

    (D) evaluate the United States' current situation involving natural gas

    (E) challenge the popular opinion that natural gas is an unreliable source of energy

2. It can be inferred from the passage that liquid natural gas is an undependable resource for the United States because

   (A) there is competition to secure liquid natural gas from other countries

   (B) liquid natural gas is too expensive to produce in large quantities

   (C) there are no operating facilities in the United States to process or receive liquid natural gas

   (D) Canada is the United States' only supplier of liquid natural gas and Canada's supplies are limited

   (E) technology is unable to produce the high temperatures needed to convert liquid natural gas into natural gas

3. According to the passage, which of the following is a reason that the United States is unable to depend on liquid natural gas to solve its energy crisis?

   (A) Politicians and business leaders are unwilling to invest money into creating new liquid natural gas facilities.

   (B) Existing liquid natural gas facilities in the United States are not capable of converting large amounts of liquid natural gas at a time.

   (C) The vessels used to transport liquid natural gas are difficult and expensive to construct.

   (D) Natural gas is always cheaper to obtain than liquid natural gas.

   (E) The United States has no domestic stores of natural gas to convert into liquid natural gas.

4. The author argues which of the following about liquid natural gas?

   (A) Liquid natural gas is an unacceptable substitute for oil and gasoline.

   (B) Liquid natural gas should not be viewed as a plentiful source of natural gas.

   (C) Liquid natural gas carries an increased risk of flammability because of the high temperatures required to heat it.

   (D) Liquid natural gas should be seen as an alternative to oil or gasoline because imports of liquid natural gas are expected to increase 500%.

   (E) Liquid natural gas should be left in its liquid form rather than being reconverted into a gas.

5. It can be inferred from the passage that the author would be most likely to agree with which of the following statements?

(A) Politicians and business leaders should support the production of natural gas because it is the only clean fuel that can be used to produce electricity.

(B) There are other energy resources that are able to produce a cleaner fuel than natural gas or liquid natural gas.

(C) At the current rate of usage, the United States has enough natural gas supplies for only another five years.

(D) Currently, the United States imports far too much liquid natural gas and should increase its importation of natural gas.

(E) Supplies of both liquid natural gas and natural gas are dwindling faster than they can be replaced.

6. The author's attitude toward liquid natural gas can best be described as

(A) unconditionally approving and optimistic

(B) hostile and antagonistic

(C) hopeful and confident

(D) cautious and pragmatic

(E) frustrated and perturbed

Answers to Exam Prep Questions

1. **The best answer is D**. The passage explores the United States'
   dependency on natural gas and discusses ways that the United States
   supplies its consumers with natural gas. This best supports answer
   choice D. Answer choice A is incorrect because the passage does not
   focus on the benefits of using natural gas over oil or gasoline; rather,
   the focus of the passage is on the United States' current position
   regarding the production and use of natural gas. Answer choice B may
   have appeared to be correct because the passage does explain how natural gas is converted into liquid natural gas. However, this is not the
   focus of the passage. Answer choice C is beyond the scope of the passage; although there is a discussion of how natural gas is converted
   into liquid natural gas, there is no suggestion of any better way to
   make the conversion. Answer choice E is incorrect because it is con-
   tradictory to information in the passage. The passage states that
   "Natural gas demand is increasing at phenomenal rates…," which suggests that the popular opinion of natural gas is positive, not negative.

2. **The best answer is A**. The passage states, "The United States also
   faces competition from Asia in securing liquid natural gas.
   Competition for liquid natural gas will most likely become even more
   ferocious as other large countries such as Japan and China become
   more desperate for fuel sources." This best supports answer choice A.
   Answer choice D may have appeared to be correct. However, the passage states that Canada is the largest supplier to the United States, not
   that Canada is the only supplier. Likewise, the other answer choices
   are not supported by the passage.

3. **The best answer is A**. The passage states, "Most business leaders and
   politicians are reluctant to create new facilities to process liquid natural gas because they are expensive and risky. This limits the capacity to
   process liquid natural gas even if it becomes more readily available."
   This best supports answer choice A. Answer choice D may have
   appeared to be correct. The passage does state, "Even when liquid
   natural gas is obtainable, there is a fear that low natural gas prices in
   the United States will make liquid natural gas uneconomical."
   However, the passage does not suggest that natural gas prices are
   always lower than liquid natural gas prices. Answer choice E is incorrect because the passage indicates that there are natural gas reserves in
   the United States, but that they are being quickly depleted. Likewise,
   the other answer choices are not supported by the passage.

4. **The best answer is B**. The passage states, "It is a common misconception that there are abundant sources of natural gas." This best supports answer choice B. According to the passage, natural gas is a popular and important energy source, so it is likely that the author would disagree with answer choice A. Answer choice C is incorrect because nothing in the passage suggests that the temperatures required to convert liquid natural gas into natural gas are too high. Answer choice D may have appeared to be correct because the passage states that liquid natural gas imports will likely increase by 500%. However, the author does not suggest that liquid natural gas or natural gas should be used as a substitute for oil or gasoline. In fact, the author would most likely argue that doing this would cause the United States to run out of natural gas even sooner than otherwise expected. According to the passage, if the natural gas was not converted back into its gaseous state, it could not be used by consumers; therefore, answer choice E is incorrect.

5. **The best answer is E**. The author begins the passage by discussing the shortage of natural gas. At the end of the passage, the author also speaks about the shortage of liquid natural gas. These discussions best support answer choice E. Answer choice A is incorrect because, although the passage indicates that natural gas is a clean fuel, the passage does not suggest that it is the only clean fuel. Likewise, answer choice B is incorrect because the passage does not mention other energy sources that are able to produce cleaner fuel. Answer choice C may have appeared to be correct. However, the passage states that when the United States uses 32 TCF a year, it will most likely have a only five-year supply left. The passage states that currently, the United States consumes 22 TCF annually.

6. **The best answer is D**. The author warns the reader that supplies of natural gas and liquid natural gas are far from endless. The author also points out the difficulties in trying to satisfy natural gas and liquid natural gas demands. The author does not express either anger or hope in this passage. He or she wants only to warn readers about the shortage and practical issues surrounding the production and use of natural gas. The remaining answer choices contain descriptions that are either too positive or too negative.

5

GMAT Quantitative Section

Terms You Need to Know

- ✓ Absolute value
- ✓ Acute angle
- ✓ Adjacent angle
- ✓ Arc
- ✓ Area
- ✓ Associative property
- ✓ Average
- ✓ Base of a triangle
- ✓ Circumference
- ✓ Commutative property
- ✓ Complementary angle
- ✓ Congruent
- ✓ Coordinate plane
- ✓ Denominator
- ✓ Diameter
- ✓ Distributive property
- ✓ Divisible
- ✓ Domain
- ✓ Equilateral triangle
- ✓ Exponent
- ✓ Factor

- ✓ Function
- ✓ Greatest Common Factor (GCF)
- ✓ Hypotenuse
- ✓ Inequality
- ✓ Integer
- ✓ Intersection
- ✓ Isosceles triangle
- ✓ Least Common Multiple (LCM)
- ✓ Line
- ✓ Line segment
- ✓ Median
- ✓ Midpoint
- ✓ Mode
- ✓ Numerator
- ✓ Obtuse angle
- ✓ Parallel
- ✓ Perimeter
- ✓ Percent
- ✓ Point

- ✓ Prime number
- ✓ Proportion
- ✓ Pythagorean theorem
- ✓ Quadrilateral
- ✓ Radius
- ✓ Range
- ✓ Ratio
- ✓ Reciprocal
- ✓ Right angle
- ✓ Sequence
- ✓ Set
- ✓ Similar triangles
- ✓ Slope
- ✓ Square root
- ✓ Standard deviation
- ✓ System of equations
- ✓ Transversal
- ✓ Vertical angle
- ✓ Volume

Concepts You Need to Master

- ✓ Analyzing properties of triangles, polygons, and circles, including perimeter, area, and circumference
- ✓ Calculating averages and determining median and mode
- ✓ Factoring polynomials
- ✓ Identifying properties of parallel and perpendicular lines
- ✓ Identifying relationships between angles in geometric figures

- ✓ Recognizing the sufficiency and relevance of information given to answer a question
- ✓ Simplifying algebraic expressions
- ✓ Solving algebraic equations and inequalities
- ✓ Translating word problems
- ✓ Understanding basic arithmetic operations on real numbers, including integers and fractions
- ✓ Understanding properties of integers
- ✓ Understanding simple coordinate geometry, including using slope and midpoint formulas
- ✓ Working with number sets and sequences

The GMAT Quantitative questions are designed to measure your basic mathematical skills, as well as your ability to reason mathematically. You should be able to solve problems and apply relevant mathematics concepts in arithmetic, algebra, geometry, and data analysis. The GMAT Quantitative Section includes both problem solving and data sufficiency multiple-choice questions. Each question type is covered later in the chapter. We begin with a review of the math concepts tested on the GMAT.

Familiarize yourself with the basic mathematical concepts included in this chapter and be able to apply them to a variety of math problems. Remember that you cannot use a calculator on this section, so you will not be required to perform any elaborate computations, but you should be able to recognize the underlying math concept being tested.

Arithmetic

This book assumes that you have a basic understanding of arithmetic. Therefore, our focus is on reviewing some general concepts and applying those concepts to simulated GMAT questions.

The GMAT Quantitative Sections require you to add, subtract, multiply, and divide whole numbers, fractions, and decimals. When performing these operations, be sure to keep track of negative signs and line up decimal points to eliminate careless mistakes. We include a review of the arithmetic concepts generally tested on the GMAT, along with sample questions:

Understanding Operations Using Whole Numbers, Decimals, and Fractions

The following list includes some simple rules to keep in mind regarding whole numbers, fractions, and decimals:

1. An *integer* is a positive or negative counting number, including zero.

2. *Ordering* is the process of arranging numbers from smallest to greatest or from greatest to smallest. The symbol > is used to represent "greater than," and the symbol < is used to represent "less than." To represent "greater than and equal to," use the symbol ≥; to represent "less than and equal to," use the symbol ≤.

3. The *Commutative Property of Multiplication* can be expressed as $a \times b = b \times a$, or $ab = ba$.

4. The *Distributive Property of Multiplication* can be expressed as
   a(b + c) = ab + ac.

5. The *Associative Property of Multiplication* can be expressed as $(a \times b) \times c = a \times (b \times c)$.

6. The Order of Operations for whole numbers can be remembered by using the acronym **PEMDAS**:

   P: First, do the operations within the *parentheses*, if any.

   E: Next, do the *exponents*, if any.

   M: Next, do the *multiplication*, in order from left to right.

   D: Next, do the *division*, in order from left to right.

   A: Next, do the *addition*, in order from left to right.

   S: Finally, do the *subtraction*, in order from left to right.

   Consider the following example:

   $$\frac{2(5 - 3)2 + 16}{4} =$$

   First, perform the operation inside the parentheses: (5 – 3) = 2

   Next, work with the exponent: $2(2)^2 = 2 \times 4 = 8$

   Next, perform the multiplication: 2(8) = 16

   Now perform the addition: 16 + 16 = 32

   Finally, perform the division: $\frac{32}{4} = 8$

7. When a number is expressed as the product of two or more numbers, it is in *factored form*. *Factors* are all the numbers that will divide evenly into one number. For example, 1, 3, and 9 are factors of 9: 9 ÷ 1 = 9; 9 ÷ 3 = 3; 9 ÷ 9 = 1.

8. A number is called a *multiple* of another number if it can be expressed as the product of that number and a second number. For example, the multiples of 4 are 4, 8, 12, 16, and so on because 4 × 1 = 4, 4 × 2 = 8, 4 × 3 = 12, 4 × 4 = 16, and so on. Consider the following sample question:

   How many multiples of 3 are there between 15 and 87, inclusive?
   (A) 22
   (B) 23
   (C) 24
   (D) 25
   (E) 26

One way to solve this problem is to write every multiple of 3 starting with 15 ($3 \times 5 = 15$, $3 \times 6 = 18$, and so on). However, this is time consuming and leaves opportunity for error. A better way to solve this problem is to recognize that $3 \times 5 = 15$ and $3 \times 29 = 87$; the number of multiples of 3 between 15 and 87, inclusive, is the same as the number of integers between 5 and 29, inclusive, which is 25.

9. The *Greatest Common Factor* (GCF) is the largest number that will divide evenly into any two or more numbers. *The Least Common Multiple* (LCM) is the smallest number that any two or more numbers will divide into evenly. For example, the GCF of 24 and 36 is 12 because 12 is the largest number that will divide evenly into both 24 and 36. The LCM of 24 and 36 is 72 because 72 is the smallest number that both 24 and 36 will divide into evenly.

10. Multiplying and dividing both the numerator and the denominator of a fraction by the same nonzero number will result in an *equivalent fraction*. For example, $\frac{1}{4} \times \frac{3}{3} = \frac{3}{12}$, which can be reduced to $\frac{1}{4}$. This works because any nonzero number divided by itself is always equal to 1.

11. When multiplying fractions, multiply the numerators to get the numerator of the product, and multiply the denominators to get the denominator of the product. For example, $\frac{1}{4} \times \frac{5}{6} = \frac{5}{24}$.

12. To divide fractions, multiply the first fraction by the *reciprocal* of the second fraction. In mathematics, the reciprocal of any number is the number that, when multiplied by the first number, will yield a product of 1. For example: The reciprocal of $\frac{1}{4}$ is $\frac{4}{1}$ because $\frac{1}{4} \times \frac{4}{1} = 1$. So, $\frac{1}{3} \div \frac{1}{4} = \frac{1}{3} \times \frac{4}{1}$, which equals $\frac{4}{3}$. This concept might be tested on the GMAT with questions similar to the following:

➤ Which of the following pairs are reciprocals of each other?

    I. $\frac{1}{5}$ and $-\frac{1}{5}$

    II. $\frac{\sqrt{5}}{5}$ and $\sqrt{5}$

    III. 5 and $\frac{1}{5}$

    IV. $\sqrt{5}$ and 5

(A) I only

(B) III only

(C) I and II

(D) II and III

(E) III and IV

Two numbers are reciprocals only when their product equals one.

Because $\frac{1}{5} \times -\frac{1}{5} = -\frac{1}{25}$ and $\sqrt{5} \times 5$ is approximately 11, answer

choices A, C, and E can be eliminated. Because $\frac{\sqrt{5}}{5} \times \sqrt{5} = \frac{5}{5} = 1$
and

$5(\frac{1}{5}) = \frac{5}{5} = 1$, D is the correct answer choice.

➤ $\dfrac{50 - 2(12 \div 3)}{\frac{1}{2}} =$

(A) 9

(B) 11

(C) 22

(D) 42

(E) 84

First, perform the calculations in the numerator (remember the order of operations!)

$50 - 2(4) =$

$50 - 8 = 42$

The next step in solving this problem is to get rid of the fraction in the denominator. To do this, multiply the entire fraction by the reciprocal of the fraction in the denominator:

$\dfrac{42}{\frac{1}{2}} \times \dfrac{2}{1} =$

$(42)(2) = 84$

13. When adding and subtracting like fractions (fractions with the same denominator), add or subtract the numerators and write the sum or difference over the denominator. So, $\frac{1}{8} + \frac{2}{8} = \frac{3}{8}$, and $\frac{4}{7} - \frac{2}{7} = \frac{2}{7}$.

14. When adding or subtracting unlike fractions, first find the *Least Common Denominator* (LCD). The LCD is the smallest number that all of the denominators will divide into evenly. For example, to add $\frac{3}{4}$ and $\frac{5}{6}$, find the smallest number that both 4 and 6 will divide into evenly. That number is 12, so the LCD of 4 and 6 is 12. Multiply $\frac{3}{4}$ by $\frac{3}{3}$ to get $\frac{9}{12}$, and multiply $\frac{5}{6}$ by $\frac{2}{2}$ to get $\frac{10}{12}$. Now add the fractions: $\frac{9}{12} + \frac{10}{12} = \frac{19}{12}$, which can be simplified to $1\frac{7}{12}$.

15. To convert a mixed number into an *improper fraction*, first multiply the whole number by the denominator, add the result to the numerator, and place that quantity over the denominator. For example: $1\frac{7}{12} = (1 \times 12) + \frac{7}{12}$, or $\frac{19}{12}$.

16. When converting a fraction to a decimal, divide the numerator by the denominator. For example, $\frac{3}{4} = 3 \div 4$, or .75.

17. *Place value* refers to the value of a digit in a number relative to its position. Starting from the left of the decimal point, the values of the digits are ones, tens, hundreds, and so on. Starting to the right of the decimal point, the values of the digits are tenths, hundredths, thousandths, and so on.

Understanding Squares and Square Roots

In mathematics, a square is the product of any number multiplied by itself, and is expressed as $a^2 = n$. A square root is written as $\sqrt{n}$, and is the non-negative value a that fulfills the expression $a^2 = n$. For example, the square root of 25 would be written as $\sqrt{25}$. The square root of 25 is 5, and 5-squared, or 5^2, equals 5×5, or 25. A number is considered a perfect square when the square root of that number is a whole number. So, 25 is a perfect square because the square root of 25 is 5, which is a whole number.

When you square a fraction, simply calculate the squares of both the numerator and the denominator, as follows:

➤ $(\frac{3}{5})^2 =$

➤ $\frac{3}{5} \times \frac{3}{5} = \frac{9}{25}$

Consider the following simulated GMAT question:

When $a = -2$, what is the value of $-4a^2$?

(A) −16
(B) −8
(C) 16
(D) 32
(E) 64

To solve this problem, first substitute −2 for a and then square −2. Remember that a negative number squared results in a positive number. Therefore, $-2^2 = 4$. Now, simply multiply -4×4 to get −16.

Understanding Exponents

When a whole number is multiplied by itself, the number of times it is multiplied is referred to as the *exponent*. As shown previously with square roots, the exponent of 5^2 is 2, and it signifies 5×5. Any number can be raised to any exponential value.

$7^6 = 7 \times 7 \times 7 \times 7 \times 7 \times 7 = 117,649$.

Remember that when you multiply a negative number by a negative number, the result will be a positive number. When you multiply a negative number by a positive number, the result will be a negative number. These rules should be applied when working with exponents, too:

➤ $-3^2 = -3 \times -3$

➤ $-3 \times -3 = 9$

➤ $-3^3 = -3 \times -3 \times -3$

➤ $(-3 \times -3) = 9$

➤ $9 \times -3 = -27$

Remember the Order of Operations mentioned previously, especially when you are working with negative numbers. For example, $-4^2 = 16$, but $-(4^2) = -16$ because you must perform the operation within the parentheses first.

The basic rules of exponents follow:

➤ $a^m \times a^n = a^{(m+n)}$

➤ $(a^m)^n = a^{mn}$

➤ $(ab)^m = a^m \times b^m$

➤ $\left[\dfrac{a}{b}\right]^m = \dfrac{a^m}{b^m}$

➤ $a^0 = 1$, when $a \neq 0$

➤ $a^{-m} = \dfrac{1}{am}$, when $a \neq 0$

➤ $\dfrac{a}{b}^{-m} = ab^m$, when $b \neq 0$

Consider the following simulated GMAT questions:

1. What is the value of $-2x^3$ if x equals -2?

    (A) 12

    (B) −12

    (C) 16

    (D) −16

    (E) 64

The PEMDAS order of operations must be followed to obtain the correct answer for this problem, with exponents being solved before multiplication. Because $x = -2$, the value of $-2x^3$ is $-2(-2)^3 = -2(-8) = 16$.

2. $(0.1^2)^3 =$

    (A) .001

    (B) .0001

    (C) .00001

    (D) .000001

    (E) .0000001

In multiplying exponents, $(a^m)^n = a^{m \times n}$, which in this case yields $0.1^{2 \times 3} = 0.1^6$. $0.1 \times 0.1 \times 0.1 \times 0.1 \times 0.1 \times 0.1 = .000001$. Thus, the correct answer is D.

Understanding Ratios and Proportions

A *ratio* is the relationship between two quantities expressed as one divided by the other. For example:

Jordan works 2 hours for every 3 hours that Al works. This can be expressed as $\frac{2}{3}$ or 2:3, and is known as a part-to-part ratio. If you compared the number of hours that Jordan works in one week to the total number of hours that every employee works in one week, that would be a part-to-whole ratio.

A *proportion* is an equation in which two ratios are set equal to each other. For example:

Jordan worked 30 hours in one week and earned $480. If he received the same hourly rate the next week, how much would he earn for working 25 hours that week?

➤ $\frac{480}{30} = \frac{x}{25}$;cross-multiply and solve for x.

➤ $30x = 12{,}000$

➤ $x = 400$

Jordan would earn $400 that week.

Consider the following simulated GMAT question:

> Three business partners, R, S, and T, agree to divide their total profit for one year in the ratios 3:4:5, respectively. If R's share was $5,000, what was the total profit of the business partners for the year?
> (A) $15,000
> (B) $20,000
> (C) $60,000
> (D) $125,000
> (E) $200,000

To solve this problem, first recognize that the whole is equal to the sum of the parts: $3 + 4 + 5 = 12$. Therefore, the ratio of R's share of the profits is 3:12, or 1:4. R's share ($5,000) is equivalent to $\frac{1}{4}$ of the total profit (x), Set up a proportion and solve for x:

➤ $\frac{\$5{,}000}{x} = \frac{1}{4}$

➤ $x = \$20{,}000$

Understanding Percent and Percentages

A *percent* is a fraction whose denominator is 100. The fraction $\frac{55}{100}$ is equal to 55%. *Percentage* problems often deal with calculating an increase or a decrease in number or price. Consider the following example:

A jacket that originally sells for $90 is on sale for 30% off. What is the sale price of the jacket (not including tax)?

➤ 30% of $90 =

➤ $\frac{30}{100} \times \$90 =$

➤ $.30 \times \$90 = \$27$

The discount is equal to $27, but the question asked for the sale price. Therefore, you must subtract $27 from $90 to get $63.

You could also more quickly solve a problem like this by recognizing that, if the jacket is 30% off of the regular price, the sale price must be equal to 100% – 30%, or 70% of the original price.

➤ 70% of $90 =

➤ $\frac{70}{100} \times \$90 =$

➤ $.70 \times \$90 = \$63$

 Remember to answer the question that is asked. You can be certain that $27 would have been an answer choice if the above problem had appeared on your test, but it is not the correct answer!

Understanding Number Lines and Sequences

A *number line* is a geometric representation of the relationships between numbers, including integers, fractions, and decimals. The numbers on a number line always increase as you move to the right and decrease when you move to the left. Number line questions typically require you to determine the relationships among certain numbers on the line. Consider the following simulated GMAT question:

On the number line, if $a > b$, if c is halfway between a and b, and if d is halfway between c and b, $\frac{b\text{-}d}{d\text{-}a}$ =

(A) $\frac{1}{4}$

(B) $\frac{1}{3}$

(C) $\frac{4}{3}$

(D) 3

(E) 4

To solve this problem, draw a number line and indicate the relative positions of points a, b, c, and d:

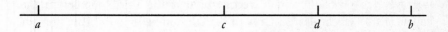

Because the positions are relative to each other, you can pick any number for each of the variables as long as the numbers meet the criteria. For example, when $a = 2$, $b = 4$, $c = 3$, and $d = 3\frac{1}{2}$. Now plug these values into the fraction:

➤ $\frac{b\text{-}d}{d\text{-}a}$ =

➤ Numerator: $4 - 3\frac{1}{2} = \frac{1}{2}$

➤ Denominator: $3\frac{1}{2} - 2 = 1\frac{1}{2}$, or $\frac{3}{2}$

To get rid of the fraction in the denominator, multiply the numerator by the reciprocal of the fraction in the denominator:

➤ $\frac{1}{2} \times \frac{2}{3} = \frac{2}{6} = \frac{1}{3}$, answer choice B.

 Remember that the distance between points on the number line does not always have to be measured in whole units. Sometimes the distance between points is a fraction of a number.

An *arithmetic sequence* is one in which the difference between consecutive terms is the same. For example, 2, 4, 6, 8..., is an arithmetic sequence where 2 is the constant difference. In an arithmetic sequence, the nth term can be found using the formula $a_n = a_1 + (n - 1)d$, where d is the common difference.

A *geometric sequence* is one in which the ratio between two terms is constant. For example, $\frac{1}{2}$, 1, 2, 4, 8..., is a geometric sequence where 2 is the constant ratio. With geometric sequences, you can find the *n*th term using the formula $a_n = a_1(r)^{n-1}$, where *r* is the constant ratio.

Typically, if you can identify the pattern or the relationship between the numbers, you will be able to answer the question. The following is an example of a sequence question similar to one you might find on the GMAT:

$$0,1,2,0,1,2,...$$

The numbers 0, 1, and 2 repeat in a sequence, as shown. If this pattern continues, what will be the sum of the 9th and 12th numbers in the sequence?

To solve this problem, simply recognize that the third number in the sequence is 2, which means that both the 9th number and the 12th number in the sequence will also be 2. Therefore, the sum of the 9th and 12th numbers is 2 + 2, or 4.

Understanding Absolute Value

The *absolute value* of a number is indicated by placing that number inside two vertical lines. For example, the absolute value of 10 is written as follows: | 10 |. Absolute value can be defined as the numerical value of a real number without regard to its sign. This means that the absolute value of 10, | 10 |, is the same as the absolute value of –10, | –10 | because they both equal 10. Think of it as the distance from –10 to 0 on the number line, and the distance from 0 to 10 on the number line...both distances equal 10 units (see Figure 5.1).

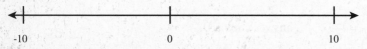

-10   0   10

Figure 5.1 Demonstrating absolute value.

Note the following example:

➤ | 3 – 5 | =

➤ | –2 | = 2

Consider this simulated GMAT question:

If a and b are integers and $b = |a + 3| + |4 - a|$, does $b = 7$?

(1) $a < 4$

(2) $a > -3$

This is a data sufficiency problem, which requires you to determine whether the information in statements (1) and/or (2) is sufficient to answer the question. Substitute the information in statement (1) into the given equation:

➤ Set a equal to 3: $b = |3 + 3| + |4 - 3|$

➤ $b = |6| + |1| = 7$

However, when $a = -4$, $b = |-4 + 3| + |4 - (-4)|$, or $|-1| + |8|$, which is equivalent to $1 + 8$, or 9. This means that the information in statement (1) alone is not sufficient to answer the question.

Now substitute the information in statement (2) into the given equation. You already know that when $a = 3$, $b = 7$.

➤ Set a equal to 5: $b = |5 + 3| + |4 - 5|$

➤ $b = |8| + |-1|$, which is equivalent to $8 + 1$, or 9.

This means that the information in statement (2) alone is not sufficient to answer the question. However, if you take both statements together, you can determine values of a for which $b = 7$; so the information in both statements together is sufficient to answer the question.

Understanding Mean, Median, and Mode

The *arithmetic mean* refers to the *average* of a set of values. For example, if a student received grades of 80%, 90%, and 95% on three tests, the average test grade is 80 + 90 + 95 divided by 3. The *median* is the middle value of an ordered list. If the list contains an even number of values, the median is simply the average of the two middle values. It is important to put the values in either ascending or descending order before selecting the median. The *mode* is the value or values that appear the greatest number of times in a list of values. Consider the following question:

A poll reveals that the average (arithmetic mean) income of 7 households is $30,000. If 4 of the households have an average income of $40,000 each, what is the average income of the other 3 households?

(A) $10,000

(B) $12,500

(C) $30,000

(D) $42,500

(E) $70,000

To calculate the average income, divide the number of households (7) by the total income. Because 4 of the households have an average income of $40,000, you know that the total income is at least 4(40,000), or $160,000. Set the average income of each of the remaining households at x; now the total income of the 7 households is $160,000 + 4x$. Set up the following equation and solve for x:

➤ $\dfrac{\$160{,}000 + 4x}{7} = \$30{,}000$

➤ $\$160{,}000 + 4x = \$210{,}000$

➤ $4x = \$50{,}000$

➤ $x = \$12{,}500$

Algebra

This book assumes that you have a basic understanding of algebra. Our focus will be on reviewing some general concepts and applying those concepts to questions that might appear on the GMAT.

Understanding Linear Equations with One Variable

In a *linear equation* with one variable, the variable cannot have an exponent or be in the denominator of a fraction. An example of a linear equation is $2x + 13 = 43$. The GMAT will most likely require you to solve for x in that equation. Do this by isolating x on the left side of the equation, as follows:

➤ $2x + 13 = 43$

➤ $2x = 43 - 13$

➤ $2x = 30$

➤ $x = \dfrac{30}{2}$, or 15.

Understanding Systems of Equations

A system of equations refers to a number of equations with an equal number of variables. To solve a system of equations you must find the values of the variables that make both equations true at the same time.

The two most common ways to solve systems of equations are the Substitution method and the Addition-Subtraction method. In the Substitution method, simply solve the first equation for one of the variables and substitute the result into the second equation wherever that variable appears. This method is generally suitable when either one or both of the variables does not have a coefficient.

On the GMAT, a system of equations generally take the form of two linear equations with two variables. The following is an example of a system of equations, solved using the Addition-Subtraction method:

➤ $4x + 5y = 21$

➤ $5x + 10y = 30$

With the Addition-Subtraction method, the first step will be to make one set of values—either the x-values or the y-values in this example—cancel the other out. To do this, make the coefficient of one of the variables in one of the equations negative. In the preceding system you can see it will be easier to work with the y-values ($5y$ and $10y$) because 5 is a factor of 10. Therefore, you can multiply each element in the first equation by -2 so that the y values cancel out, as shown in the following steps:

➤ $-2(4x) + -2(5y) = -2(21)$

➤ $-8x - 10y = -42$

The first equation is now $-8x - 10y = -42$, which is equivalent to the original first equation because you did the same thing to each term. Now, you can add the like terms in each equation:

➤ $(-8x + 5x) = -3x$

➤ $(-10y + 10y) = 0$

➤ $-42 + 30 = -12$

➤ $3x = -12$

Notice that the two y-terms cancel each other out. Solving for x, you get $x = 4$. Now, choose one of the original two equations, plug 4 in for x, and solve for y:

➤ $4(4) + 5y = 21$

➤ $16 + 5y = 21$

➤ $5y = 5$

➤ $y = 1$

The solutions for the system of equations are $x = 4$ and $y = 1$, which means that when $x = 4$ and $y = 1$, both equations will be true.

Consider the following simulated GMAT question:

If $a = 1 + 3c$ and $b = 2c - 1$, for what value of c does $a = b$?

(A) -2

(B) -1

(C) 0

(D) 2

(E) 3

In this system of equations, you are looking for the value of c that makes a equal to b, so set the expressions for a and b equal to each other and solve for c, as follows:

➤ $1 + 3c = 2c - 1$

➤ $3c = 2c - 2$

➤ $c = -2$

Understanding Polynomial Operations and Factoring Simple Quadratic Expressions

A *polynomial* is the sum or difference of expressions such as $2x^2$ and $14x$. The most common polynomial takes the form of a *simple quadratic expression*, such as: $2x^2 + 14x + 8$, with the terms in decreasing order. The standard form of a simple quadratic expression is $ax^2 + bx + c$, where a, b, and c are whole numbers. When the terms include both a number and a variable, such as x, the number is called the *coefficient*. For example, in the expression $2x$, 2 is the coefficient of x.

The GMAT will often require you to evaluate, or solve, a polynomial by substituting a given value for the variable.

For example: If $x = -2$, what is the value of $2x^2 + 14x + 8 = ?$

➤ $2(-2)^2 + 14(-2) + 8 =$

➤ $2(-2 \times -2) + 14(-2) + 8$

➤ $2(4) + (-28) + 8 =$

➤ $8 - 28 + 8 = -12$

You will also be required to add, subtract, multiply, and divide polynomials. To add or subtract polynomials, simply combine like terms, as in the following examples:

$(2x^2 + 14x + 8) + (3x^2 + 5x + 32) = 5x^2 + 19x + 40$

Add the like terms:

➤ $2x^2 + 3x^2 = 5x^2$

➤ $14x + 5x = 19x$

➤ $8 + 32 = 40$

The same steps apply when subtracting polynomials:

$(8x^2 + 11x + 23) - (7x^2 + 3x + 13) = x^2 + 8x + 10$

Add like terms:

➤ $8x^2 - 7x^2 = x^2$

➤ $11x - 3x = 8x$

➤ $23 - 13 = 10$

To multiply polynomials, use the *Distributive Property* to multiply each term of one polynomial by each term of the other polynomial. Following are some examples:

$(3x)(x^2 + 4x - 2) = (3x^3 + 12x^2 - 6x)$

Let's break this example down:

➤ $3x \times x^2 = 3x^3$

➤ $3x \times 4x = 12x^2$

➤ $3x \times -2 = -6x$

Remember the *FOIL* method for problems like the one that follows. In the FOIL method, multiply the first terms of each polynomial, and then multiply the outside terms, and then multiply the inside terms, and finally multiply the last terms. Consider this question:

If $(2x + 5)(x - 3) = ax^2 + bx + c$ for all values of x, what is the value of b?

To solve this problem, apply the FOIL method:

➤ Multiply the *F*irst terms: $(2x)(x) = 2x^2$

➤ Multiply the *O*utside terms: $(2x)(-3) = -6x$

➤ Multiply the *I*nside terms: $(5)(x) = 5x$

➤ Multiply the *L*ast terms: $(5)(-3) = -15$

Now put the terms in decreasing order:

➤ $2x^2 + (-6x) + 5x + (-15) =$

➤ $2x^2 - x - 15$

Therefore, because the middle term has a coefficient of -1, the value of b is -1.

You may also be asked to find the factors or *solution sets* of certain simple quadratic expressions. A factor or solution set takes the form, $(x \pm$ some number$)$. Simple quadratic expressions will usually have 2 of these factors or solution sets. The GMAT might require you to calculate the values of the solution sets. The following example shows you how to work through these problem types:

If $(2x + 5)(x - 3) = 0$, what are all the possible values of x?

Set both elements of the equation equal to zero:

➤ $(2x + 5) = 0$

➤ $(x - 3) = 0$

Now solve for x:

➤ $2x + 5 = 0$

➤ $2x + 5 - 5 = 0 - 5$

➤ $2x = -5$

➤ $x = -\dfrac{5}{2}$

and

➤ $x - 3 = 0$

➤ $x - 3 + 3 = 0 + 3$

➤ $x = 3$

The possible values of x are $-\dfrac{5}{2}$ and 3.

Following are some general factoring rules that might prove useful for answering GMAT quantitative questions:

➤ Finding the difference between two squares: $a^2 - b^2 = (a + b)(a - b)$

➤ Finding common factors, such as: $x^2 - 2x = x(x + 2)$

➤ Factoring quadratic equations, such as: $x^2 + 2x - 8 = (x + 4)(x - 2)$

The GMAT might ask you to solve one variable in terms of another variable. You may not be able to find a specific numerical value for the variables, but generally you won't need to. Your job will be to manipulate the given expression so that you can isolate one variable on one side of the equation.

Understanding Linear Inequalities with One Variable

Linear inequalities with one variable are solved in almost the same manner as linear equations with one variable, by isolating the variable on one side of the inequality. Remember, though, that when multiplying both sides of an inequality by a negative number, the direction of the sign must be reversed, as follows:

If $3x + 4 > 5x + 1$, $x =$

First, isolate x on one side of the inequality.

➤ $3x - 5x > 1 - 4$

➤ $-2x > -3$

Because you have to divide both sides by -2, remember to reverse the inequality sign.

$x < \dfrac{3}{2}$

The GMAT might test inequalities in the following way:

> Alan's school is 10 miles from his home. He travels 4 miles from school to baseball practice and then 2 miles to the library. If he is then x miles from home, what is the range of possible values for x?
>
> (A) $2 \leq x > 10$
> (B) $4 \leq x > 10$
> (C) $4 \leq x > 12$
> (D) $4 \leq x > 16$
> (E) $10 \leq x > 16$

This problem requires you to find the minimum and maximum values for x. The value of x will be greatest if the practice field and the school are between Alan's house and the library. In other words, $x = 10 + 4 + 2$, or 16 miles. Therefore, you can eliminate answer choices A, B, and C. The value of x will be least if the practice field and the library are between Alan's home and the school. In other words, $x = 10 - 6$, or 4. Answer choice D is correct.

 Remember that when you multiply or divide both sides of an inequality by a negative number, you must reverse the direction of the inequality. This applies to operations involving the greater than or equal to symbol ($\geq$) and the less than or equal to symbol ($\leq$) as well.

Understanding Functions

A *function* is a set of ordered pairs in which no two of the ordered pairs has the same x-value. In a function, each input (x-value) has exactly one output (y-value). An example of this relationship is $y = x^2$. Here, y is a function of x because for any value of x, there is exactly one value of y. For example, when x = either 4 or –4, y equals 16. However, x is not a function of y because for certain values of y, there is more than one value of x, as we just showed. The *domain* of a function refers to the x-values, and the *range* of a function refers to the y-values, or the $f(x)$ values. If the values in the domain correspond to more than one value in the range, the relation is not a function.

For example: Let the function f be defined by $f(x) = x^2 - (3x)$. What is the value of $f(5)$?

Solve this problem by substituting 5 for x wherever x appears in the function:

➤ $f(x) = x^2 - 3x$

➤ $f(5) = (5)^2 - (3)(5)$

➤ $f(5) = 25 - 15$

➤ $f(5) = 10$

In this example, whenever $x = 5$, $f(5) = 10$.

Understanding Simple Probability

Probability is used to measure how likely an event is to occur. It is always between 0 and 1; an event that will definitely not occur has a probability of 0, whereas an event that will certainly occur has a probability of 1.

To determine probability, divide the number of outcomes that fit the conditions of an event by the total number of outcomes. Take the following example:

The chance of getting heads when flipping a coin is 1 out of 2, or $\frac{1}{2}$. There are 2 possible outcomes (heads or tails) but only 1 outcome (heads) that fits the conditions of the event. Therefore, the probability of the coin toss resulting in heads is $\frac{1}{2}$ or .5.

When two events are *independent*, meaning the outcome of one event does not affect the other, you can calculate the probability of both occurring by multiplying the probabilities of each of the events together. For example

The probability of flipping a coin and getting three heads in a row would be $\frac{1}{2} \times \frac{1}{2} \times \frac{1}{2}$, or $\frac{1}{8}$.

Consider the following simulated GMAT question:

> A management team is composed of w women and m men. If 4 women and 3 men are added to the team, and if one person is selected at random from the enlarged team to make a presentation, the probability that a woman is selected can be represented by
>
> (A) $\dfrac{w}{m}$
>
> (B) $\dfrac{w}{w+4}$
>
> (C) $\dfrac{(w+4)}{(m+3)}$
>
> (D) $\dfrac{(w+4)}{(w+m+3)}$
>
> (E) $\dfrac{(w+4)}{(w+m+7)}$

Before the addition of the new members, the management team had a total of $w + m$ members. With the addition of the new members, the total number of members is $w + 4 + m + 3$, or $w + m + 7$ members. The probability that a woman will be selected is the number of women $(w + 4)$ over the total number of team members $(w + m + 7)$: $\dfrac{(w+4)}{(w+m+7)}$.

Geometry

This book assumes you have a basic understanding of both coordinate geometry and plane geometry. The focus will be on reviewing some general concepts and applying those concepts to simulated GMAT questions.

Understanding the Coordinate Plane

The xy-coordinate plane has four separate quadrants, as shown in Figure 5.2.

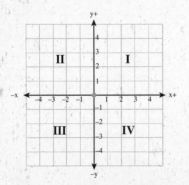

Figure 5.2 The xy-coordinate plane.

The x-coordinates in Quadrants I and IV will be positive, and the x-coordinates in Quadrants II and III will be negative. The y-coordinates in Quadrants I and II will be positive, and the y-coordinates in Quadrants III and IV will be negative.

These concepts might be test on the GMAT in the following way:

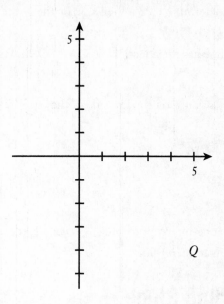

In the figure, the coordinates of point Q are

(A) $(-5, -4)$
(B) $(-4, 5)$
(C) $(4, -5)$
(D) $(5, -4)$
(E) $(5, 4)$

To answer this question, first recognize that point Q is in Quadrant IV, which means that the x-coordinate will be positive and the y-coordinate will be negative. You can eliminate answer choices A and B because the x-coordinates are negative, and you can eliminate answer choice E because the y-coordinate is positive. You are now left with answer choices C and D. Based on the figure, the x-coordinate of point Q is 5, which means that answer choice D must be correct.

Understanding the Equation of a Line

The GMAT will include questions concerning the *slope-intercept* form of a line, which is expressed as $y = mx + b$, where m is the slope of the line and b is the y-intercept (that is, the point at which the graph of the line crosses the y-axis). You might be required to put the equation of a line into the slope-intercept form to determine either the slope or the y-intercept of a line, as follows:

In the xy-plane, a line has the equation $3x + 7y - 16 = 0$. What is the slope of the line?

The first step is to isolate y on the left side of the equation:

➤ $3x + 7y - 16 = 0$

➤ $3x - 3x + 7y - 16 + 16 = 0 - 3x + 16$

➤ $7y = -3x + 16$

➤ $y = -\dfrac{3}{7}x + \dfrac{16}{7}$

According to the slope-intercept formula, $y = mx + b$, the slope of the line is $-\dfrac{3}{7}$ because $-\dfrac{3}{7}$ is in the m slot.

Understanding Slope

The *slope* of a line is commonly defined as "rise over run," and is a value that is calculated by taking the change in y-coordinates divided by the change in x-coordinates from two given points on a line. The formula for slope is

$$m = \frac{(y_2 - y_1)}{(x_2 - x_1)}$$

where (x_1, y_1) and (x_2, y_2) are the two given points. For example, if you are given (3,2) and (5,6) as two points on a line, the slope would be

$$m = \frac{(6-2)}{(5-3)} = \frac{4}{2} = 2$$

With a *positive slope*, the graph of the line goes up and to the right. With a *negative slope*, the graph of the line goes down and to the right. A horizontal line has a slope of 0, and a vertical line has an undefined slope (see Figure 5.3).

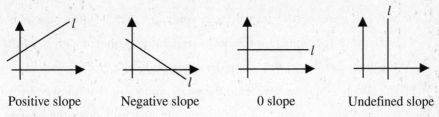

| Positive slope | Negative slope | 0 slope | Undefined slope |

Figure 5.3 Directions of slopes.

Understanding Parallel and Perpendicular Lines

Two lines are parallel if they lie in the same plane and never intersect. Two lines are perpendicular if they intersect at right angles. Figure 5.5 demonstrates this concept. Note that in the figure, the two parallel lines (*x*) intersect a third, perpendicular line to form two right angles.

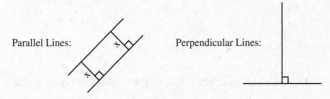

Parallel Lines: Perpendicular Lines:

Figure 5.4 Perpendicular and parallel lines.

This concept is important for GMAT quantitative questions such as the following:

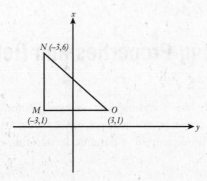

In the figure, if *MO* and *MN* are parallel to the *x* and *y* axes, respectively, what is the area of triangle *MNO*?

The area of a triangle is $\frac{1}{2}(bh)$. Because you know that *MO* (the base, *b*) is parallel to the *x*-axis, you know that it is a straight line segment with a length of 6 (the distance from −3 to 3 along the *x*-axis). Likewise, because you know that *MN* (the height, *b*) is parallel to the *y*-axis, you know that it is a straight line segment with a length of 5 (the distance from 1 to 6 along the *y*-axis). Therefore, the area of triangle *MNO* is $\frac{1}{2}$ (6 × 5), or 15.

Understanding Distance and Midpoint Formulas

To find the distance between two points on a coordinate graph, use the formula $\sqrt{([x_2 - x_1]^2 + [y_2 - y_1]^2)}$, where (x_1, y_1) and (x_2, y_2) are the two given points. For instance, the distance between (3,2) and (7,6) is calculated as follows:

➤ $\sqrt{([7-3]^2 + [6-2]^2)}$ =

➤ $\sqrt{(16+16)}$ = $\sqrt{32}$

➤ $\overline{(16)(2)}$ = $4\sqrt{2}$

To find the midpoint of a line segment given two endpoints, use the formula

$$\left(\frac{[x_1 + x_2]}{2} , \frac{[y_1 + y_2]}{2} \right)$$

For example, the midpoint between (5,4) and (9,2) is

$$\left(\frac{[5+9]}{2} , \frac{[4+2]}{2} \right), \text{ or } (7,3)$$

Understanding Properties and Relations of Plane Figures

Plane figures include *circles* and *polygons*—closed plane figures bounded by three or more line segments—such as *triangles*, *rectangles*, *squares*, and other *parallelograms*. This book assumes a basic understanding of the properties of these figures.

Triangles

A *triangle* is a polygon with three sides and three angles. If the measure of all three angles in the triangle are the same, and all three sides of the triangle are the same length, the triangle is an *equilateral triangle*. If the measure of two angles and two sides of the triangle are the same the triangle is an *isosceles triangle*. A triangle in which none of the sides are the same is called a *scalene triangle*.

The sum of the *interior angles* in a triangle is always 180°. If the measure of one of the angles in the triangle is 90° (a right angle), the triangle is a *right triangle*, as shown in Figure 5.5.

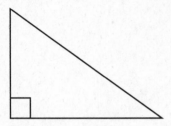

Figure 5.5   A right triangle.

Some right triangles have unique relationships between the angles and the lengths of the sides. These are called *special right triangles* (see Figure 5.6) .

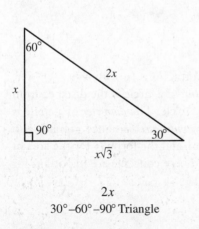
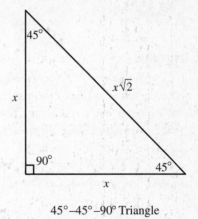

Figure 5.6   Special right triangles.

The perimeter of a triangle is the sum of the lengths of the sides. The area of a triangle is calculated by using the formula A = $\frac{1}{2}$ (base)(height). For any right triangle, the *Pythagorean theorem* states that $a^2 + b^2 = c^2$, where *a* and *b* are legs (sides) and *c* is the hypotenuse. Solve the following problem using the Pythagorean theorem:

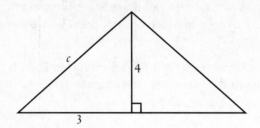

What is the value of *c* in the figure?

➤ $a^2 + b^2 = c^2$

➤ $3^2 + 4^2 = c^2$

➤ $9 + 16 = c^2$

➤ $25 = c^2$

➤ $5 = c$

 Similar triangles always have the same shape, and each corresponding pair of angles has the same measure. The lengths of the pairs of corresponding sides that form the angles are proportional.

Circles

The *equation of a circle* centered at the point (*h*,*k*) is $(x - h)^2 + (y - k)^2 = r^2$, where *r* is the radius of the circle. The *radius* of a circle is the distance from the center of the circle to any point on the circle. The *diameter* of a circle is twice the radius. The formula for the *circumference* (distance around, also called *perimeter*) of a circle is $C = 2\pi r$, or πd, and the formula for the area of a circle is $A = \pi r^2$. A circle contains 360°. These concepts are important for GMAT questions such as the following:

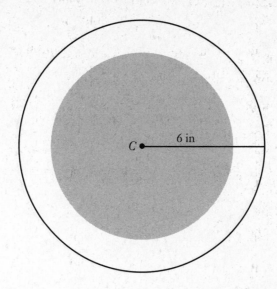

1. The figure shows a circular pendant, with its center at C, that contains a gem inlay (the shaded region) with a radius of 4 inches. What is the area of the pendant surrounding the gem inlay, in square inches?

(A) 12π
(B) 16π
(C) 20π
(D) 24π
(E) 36π

You are given that the radius of the shaded region is 4 inches, which means that the area of the shaded region must be 16π. According to the figure, the radius of the entire pendant is 6, which means that the area of the entire pendant must be 36π. Therefore, the area of the pendant surrounding the gem inlay (the shaded region) must be $36\pi - 16\pi$, or 20π.

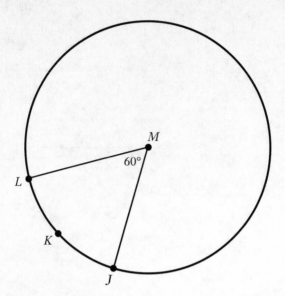

2. If the circle has a center M and circumference 24π, the perimeter of sector $JKLM$ is

(A) $4\pi + 8$

(B) $4\pi + 24$

(C) $8\pi + 8$

(D) $8\pi + 12$

(E) $8\pi + 24$

The perimeter of any object is the distance around that object. The first step in solving this problem is to determine the length of the line segments JM and LM. These segments are radii of the circle, so calculate the length of the radius. You are given that the circumference of the circle is 24π, which means that the radius must be 12. So, at this point, you know that the perimeter of sector $JKLM$ will be the length of arc RST, plus 2(12), or 24. This means that you can eliminate answer choices A, C, and D. Now, calculate the length of the arc. You are given that the interior angle is 60°, which is equal to $\frac{1}{6}$ of the total number of degrees in a circle (360°). The length of the arc, therefore, is equivalent to $\frac{1}{6}$ of the circumference of the circle (24π). Therefore, the length of the arc is 4π, so the perimeter of sector $JKLM$ is $4\pi + 24$, answer choice B.

Rectangles

A *rectangle* is a polygon with four sides (two sets of congruent, or equal, sides) and four right angles (see Figure 5.7).

Figure 5.7   A rectangle.

The sum of the angles in a rectangle is always 360°. The *perimeter* of a rectangle is:

P = 2*l* + 2*w*, where *l* is the length and *w* is the width.

The *area* of a rectangle is:

A = *lw*, where *l* is the length and *w* is the width.

The lengths of the diagonals of a rectangle are congruent, or equal.

These concepts might be tested on the GMAT as follows:

> If the length and width of a rectangular yard were each increased by 30%, what would be the percent increase in the area of the yard?
>
> (A) 30%
> (B) 33%
> (C) 60%
> (D) 69%
> (E) 90%

The first step in solving this problem is to calculate the new length (*l*) and the new width (*w*). Because each measurement is increasing by 30%, the new length will be 1.30*l* and the new width will be 1.30*w*. Now calculate the new area. The area of a rectangle is calculated by multiplying the length (*l*) by the width (*w*). Therefore, the increased area is (1.3*l*)(1.3*w*), or 1.69*lw*. The increase is 69%.

Parallelograms

A *parallelogram* is a quadrilateral with four sides and four angles. A parallelogram has two sets of congruent sides and two sets of congruent angles (see Figure 5.8).

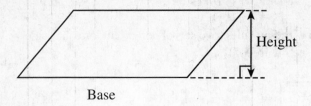

Figure 5.8 A parallelogram.

In addition, the following are special properties of parallelograms:

➤ The sum of the angles of a parallelogram is 360°.

➤ The perimeter of a parallelogram is:

$P = 2l + 2w$

➤ The area of a parallelogram is:

A = (base)(height), with the height being the vertical distance from top to bottom.

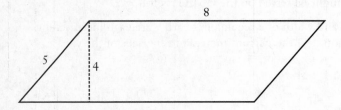

These concepts might be tested on the GMAT as follows:

What is the area of the parallelogram shown in the above figure?
(A) 20
(B) 28
(C) 32
(D) 40
(E) 160

To calculate the area of a parallelogram, multiply the base times the height. The base is given as 8, and the height is given as 4. Therefore, the area is 8 × 4, or 32. Remember that the height is the vertical distance from the top of the parallelogram to the bottom of the parallelogram

Trapezoids

A *trapezoid* is a quadrilateral with four sides and four angles (see Figure 5.9).

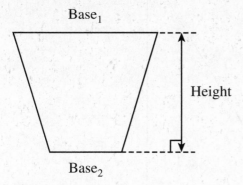

Figure 5.9   A trapezoid.

In addition, the following are special properties of trapezoids:

➤ The *bases* of the trapezoid (top and bottom) are never the same length.

➤ On the GMAT, the sides of the trapezoid are generally the same length.

➤ The *perimeter* of the trapezoid is the sum of the lengths of the sides.

➤ The *area* of a trapezoid is $A = \dfrac{1}{2}$ (base$_1$ + base$_2$)(height). Height is the vertical distance between the bases.

The following are examples of GMAT questions testing some of the concepts regarding quadrilaterals:

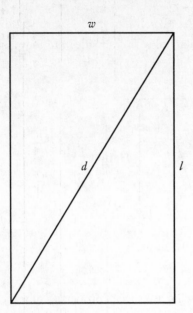

1. What is the area of the rectangular region ?

   (1) length + width = 4

   (2) $d^2 = 25$

This is an example of a data sufficiency question, which means that you don't need to answer the question; you simply need to decide whether the statements include sufficient information to lead you to an answer. Statement (1) indicates that length + width = 4, but does not include any information about what either the length or the width is. Therefore, statement (1) does not include information sufficient to determine the area of the rectangle. Likewise, you can determine the length of the diagonal from statement (2), but this information will not determine either the length or the width, both of which are necessary to calculate the area. However, you can use the Pythagorean theorem together with the information contained in both statements to answer the question, so statement (1) and statement (2) together are sufficient to answer the question.

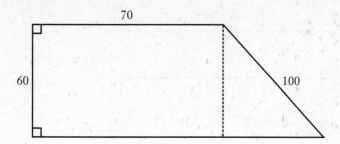

2. What is the perimeter of the figure?

(A) 380

(B) 300

(C) 270

(D) 260

(E) 240

The perimeter is the distance around an object. Because you know that opposite sides of a rectangle are congruent, you know that the side opposite the side with a measure of 60 is also 60. So you now have two sides of the right triangle shown in the figure. Therefore, you can use the Pythagorean theorem to find the distance of the third side, as follows:

➤ $100^2 = 60^2 + x^2$

➤ $10,000 - 3,600 = x^2$

➤ $6,400 = x^2$

➤ $80 = x$

The perimeter is $60 + 2(70) + 100 + 80$, or 380.

Understanding Angles

Angles can be classified as *acute*, *obtuse*, or *right*. An *acute angle* is any angle less than 90°. An *obtuse angle* is any angle that is greater than 90°. A *right angle* is a 90° angle.

When two parallel lines are cut by a perpendicular line, right angles are created, as shown in Figure 5.10.

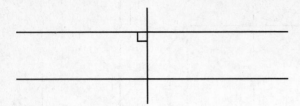

Figure 5.10 Creating right angles.

When two parallel lines are cut by a *transversal*, or intersecting line, the angles created have special properties. Each of the parallel lines cut by the transversal has four angles surrounding the intersection, which are matched in measure and position with a counterpart at the other parallel line. The *vertical* (opposite) *angles* are congruent, and the *adjacent angles* are *supplementary*; that is, the sum of the two supplementary angles is 180°. Figure 5.11 shows these special relationships, where the angles with measure *a* are congruent to each other, the angles with measure *b* are congruent to each other, and angles $a + b = 180$.

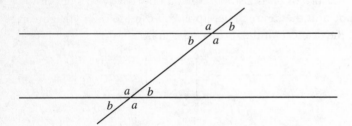

Figure 5.11 Congruent and supplementary relationships from transversals.

This concept might be tested on the GMAT as follows:

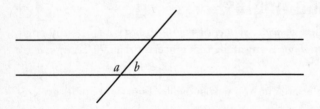

1. In the figure, if $\dfrac{a}{(a+b)} = \dfrac{3}{4}$, $a =$

    (A) 65°

    (B) 75°

    (C) 135°

    (D) 150°

    (E) 175°

You are given that $\dfrac{a}{(a+b)} = \dfrac{3}{4}$. Cross-multiply to eliminate the denominators, as follows:

➤ $\dfrac{a}{(a+b)} = \dfrac{3}{4}$

➤ $4a = 3(a + b)$

Angles a and b are supplementary, which means that $a + b = 180°$. Therefore, $4a = 3(180)$. Solve for a:

➤ $4a = 540°$

➤ $a = 135°$

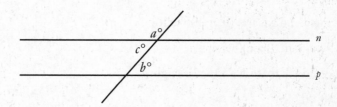

2. In the figure, if lines n and p are parallel, what is the value of b?

    (1) $a = 120$

    (2) $c = 60$

Because a and c are supplementary angles, and b and c are congruent angles, statement (1) alone indicates that angle c must be equal to 60 ($180 - 120 = 60$), and angle b is also equal to 60. Therefore, the information in statement (1) alone is sufficient to answer the question. Likewise, statement (2) alone is sufficient to answer the question because angle c and angle b are congruent.

Recapping Perimeter, Area, and Volume

The area, perimeter, and volume of geometric figures involve the size and amount of space taken up by a particular figure. The following sections are a recap of the formulas for perimeter, area, and volume of shapes that might appear on the GMAT math sections.

Perimeter

The formulas for calculating the perimeter of shapes that might appear on the GMAT math sections are as follows:

➤ Triangle: sum of the sides

➤ Rectangle and parallelogram: $2l + 2w$ (l is length and w is width)

➤ Square: $4s$ (s is the length of each side)

➤ Trapezoid: sum of the sides

➤ Circle (circumference): $2\pi r$, or πd

Area

The formulas for calculating the area of shapes that might appear on the GMAT are as follows:

➤ Triangle: $\frac{1}{2}$ (base)(height)

➤ Rectangle and square: (length)(width)

➤ Parallelogram: (base)(height)

➤ Trapezoid: $\frac{1}{2}$ (base 1 + base 2)(height)

➤ Circle: πr^2

Volume

The formulas for calculating the volume of basic three-dimensional shapes that might appear on the GMAT are as follows:

➤ Rectangular box and cube: (length)(width)(height)

➤ Sphere: $(\frac{4}{3})\pi r^3$

➤ Right circular cylinder: $\pi r^2 h$ (h is the height)

Word Problems

Many GMAT quantitative questions are presented as word problems that require you to apply math skills to everyday situations. It is important that you carefully read the questions and understand what is being asked. Some of the information given may not be relevant to answering the question. Figure 5.12 lists the relationship between some words and their mathematical counterparts:

Description	Mathematical Translation
5 more than n	$n + 5$
5 less than n	$n - 5$
2 times the quantity $(x + 3)$	$2(x + 3)$
the sum of a and b	$a + b$
the difference between a and b	$a - b$
the product of a and b	$a \times b$
the quotient of a and b	$a \div b$
50 miles per hour	50 miles/60 minutes, or 50 miles/1 hour
3 more than twice n	$2n + 3$
3 less than twice n	$2n - 3$
the average of a and b	$\frac{a+b}{2}$
20 percent of n	$n(.2)$

Figure 5.12 Relationships between words and mathematical counterparts.

It is a good idea to actually set up tables or equations based on the relevant information in word problems. Do not try to solve these problems in your head. Visualizing the situation presented in the problem helps you keep track of the important information and prevents you from making careless errors.

Consider the following simulated GMAT question:

How many ties does Jeff have?

(1) If Jeff had 10 fewer ties, he would have only half as many as he actually has.

(2) Jeff has twice as many blue ties as red ties.

To answer this question, set the number of ties that Jeff has at t. According to the information in statement (1), if Jeff had $t - 10$ ties, he would have $\frac{1}{2}$ t ties. Expressed mathematically, $t - 10 = \frac{1}{2} t$, which can be solved for t. Therefore, the information in statement (1) is sufficient to answer the question. However, because statement (2) gives only the ratio of blue to red ties and does not provide any information about the number of red or blue ties, the information in statement (2) is not sufficient.

Data Interpretation

Data Interpretation questions require you to interpret information that is presented in charts, graphs, or tables; compare quantities; recognize trends and changes in the data; and perform basic calculations based on the information contained in the figures.

Get a general understanding of the charts, graphs, or tables before you look at the questions. If you can determine the relationships between the data elements, the questions will be much easier to answer.

The GMAT Data Interpretation questions also include analysis of measurement, such as average, median, and percent, which was discussed previously in this chapter.

The best approach to Data Interpretation questions is to gain an understanding of how the data is represented and then look for patterns or trends in the data. When there are charts or graphs given, take a moment to figure out which variables are being charted and note any apparent relationships between them. For example, a *direct relationship* is when one variable increases as the other increases. An *inverse relationship* is when one variable decreases as another increases.

Remember that these questions test your ability to interpret and understand relationships and trends in data and that most of the math calculations will be fairly simple. Read the questions carefully and let the answer choices guide you.

The following are examples of data interpretation questions that you might encounter on the GMAT, followed by an explanation of the answers:

Questions 1-2 refer to the following graph:

**County M's total annual expenditures compared to
County O's total annual expenditures, 1995-2000**

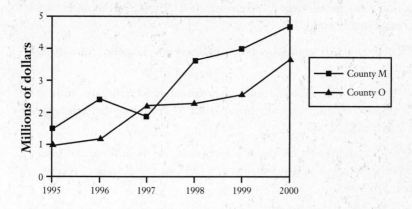

1. For which year shown on the graph did County O's annual expendi-
   tures exceed County M's annual expenditures?
   (A) 1995
   (B) 1997
   (C) 1998
   (D) 1999
   (E) 2000

According to the graph, in 1997, County O's expenditures were slightly
more than $2 million, and County M's expenditures were slightly less than
$2 million. For every other year, County M's expenditures were higher than
County O's expenditures. Therefore, answer choice B is correct.

2. For how many years shown on the graph did County M's expenditures
   exceed County O's expenditures by more than $750,000?
   (A) 2
   (B) 3
   (C) 4
   (D) 5
   (E) 6

You can eliminate answer choice E immediately because you already know
that during at least one year, County O's expenditures exceeded County M's
expenditures (refer to the previous question). Because only 6 years are shown
on the graph, County M's expenditures could not have exceeded County O's
expenditures in any amount for 6 years. The next step is to look carefully at
the amounts of the expenditures for each year:

1995: County M's expenditures = approximately $1.5 million, and County O's expenditures = approximately $1 million; the difference is less than $750,000.

1996: County M's expenditures = approximately $2.3 million, and County O's expenditures = approximately $1.2 million; the difference is more than $750,000.

1997: During this year, County O's expenditures exceeded County M's expenditures.

1998: County M's expenditures = approximately $3.6 million, and County O's expenditures = approximately $2.2 million; the difference is more than $750,000.

1999: County M's expenditures = approximately $4 million, and County O's expenditures = approximately $2.5 million; the difference is more than $750,000.

2000: County M's expenditures = approximately $4.7 million, and County O's expenditures = approximately $3.5 million; the difference is more than $750,000.

You can see that during 4 years as shown on the graph, County M's expenditures exceeded County O's expenditures by more than $500,000, answer choice C.

Question 3 refers to the following graph:

SOURCES OF SCHOOL S FUNDING, 1997

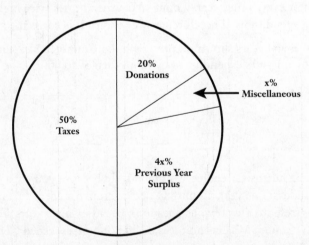

3. According to the graph, what percent of the funds for School S in 1997 came from the previous year's surplus?

(A) 27%

(B) 24%

(C) 20%

(D) 6%

(E) 3%

Based on the graph, the total of Donations, Miscellaneous, and Surplus funds is equivalent to 50% of the funds in 1997. Therefore, $20 + x + 4x = 50$. Solve for x:

➤ $20 + x + 4x = 50$

➤ $20 + 5x = 50$

➤ $5x = 30$

➤ $x = 6$

Therefore, the surplus from the previous year accounted for (4)(6)%, or 24% of the funds for School S in 1997.

Understanding Measures of Dispersion and Distribution

Discrete sets of numerical values can be measured in many ways. The GRE data interpretation questions commonly test the simplest measure of dispersion, known as *range*. Range is defined as the greatest measured value minus the least measured value. Consider the following example:

Week 1 Temperatures	72°	74°	76°	80°	80°	74°	78°
Week 2 Temperatures	68°	70°	70°	72°	76°	74°	72°

1. In the table shown, the difference between the highest and lowest temperatures is what percent of the highest temperature?

(A) 10%

(B) 12%

(C) 15%

(D) 68%

(E) 80%

The first step in answering this question is to find the highest and lowest temperatures recorded in the table. The highest recorded temperature is 80°, and the lowest recorded temperature is 68°. Now, find the difference: 80 − 68 = 12. Next, divide the difference (12) by the highest temperature (80) to calculate the percent:

➤ 12 ÷ 80 = .15

➤ .15 = $\frac{15}{100}$, or 15%

Frequency distribution is often a more convenient way to express a set of measurements. A frequency distribution table or graph shows the frequency of occurrence of each value in the set. Consider the following example:

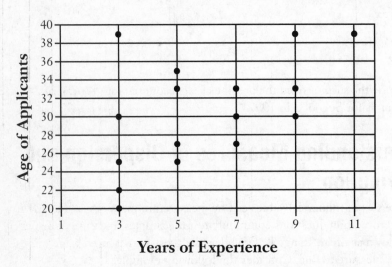

Years of Experience

2. The dots on the graph represent the ages and years of experience of 16 job applicants. How many of the applicants have more than 5 years of experience?

 (A) 5

 (B) 7

 (C) 8

 (D) 10

 (E) 11

To answer this question, count the number of dots to the right of the 5-year mark. Do not include the dots on the 5-year mark because the question asks for the number of applicants with *more* than 5 years of experience. There are 7 dots to the right of the 5-year mark for answer choice B. If you counted the dots on the 5-year mark, you would have arrived at answer choice E, which is incorrect.

Answering the Questions

As mentioned previously, the GMAT Quantitative questions come in two forms: Problem Solving and Data Sufficiency. Each question type requires its own set of strategies, outlined in the following sections.

Problem Solving

The Problem Solving questions on the GMAT are multiple choice questions, and you select the correct answer from five possible answer choices. Remember the following general strategies when approaching GMAT Problem Solving questions. We have included examples for some of the strategies to help you understand how to correctly apply them:

1. **Draw pictures**. It really helps sometimes to visualize the problem. This strategy should not take a lot of time and can prevent careless errors. Sometimes, you are given a figure or a table that you can work with; sometimes, you just have to make your own.

2. **Apply logic**. You cannot use a calculator, so most of the actual calculations are fairly simple. In fact, the GMAT test-writers are just as likely to test your logical reasoning ability or your ability to follow directions as they are to test your ability to plug numbers into an equation.

3. **Answer the question that they ask you**. If the problem requires three steps to reach a solution and you only completed two of the steps, it is likely that the answer you arrived at will be one of the choices. However, it will not be the correct choice!

4. **Don't quit early**. Reason your way through the problem so that it makes sense. Keep in mind, though, that these questions do not usually involve intensive calculations or complicated manipulations.

5. **Check the choices**. Take a quick look at the answer choices as you read the problem for the first time. They can provide valuable clues about how to proceed. For example, many answer choices will be in either ascending or descending order. If the question asks you for the least possible value, try the smallest answer choice first. If it does not correctly answer the question, work through the rest of the answer choices from smallest to largest. Remember that one of them is the correct choice. Consider the following example:

If x is an integer and $y = 7x + 11$, what is the greatest value of x for which y is less than 50?

(A) 7
(B) 6
(C) 5
(D) 4
(E) 3

Because the question asks for the greatest value of x, start with answer choice A:

➤ $y = 7(7) + 11 = 60$. This is not less than 50, so eliminate answer choice A.

➤ $y = 7(6) + 11 = 53$. This is not less than 50, so eliminate answer choice B.

➤ $y = 7(5) + 11 = 46$. This is the greatest of the remaining answer choices, so it must be correct.

6. **Pick numbers for the variables**. You can sometimes simplify your work on a given problem by using actual numbers as "stand-ins" for variables. This strategy works when you have variables in the question and the same variables in the answer choices. You can simplify the answer choices by substituting actual numbers for the variables. Pick numbers that are easy to work with and that meet the parameters of the information given in the question. If you use this strategy, remember that numbers on the GMAT can be either positive or negative and are sometimes whole numbers and sometimes fractions. You should also be careful not to use 1 and 0 as your "stand-ins" because they can create "identities," which can lead to more than one seemingly correct answer choice. In addition, it is sometimes necessary to try more than one number to see whether the result always correctly responds to the question. If the numbers that you pick work for more than one answer choice, pick different numbers and try again, focusing on the remaining answer choices.

Consider the following example:

If positive integers a and b are not both even, which of the following must be odd?

(A) ab
(B) $a + b$
(C) $a - b$
(D) $a - b + 1$
(E) $2(a + b) - 1$

The word "must" in the question indicates that the correct answer choice will always be odd. You are given that a and b are not both even, which means that one or the other must be odd, or they must both be odd. Pick numbers that fit the criteria: $a = 2$ and $b = 3$; $a = 3$ and $b = 3$. Now, substitute these numbers into each of the answer choices, as follows:

➤ Answer choice A: When $a = 2$ and $b = 3$, $ab = 6$; when $a = 3$ and $b = 3$, $ab = 9$. Therefore, ab is not always odd, and answer choice A is incorrect.

➤ Answer choice B: When $a = 2$ and $b = 3$, $a + b = 5$; when $a = 3$ and $b = 3$, $a + b = 6$. Therefore, $a + b$ is not always odd, and answer choice B is incorrect.

➤ Answer choice C: When $a = 2$ and $b = 3$, $a - b = -1$; when $a = 3$ and $b = 3$, $a - b = 0$. Therefore, $a - b$ is not always odd, and answer choice C is incorrect.

➤ Answer choice D: When $a = 2$ and $b = 3$, $a - b + 1 = 0$; when $a = 3$ and $b = 3$, $a - b + 1 = 1$. Therefore, ab is not always odd, and answer choice D is incorrect.

➤ Answer choice E : When $a = 2$ and $b = 3$, $2(a + b) - 1 = 9$; when $a = 3$ and $b = 3$, $2(a + b) - 1 = 11$. Therefore, $2(a + b) - 1$ is always odd, and answer choice E is correct.

Data Sufficiency Questions

The GMAT Quantitative Section includes a type of question called *Data Sufficiency*, which consists of a question, sometimes accompanied by additional information, and two statements, labeled (1) and (2). You must decide whether sufficient information or data to answer the question is given by either statement alone, by both statements combined, or by neither statement (additional data is required to answer the question). These questions are designed to measure your ability to analyze a problem, to determine which information is relevant, and to make a decision regarding the sufficiency of the information presented. Select an answer choice based on the following criteria:

A   Statement (1) ALONE is sufficient, but statement (2) alone is not sufficient to answer the question.

B   Statement (2) ALONE is sufficient, but statement (1) alone is not sufficient to answer the question.

C   BOTH statements (1) and (2) TOGETHER are sufficient to answer the question asked; but NEITHER statement ALONE is sufficient.

D   EACH statement ALONE is sufficient to answer the question.

E   Statements (1) and (2) TOGETHER are NOT sufficient to answer the question, and additional information specific to the problem is needed.

For example:

How many of the girls in a group of 200 children have blue eyes?
(1) Of the children in the group, 40% have blue eyes.
(2) Of the children in the group, 80 are girls.

From statement (1) alone, only the total number of children who have blue eyes can be determined, so statement (1) alone is not sufficient. Statement (2) alone is not sufficient because nothing is said about how many of those girls have blue eyes. Statements (1) and (2) together do not tell us how any girls in the group have blue eyes, so more information is needed to answer this question, which means answer choice E is correct.

The GMAT is a filter for potential managers, not potential mathematicians. This means that the test is trying to measure how well you are able to decide *when and if* you have enough information to answer a question. On this section, they are not as interested in whether you *can* actually answer the question.

Remember these general strategies when approaching GMAT Data Sufficiency questions:

1. **Understand the answer choices**. The answer choices are always the same for every Data Sufficiency question. You choose A if statement (1) contains enough information on its own for you to answer the question. You choose B if statement (2) alone has enough information. Choose C if neither statement alone is enough to answer the question, but you can answer it if you combine the information from the two statements. Select answer choice D if either of the two statements has enough information, on its own, to answer the question. Choose E if there is not enough information to answer the question, even after considering both statements together.

2. **Don't over-choose E**. There is a tendency among test-takers to choose E more often than the other choices, especially on the more difficult questions. Remember that choosing E means that you have decided that *no one* could answer the question posed based on information in the two statements, even when the statements are taken together. It doesn't mean that *you* don't know the answer to that particular problem on test day.

3. **An answer to the question posed means one distinct value**. Being able to determine upper or lower limits based on one or both of the statements is not the same as being able to answer the question posed, if the question is asking for a specific value.

4. **Figures are not necessarily drawn to scale**. For example, if you think that you are looking at a drawing of an equilateral triangle, but there aren't any notes on the figure to confirm that all the sides are equal, you have to proceed on the basis that the triangle could be either an isosceles or scalene triangle.

5. **Consider the statements separately and eliminate answer choices as you do so**. If you decided that statement (1) does not contain enough information to answer the question, you can certainly eliminate answer choices A and D. If you determine that statement (1) is sufficient on its own, you can eliminate choices B, C, and E. Similarly, if you can determine that statement (2) is not sufficient on its own, you can eliminate B and D. If it is sufficient to answer the question alone, you can eliminate choices, A, C, and E. Because, on the real GMAT, you have to answer each question that comes along before you can move ahead, eliminating some choices so that you can make intelligent guesses can be a real benefit.

Putting It to Practice

The following section contains simulated GMAT Quantitative questions. Read the directions carefully before you begin to answer the questions. When you select an answer, circle it in the book. Make guesses as necessary. Remember that on the actual computer-adaptive exam, you will be required to select an answer before you can move on to the next question. Be sure to read the explanations to help you gain a better understanding of why the correct answer is correct.

Exam Prep Questions

This section consists of two different types of questions. To answer the questions, select the best answer from the answer choices given.

The *Problem-Solving* questions require you to solve the problem and select the best answer choice.

Each *Data Sufficiency* problem contains a question followed by two statements, (1) and (2). You are asked to determine whether the statements are sufficient to answer the question. You will need to use the information given in the statements along with your knowledge of general mathematics and other common facts (such as the number of minutes in an hour or the number of days in a year) to determine whether:

A   Statement (1) ALONE is sufficient, but statement (2) alone is not sufficient to answer the question.

B   Statement (2) ALONE is sufficient, but statement (1) alone is not sufficient to answer the question.

C   BOTH statements (1) and (2) TOGETHER are sufficient to answer the question asked; but NEITHER statement ALONE is sufficient.

D   EACH statement ALONE is sufficient to answer the question.

E   Statements (1) and (2) TOGETHER are NOT sufficient to answer the question, and additional information specific to the problem is needed.

Numbers: All of the numbers used are real numbers.

Figures: Any figure given with a problem refers to the information in the question, but will not always refer to the information in statements (1) and (2). A line that appears straight should be considered a straight line. The points, angles, and so forth used in this section can be assumed to be in the order that they appear. The measures of all angles used are never below zero.

In any Data Sufficiency problem that asks for the value of an unknown quantity, the statements are sufficient to answer the question only when you can determine exactly one value.

1. What is the number of 360° rotations that an automobile tire makes while traveling 500 feet in a straight line without stopping?
   (1) The diameter of the automobile tire, including the rim, is 2 feet.
   (2) The automobile tire makes thirty 360° rotations per minute.

2. A bookstore owner ordered 125 paperback copies of a certain book and 125 hardcover copies of the same book. If the total cost to the bookseller was $3,500.00 (excluding tax) and the price of each paperback was $8.00 (excluding tax), what was the price of each hardcover (excluding tax)?
   (A) $8.00
   (B) $12.00
   (C) $16.00
   (D) $20.00
   (E) $35.00

3. If $a = -5$, what is the value of $2a^2$?

   (A) –25
   (B) –10
   (C) 10
   (D) 20
   (E) 50

4. If a certain animated television show consists of a total of 22,240 frames on film, how many minutes will it take to run the animated show?

   (1) The animated television show runs without any interruption at the rate of 20 frames per second.

   (2) It takes four times as long to run the animated television show as it takes to rewind the film, and it takes a total of 25 minutes to do each.

5. What is the average number of miles per gallon of gasoline used by a motorcycle during a certain trip?

   (1) The total cost of the gasoline used by the motorcycle for the 120-mile trip was $14.00.

   (2) The cost of the gasoline used by the motorcycle for the trip was $1.40 per gallon.

6. The only contents of a box are 15 folders and 26 pieces of paper. What is the total weight, in ounces, of the box's contents?

   (1) The weight of each folder is four times the weight of each piece of paper.

   (2) The total weight of one piece of paper and two folders is $\frac{1}{2}$ ounce.

7. The annual budget of a small business is shown on a circle graph. If the size of each sector of the graph is proportional to the amount of the budget it represents, how many degrees of the circle should be used to represent 25% of the budget?

   (A) 25
   (B) 45
   (C) 75
   (D) 90
   (E) 270

8. If 24 is 15% of 40% of a certain number, what is the number?

   (A) 15
   (B) 64
   (C) 79
   (D) 160
   (E) 400

> Today Only! Everything in the store is half-off!

9. If l and w represent the length and width, respectively, of the rectangular sign, what is the perimeter?

   (1) $2l + w = 60$

   (2) $l + w = 35$

10. If r is an even integer and s is an odd integer, which of the following must be an even integer?

   (A) $\dfrac{s}{r}$

   (B) rs

   (C) $r + s$

   (D) $\dfrac{3s}{r}$

   (E) $3(r + s)$

11. Last year Kate received 50 paychecks. Each of her first 10 paychecks was $500; each of her remaining paychecks was $75 more than each of her first 10 paychecks. To the nearest dollar, what was the average (arithmetic mean) amount of her paychecks for the year?

   (A) $100

   (B) $175

   (C) $500

   (D) $560

   (E) $575

12. If the length of an edge of Cube Y is three times the length of an edge of Cube Z, what is the ratio of the volume of Cube Z to the volume of Cube Y?

   (A) 1:27

   (B) 1:9

   (C) 1:3

   (D) 9:1

   (E) 27:1

13. What is the ratio of m to n?

   (1) m is 6 times more than twice n.

   (2) The ratio of $0.5m$ to $2n$ is 4 to 5.

14. What is the value of n?

   (1) $-(n + m) = n - m$

   (2) $n + m = 6$

15. A sum of $400,000 was divided among a parent and three children. How much of the money did the youngest child receive?

(1) The parent received $\frac{1}{2}$ of the sum, and the oldest child received $\frac{1}{4}$ of the remainder.

(2) Each of the two younger children received $25,000 more than the oldest child, and $125,000 less than the parent.

16. If a 20% deposit that has been paid toward the purchase of a certain product is $150, how much more remains to be paid (excluding tax)?

(A) $170
(B) $300
(C) $430
(D) $600
(E) $750

17. If $y = 3 + (x - 2)^2$, then y is the least when $x =$

(A) –2
(B) 0
(C) 2
(D) 3
(E) 6

18. If the local library's total expenditure for salaries, grounds maintenance, and books last year was $700,000, how much of the expenditure was for salaries?

(1) The expenditure for books was 30% greater than the expenditure for ground maintenance.

(2) The total of the expenditure for grounds maintenance and books was 20% less than the expenditure for salaries.

19. The symbol ¤ represents one of the following operations: addition, subtraction, multiplication, or division. What is the value of 4 ¤ 3?

(1) 0 ¤ 1 = 1
(2) 1 ¤ 0 = 1

Container	Number of Quarters	Number of Nickels	Total Number of Quarters and Nickels
X	a	b	80
Y	b	c	120
Z	a	c	160

20. In the table, what is the number of nickels in container Z?
    (A) 70
    (B) 80
    (C) 90
    (D) 100
    (E) 110

Answers to Exam Prep Questions

1. **The correct answer is A.** For each 360° rotation, the tire has traveled a distance equal to its circumference. Therefore, it is important to know the size of the tire. From statement (1), the circumference of the tire can be determined and statement (1) alone is sufficient. Statement (2) gives the speed at which the tire rotated, but the size of the tire cannot be determined. Therefore, statement (2) alone is not sufficient and the correct answer is A.

2. **The correct answer is D.** To solve this problem, first set the number of paperbacks to p and the number of hard covers to h. You are given that the bookstore owner ordered 125 copies of each type of book and that the total cost was \$3,500. Therefore, $125p + 125h = 3,500$. You are also given that the price of each paperback was \$8.00, so replace p with 8 in the equation and solve for h, as follows:

   ➤ $125(8) + 125h = 3,500$

   ➤ $1,000 + 125h = 3,500$

   ➤ $125h = 2,500$

   ➤ $h = 20$

   The price of each hardcover was \$20.00.

3. **The correct answer is E.** To solve this problem, replace a with -5, making sure that you keep track of the negative signs.

➤ $2(-5)^2 =$

➤ $2(25) = 50$

4. **The correct answer is D.** From statement (1), it can be determined that it takes $\dfrac{22,240}{(20 \times 60)}$ minutes to run the animated television show. Therefore, statement (1) alone is sufficient. From statement (2), the time it takes to run the animated television show can be determined as well: $25 = x + 4x$ (– solve for x). Therefore, the correct answer is D.

5. **The correct answer is C.** Statement (1) gives the number of miles the motorcycle traveled, but the number of gallons of gasoline used cannot be determined because only the total cost of the gasoline is known. Statement (1) alone is not sufficient. Statement (2) alone is also not sufficient, but combined with the information given in statement (1) you can determine the number of gallons of gasoline used. When you know the number of miles traveled and the number of gallons of gasoline used, you can determine the average number of miles per gallon. Therefore, the correct answer is C.

6. **The correct answer is C.** Let f and p denote the weight, in ounces, of a folder and piece of paper, respectively. The total weight of the box is $15f + 26p$. The information in statement (1) can be written as $f = 4p$. Even when you substitute this into the original expression, you still do not know p. Therefore, statement (1) alone is insufficient. Similarly, statement (2) is insufficient. However, if you solve the two linear equations summarizing the information given in statements (1) and (2) simultaneously for f and p, you are able to determine the weight of the box's contents. Therefore, the best answer is C.

7. **The correct answer is D**. To solve this problem, it might be helpful to draw a diagram, as shown in the following figure:

The diagram shows a circle divided into four equal sections. Each section is equivalent to 25% of the circle, so the total budget is represented by four sections. There are 360° in a circle, so the number of degrees of the circle that represents 25% of the budget will be 360 ÷ 4 (or 25% of 360), which is 90.

8. **The correct answer is E**. There are two ways to solve this problem easily. First, you can answer the question "24 is 15% of what?" by setting up a proportion, as follows:

➤ 24 is to 15 as x is to 100

➤ $\frac{24}{15} = \frac{x}{100}$; cross-multiply and solve for x

➤ $15x = 2,400$

➤ $x = 160$

Next, answer the question "160 is 40% of what number?" by setting up a proportion, as follows:

➤ 160 is to 40 as x is to 100

➤ $\frac{160}{40} = \frac{x}{100}$; cross-multiply and solve for x

➤ $40x = 16,000$

➤ $x = 400$

You can also convert the percentages to their decimal equivalents and set up an equation to solve for x, as follows:

➤ $24 = (.15)(.4x)$

➤ $24 = .06x$

➤ $400 = x$

9. The correct answer is B. The formula used to determine the perimeter of a rectangle is P = $2l$ + $2w$ or $2(l + w)$ when l = length and w = width. The perimeter can be found when the length and the width of a rectangle are known. The length and width cannot be determined from statement (1) alone. However, statement (2) alone is sufficient because you know $l + w$. Therefore, the correct answer is B.

10. The correct answer is B. The best way to solve this problem is to pick numbers for r and s and substitute those values for r and s in each of the answer choices. If the result is an odd integer, eliminate the answer choice. Pick easy numbers to work with, and remember that you might have to pick several numbers, as follows:

➤ Answer choice A: When $r = 2$ and $s = 3$, $\frac{s}{r} = \frac{2}{3}$, which is not an integer. Eliminate answer choice A.

➤ Answer choice B: When $r = 2$ and $s = 3$, $rs = (2)(3)$, which is an even integer. Answer choice B is correct.

➤ Work through the remaining answer choices and you will see that they will, at least sometimes, yield an odd integer, or a fraction.

11. The correct answer is D. To solve this problem, first calculate the total amount of money that Kate earned last year, using the information given, as follows:

➤ First 10 paychecks = 10(500)

➤ Remaining 40 paychecks = 40(575)

➤ 10(500) + 40(575) =

➤ 5,000 + 23,000 = 28,000

Because you are asked for the average amount of her paychecks, divide the total amount that she earned ($28,000) by the number of paychecks that she received (50):

➤ $\frac{\$28,000}{50} = \$560$

12. **The correct answer is E.** To solve, set each edge of Cube Y equal to y. The volume of Cube Y, therefore, is $(y)(y)(y)$, or y^3. You are given that each edge of Cube Z is three times that of Cube Y, so each edge of Cube Z is $3y$. Therefore, the volume of Cube Z is $(3y)(3y)(3y)$, or $27y^3$. The ratio of the volume of Cube Z to Cube Y, then, is 27:1 because the volume of Cube Z is 27 times the volume of Cube Y.

13. **The correct answer is B.** Statement (1) can be expressed as $m = 2n + 6$. This is insufficient because you need to know n to solve this equation. Statement (2) can be expressed as $\frac{0.5m}{2n} = \frac{4}{5}$ ($\frac{m}{n} = \frac{4}{5}$ divided by $\frac{0.5}{2}$). Therefore, statement (2) alone is sufficient, and the correct answer is B.

14. **The correct answer is A.** In statement (1) the equation $-(n + m) = n - m$ can be reduced to $-n = n$. Zero (0) is the only number whose value would not change if a negative sign were placed in front of it. Therefore, statement (1) alone is sufficient. In statement (2) the value of n would depend on the value of m, (unknown) so statement (2) alone is not sufficient. The correct answer is A.

15. **The correct answer is B.** From statement (1) the combined amount that the two younger children received can be determined, but you cannot determine the individual amount that each younger child received. Therefore, statement (1) alone is insufficient. In statement (2) the amount of money received by the oldest child and the parent can be expressed in terms of the known amount. An equation can be set up to determine how much each of the younger children received. Statement (2) alone is sufficient, so the correct answer is B.

16. **The correct answer is D.** There are two ways to solve this problem. First, you can answer the question "$150 is 20% of what number" by setting up a proportion, as follows:

   ➤ 150 is to 20 as x is to 100

   ➤ $\frac{150}{20} = \frac{x}{100}$; cross-multiply and solve for x

   ➤ $20x = 15,000$

   ➤ $x = 750$

This is the total purchase price, so now you must subtract $150 from $750 to find the amount that remains to be paid:

➤ $750 – $150 = $600

You could also set up the original proportion based on the fact that 80% of the total price remains to be paid, as follows:

➤ 150 is to 20 as x is to 80

➤ $\frac{150}{20} = \frac{x}{80}$; cross-multiply and solve for x

➤ $20x = 1,200$

➤ $x = 600$

17. **The correct answer is C.** To solve, substitute the values in each answer choice for x in the equation, and solve for y as follows:

➤ Answer choice A: $y = 3 + (-2 - 2)^2 = 3 + 16 = 19$.

➤ Answer choice B: $y = 3 + (0 - 2)^2 = 3 + 4 = 7$.

➤ Answer choice C: $y = 3 + (2 - 2)^2 = 3 + 0 = 3$.

➤ Answer choice D: $y = 3 + (3 - 2)^2 = 3 + 1 = 4$.

➤ Answer choice E: $y = 3 + (6 - 2)^2 = 3 + 16 = 19$.

Based on these calculations, y is least when $x = 2$.

18. **The correct answer is B.** Let s, g, and b denote the expenditure, in dollars, for salaries, grounds maintenance, and books, respectively. You know that $s + g + b =$ $700,000. In statement (1) it can be determined that $b = 1.3g$, so $s + 2.3g =$ $700,000. However, the value for s cannot be determined and statement (1) alone is not sufficient. In statement (2) it follows that $g + b = .80s$. Then, $.80s$ can be substituted for g and b in the $s + g + b =$ $700,000 equation. From here, you can determine the value of s, so statement (2) alone is sufficient. The correct answer is B.

19. **The correct answer is A.** To solve, perform each of the calculations indicated by the operators given: $0 + 1 = 1$, $0 - 1 = -1$, $0 \times 1 = 0$, and $0 \div 1 = 0$. Therefore, it follows from statement (1) that ¤ represents addition, so the value of 4 ¤ 3 can be determined; statement (1) alone is sufficient. It follows from statement (2) that ¤ could be either addition or subtraction, so statement (2) alone is not sufficient. The correct answer is A; only the information in statement (1) is sufficient.

20. The correct answer is D. To solve this problem, set up equations for each of the containers, solving for a, b, and c as follows:

➤ Container X: $a + b = 80$; $a = 80 - b$

➤ Container Y: $b + c = 120$; $b = 120 - c$

➤ Container Z: $a + c = 160$; $c = 160 - a$

Now you can substitute to find the value of c in Container Z, as follows:

➤ First, solve for a in the first equation: $a = 80 - (120 - c)$ $a = -40 - c$

➤ Next, solve for c in the third equation (Container Z):
$c = 160 - (-40 - c)$

➤ $c = 200 - c$

➤ $2c = 200$

➤ $c = 100$

You could also use the total number of coins in each container guide you. Because $a = 80 - b$, $b = 120 - c$, and $c = 160 - a$, a must equal 60, b must equal 20, and c must equal 100 for each container.

GMAT Practice Test 1

This practice GMAT consists of 78 multiple-choice questions and 2 essay tasks, divided into four sections. Please allow approximately 3 hours and 30 minutes to complete the practice test. Each of the test sections should be taken in the time indicated at the beginning of the sections, and in the order in which they appear on this test. There are several different types of questions within each section. Answer each question in order before you move on to the next question. You will not be able to skip around and come back to any questions on the actual computer-adaptive GMAT. Make sure that you read and understand all directions before you begin. To achieve the best results, time yourself strictly on each section. Use the Answer Sheet at the end of the chapter to mark your answers.

We suggest that you make this practice test as much like the real test as possible. Find a quiet location, free from distractions, and make sure that you have pencils and a timepiece. You should read the chapters for each specific section of the GMAT prior to taking this practice test.

Your score on the actual GMAT depends on many factors, including your level of preparedness and your fatigue level on test day.

SECTION 1

30 Minutes

1 Question

Analysis of an Argument

Directions: This section asks you to analyze and critique an argument that is presented. This section is NOT asking you to respond with your perspective on the topic.

Before you begin to write, you should organize your thoughts and plan out your response. Make sure to develop your points fully, but save some time to read over your response and make any necessary revisions.

Your response will be evaluated on your ability to express your ideas clearly, to support your reasoning appropriately, and to apply the standards of written English.

> "Mama Bellamy's pizza has been a local favorite for years. Now she has sold her recipe to Giant Frozen Foods and they will be offering Mama Bellamy's Pizza in the freezer cases of grocery stores nationwide. Clearly, there is no reason to visit Mama Bellamy's restaurant anymore."

SECTION 2

30 Minutes

1 Question

Analysis of an Issue

Directions: This section asks you to analyze an issue and offer your perspective on it. There is no correct answer, so consider all of the possible viewpoints as you develop your own.

Before you begin to write, you should organize your thoughts and plan out your response. Make sure to develop your points fully, but save some time to read over and revise your response.

Your response will be evaluated on your ability to express your ideas clearly, to support your reasoning appropriately, and to apply the standards of written English.

"The success of any culture should be measured more by the health of its citizens than by its artistic, musical, or architectural achievements."

SECTION 3

75 Minutes

37 Questions

Quantitative

This section consists of two different types of questions. To answer the questions, select the best answer from the answer choices given.

The *Problem-Solving* questions require you to solve the problem and select the best answer choice.

Numbers: All of the numbers used are real numbers.

Figures: A figure given for a question provides information that can be used to solve the problem. Figures are drawn to scale, as accurately as possible, unless it is stated otherwise. A line that appears straight should be considered a straight line. All figures given in this section lie in a plane unless it is stated otherwise.

Each *Data Sufficiency* problem contains a question followed by two statements, (1) and (2). You are asked to determine whether the statements are sufficient to answer the question. You will need to use the information given in the statements along with your knowledge of general mathematics and other common facts (such as the number of minutes in an hour or the number of days in a year) to determine whether

A   Statement (1) ALONE is sufficient, but statement (2) alone is not sufficient to answer the question.

B   Statement (2) ALONE is sufficient, but statement (1) alone is not sufficient to answer the question.

C   BOTH statements (1) and (2) TOGETHER are sufficient to answer the question asked, but NEITHER statement ALONE is sufficient.

D   EACH statement ALONE is sufficient to answer the question.

E   Statements (1) and (2) TOGETHER are NOT sufficient to answer the question, and additional information specific to the problem is needed.

In any Data Sufficiency problem that asks for the value of an unknown quantity, the statements are sufficient to answer the question only when you can determine exactly one value.

1. If Jennifer was 23 years old 7 years ago, how old was she x years ago?

   (A) $x - 30$
   (B) $x - 16$
   (C) $30 - x$
   (D) $16 - x$
   (E) $16 + x$

2. Running at the same constant rate, 12 identical machines can produce a total of 540 containers per minute. At this rate, how many containers could 20 of these machines produce in 8 minutes?

   (A) 1,296
   (B) 7,200
   (C) 10,900
   (D) 14,200
   (E) 14,400

3. A park ranger wants to put up fencing around three sides of a rectangular portion of a national park and leave 40 feet unfenced. If the rectangular portion of the park being fenced has an area of 1,360 square feet, how many feet of fencing does he need?

   (A) 68
   (B) 80
   (C) 106
   (D) 108
   (E) 204

4. In a presidential election, if each of the 1,800 voters in a certain precinct voted for either O'Donnell or Johnson (but not both), what percent of the male voters in this precinct voted for Johnson?

   (1) Ninety percent of the male voters in the precinct voted for O'Donnell.
   (2) Seventy percent of the female voters voted for Johnson.

5. During week T, how much did it cost, per mile, for the gasoline used by bus R?

   (1) During week T, bus R used gasoline that cost $2.48 per gallon.
   (2) During week T, bus R was driven 540 miles.

6. If x and y are integers, is x divisible by 3?

   (1) The product xy is divisible by 3.
   (2) y is not divisible by 3.

7. The average (arithmetic mean) of 4 numbers is 9. When one number is discarded, the average of the remaining numbers becomes 6. What is the discarded number?

(A) 11
(B) 13
(C) 14
(D) 16
(E) 18

8. During the first week of December, a ski retailer sold 10 pairs of a certain brand of skis at $95.00 a pair. If, during the second week of December, 15 pairs were sold at the sale price of $75.50 a pair, by what amount did the revenue from weekly sales of these skis increase during the second week?

(A) $182.50
(B) $195.50
(C) $255.50
(D) $285.50
(E) $290.50

9. A sorority collected exactly $699 dollars in dues from its members. If each member contributed at least $12.00, what is the greatest number of members the sorority could have?

(A) 39
(B) 47
(C) 58
(D) 59
(E) 65

10. If $st = \frac{7}{4}$, what is the value of $s + t$?

(1) $s > 0$
(2) $3s + t = 38$

11. Is x less than 0?

(1) $vw > 0$ and $wx < 0$
(2) $v > 0$

12. What is Kevin's age now?

(1) Kevin is now twice as old as he was exactly 4 years ago.
(2) Kevin's sister Lynn is now 3 times as old as Kevin was exactly 4 years ago.

13. Diana purchased brand *P* candy for $4.00 per box and brand *Q* candy for $2.50 per box. If Diana purchased a total of 12 boxes of candy for $42.00, how many boxes of brand *P* candies did she purchase?

(A) 3
(B) 4
(C) 5
(D) 7
(E) 8

14. If the length and the width of a garage floor were each increased by 30%, what would be the percent increase in the area of the garage floor?

(A) 20%
(B) 26%
(C) 43%
(D) 54%
(E) 69%

15. If *s* and *t* are prime numbers, which of the following CANNOT be the sum of *s* and *t*?

(A) 5
(B) 8
(C) 14
(D) 16
(E) 27

16. In year *T*, 7.4% of the women in the work force were unemployed in April compared with 7.1% in March. If the number of women in the work force was the same for both months, how many women were unemployed in April of that year?

(1) In March of year *T*, the number of unemployed women in the work force was 4.42 million.

(2) In year *T*, 240,000 more women in the work force were unemployed in April than in March.

17. If the average (arithmetic mean) of 5 numbers is 60, how many of the numbers are greater than 60?

(1) None of the five numbers is equal to 60.

(2) Two of the number are equal to 30.

18. On Friday afternoon, a certain printer ran continuously at a consistent rate to fill a production order. At what time did it completely fill the order that afternoon?

   (1) The printer began filling the order at 12:30 p.m.

   (2) The printer had filled $\frac{1}{2}$ of the order by 1:30 p.m. and $\frac{5}{6}$ of the order by 2:10 p.m.

19. Of the 2,400 employees of Company Y, $\frac{1}{4}$ are union workers. If the number of union workers were to be reduced by $\frac{1}{4}$, and no nonunion workers are hired or fired, what percent of the total number of the remaining employees would then be union workers?

   (A) 20%

   (B) 22.5%

   (C) 25%

   (D) 40%

   (E) 42.5%

20. In which of the following pairs are the two numbers reciprocals of each other?

   I. 4 and $\frac{1}{4}$

   II. $\frac{1}{15}$ and $-\frac{1}{15}$

   III. $\sqrt{3}$ and $\frac{\sqrt{3}}{3}$

   (A) I only

   (B) II only

   (C) I and II

   (D) I and III

   (E) II and III

21. If x folders cost $4.00 each and y folders cost $7.00 each, the average (arithmetic mean) cost in dollars per folder is equal to

   (A) $\dfrac{4x + 7y}{x + y}$

   (B) $\dfrac{4x + 7y}{xy}$

   (C) $\dfrac{4x + 7y}{11}$

   (D) $\dfrac{21xy}{x + y}$

   (E) $\dfrac{21xy}{11}$

22. If $s + m = p$, what is the value of m?

    (1) $s = 12$

    (2) $p + 12 = s$

23. Town C has 40,000 residents, 40% of whom are male. What percent of the residents were born in Town C?

    (1) The number of male residents who were born in Town C is twice the number of female residents who were *not* born in Town C.

    (2) The number of male residents who were *not* born in Town C is twice the number of male residents who were born in Town C.

24. If $\frac{1}{2}$ of the money inherited by a certain individual was invested in gold, $\frac{1}{4}$ in stocks, $\frac{1}{5}$ in government bonds, and the remaining $20,000 in real estate, what was the total amount of money inherited?

    (A) $200,000

    (B) $370,000

    (C) $400,000

    (D) $650,000

    (E) $800,000

25. Debbi rented a car for $22.00 plus $0.10 per mile driven. Tom rented a car for $28.00 plus $0.05 per mile driven. If each drove x miles and each was charged exactly the same amount for the rental, x equals

    (A) 100

    (B) 105

    (C) 115

    (D) 120

    (E) 140

26. Can the positive integer r be written as the sum of two different positive prime numbers?

    (1) r is greater than 3.

    (2) r is odd.

27. If both c and d are nonzero numbers, what is the value of $\frac{d}{c}$?

    (1) $c = 6$

    (2) $d^2 = c^2$

28. What were the gross revenues from ticket sales for a certain Broadway play during the second week that it ran?

(1) Gross revenues during the second week were $2.5 million less than during the first week.

(2) Gross revenues during the third week were $3.0 million less than during the first week.

29. Machine C produces doll parts at a uniform rate of 150 every 50 seconds, and Machine D produces doll parts at a uniform rate of 160 every 40 seconds. If the two machiness work simultaneously, how many seconds will it take for them to produce a total of 210 doll parts?

(A) 28
(B) 30
(C) 32
(D) 36
(E) 42

30. $\frac{5.005}{4.004} =$

(A) .755
(B) 1.0055
(C) 1.05
(D) 1.155
(E) 1.25

31. What is the decimal equivalent of $(\frac{1}{4})^4$?

(A) 0.0039062
(B) 0.0046420
(C) 0.0016
(D) 0.016
(E) 0.025

32. What number is 20% of r?

(1) 14 is 4% of r.
(2) $\frac{2}{3}$ of r is 200.

33. How many videocassettes does Bob have?

(1) If Bob had 15 fewer videocassettes, he would have only half as many as he actually has.

(2) Bob has twice as many action videocassettes as horror videocassettes.

34. For a company retreat, two hundred gallons of lemonade are purchased at $9.10 per gallon and are consumed at a rate of $70.00 worth of lemonade per hour. At this rate, how many hours are required to consume the 200 gallons of lemonade?

(A) 14

(B) 22

(C) 26

(D) 33

(E) 36

35. If Shirley had twice the amount of money that she has, she would have exactly the amount necessary to buy 3 hotdogs at $0.94 each and 2 soft drinks at $1.30 each. How much money does Shirley have?

(A) $2.49

(B) $2.67

(C) $2.71

(D) $2.83

(E) $2.87

36. If a fax machine can process two documents in $\frac{1}{4}$ second, then, at the same rate, how many documents can it process in 4 minutes?

(A) 1,004

(B) 1,204

(C) 1,440

(D) 1,640

(E) 1,920

37. What is the amount of money raised by a certain organization?

(1) Of the amount raised, 40% came from fundraising efforts.

(2) Of the amount raised, $150,000 came from individual donations.

SECTION 4

75 Minutes

41 Questions

Verbal

This section consists of three different types of questions.

Each *Reading Comprehension* question is based on the content of the accompanying passage. Read the passage and choose the best answer from each of the questions that follow. The correct answers will refer to information that is stated or implied in the passage.

The *Sentence Correction* questions contain a sentence that is either partially or completely underlined. Following the sentence are five answer choices, each giving you five different ways to phrase the underlined portion of the sentence. Answer choice A repeats the original sentence; choose answer choice A if you do not want to change the underlined portion at all. The remaining answer choices are all different.

Your answer choices will depend on the standards of written English, especially sentence construction, grammar, and word choice. The questions test your ability to express an idea clearly, simply, and correctly, without being awkward or redundant, while obeying all grammar rules.

To answer the *Critical Reasoning* questions, read the question and any accompanying information, and then select the best answer choice from those given.

Questions 1–3 are based on the following passage.

Eli Whitney (1765–1825) was the inventor of the cotton gin. This innovative machine enabled the American South to begin the mass production of cotton. Eli Whitney's cotton gin could produce up to 50 pounds of cleaned cotton daily; this efficient machine helped make cotton a prof-
5 itable crop for the first time.

The cotton gin is a machine that removes the seeds from the cotton fiber. Although Whitney's cotton gin was the first of its kind in America, simple devices similar to the cotton gin were used for centuries around the world. For instance, an Indian invention called a *charka* was used to sepa-
10 rate the cottonseeds from the lint when the crude fiber was pulled through the machine. This machine was not used in America because the *charka* was designed to process long-staple cotton and America produced short-

staple cotton. Before the cotton gin was invented, the cottonseed in America was removed by hand.

15   The invention of the cotton gin transformed the economy of the South. Farmers who produced other crops were displaced as cotton plantations were formed. Cotton was so profitable that many farmers stopped planting food crops. This led to a sharp decrease in food supplies.

Although the cotton gin is considered to be one of the most important
20 inventions in American history, the cotton gin also played a devastating role in causing the continuance of slavery in America. Prior to the invention of the cotton gin, slavery had become unpopular in America. The new immigrants who arrived daily to the United States made labor inexpensive enough that slavery was no longer as profitable as it had been.
25 However, when cotton plantations emerged, the need for labor skyrocketed and plantation owners became fierce advocates for slavery. The enormous plantations required a tremendous amount of labor to pick and process the cotton. While the arrival of immigrants to America brought cheap labor, the immigrants were generally unwilling to do the arduous
30 work required for cotton production. Unable to attract immigrant workers, the plantation owners relied almost solely on slave labor.

1. The passage is primarily concerned with
   - (A) evaluating the impact of slavery on American history
   - (B) comparing Eli Whitney's cotton gin with the *charka*
   - (C) contradicting historians who believe that the cotton gin was a beneficial invention
   - (D) examining the effects the cotton gin had on the economy of the South
   - (E) criticizing farmers who switched to planting cotton after the invention of the cotton gin

2. According to the passage, the cotton gin is associated with
   - (A) causing unemployment rates among immigrants to rise
   - (B) prolonging the existence of slavery in the United States
   - (C) the price of labor skyrocketing in the South
   - (D) the production of other textile crops ceasing
   - (E) eliminating the need for other machines that processed cotton

3. In the last paragraph, the author is primarily concerned with

  (A) deprecating the invention of the cotton gin

  (B) analyzing the effects of immigration on cotton production

  (C) discussing a negative impact that the cotton gin had on society

  (D) refuting an argument that immigration did not affect the American economy

  (E) citing evidence that slavery was about to be abolished prior to the invention of the cotton gin

4. The alcohol industry is still lucrative and experts believe that it will remain so. In Canada this year, the total amount of alcohol sold by manufacturers has increased, even though the number of adults who drink alcohol has decreased.

Each of the following, if true, could explain the simultaneous increase in alcohol sales and the decrease in the number of adults who drink alcohol EXCEPT:

  (A) During this year, the number of men who have begun to drink alcohol is greater than the number of men who have quit drinking alcohol.

  (B) The number of underage drinkers this year is greater than the number of adults who have quit drinking alcohol during the same period.

  (C) During this year, the number of nondrinkers who have begun to use alcohol for cooking is greater than the number of people who have quit drinking alcohol.

  (D) The people who have continued to drink consume more alcohol per person than they did in the past.

  (E) More of the alcohol produced in Canada this year was exported to other countries than was the case last year.

5. Cereal has more nutritional value than bread. But since pasta has more nutritional value than rice, it follows that cereal has more nutritional value than rice.

Any of the following, if introduced into the argument as an additional premise, makes the argument above logically correct EXCEPT:

  (A) Pasta has more nutritional value than cereal.

  (B) Bread has more nutritional value than rice.

  (C) Bread has more nutritional value than pasta.

  (D) Bread and pasta have the same nutritional value.

  (E) Cereal and pasta have the same nutritional value.

6. The Truman study indicates that even after two decades adult men and women still experience some of the effects of a traumatic incident <u>occurring when an adolescent</u>.

   (A) occurring when an adolescent
   (B) occurring when adolescents
   (C) that occurred when a adolescent
   (D) that occurred when they were adolescents
   (E) that has occurred as each was an adolescent

7. Since 1992, when the livestock depression began, the number of acres overseen by certified ranch-management companies <u>have grown from 22 million to nearly 37 million, an area that is about Maine's size</u>.

   (A) have grown from 22 million to nearly 37 million, an area that is about Maine's size
   (B) have grown from 22 million to nearly 37 million, about the size of Maine
   (C) has grown from 22 million to nearly 37 million, an area about the size of Maine
   (D) has grown from 22 million up to nearly 37 million, an area about the size of Maine
   (E) has grown from 22 million up to nearly 37 million, about Maine's size

8. The only way for farmers to recover frozen wheat crops is <u>to thresh them quickly into hay before the arrival of warmer weather causes the wheat to decompose</u>.

   (A) to thresh them quickly into hay before the arrival of warmer weather causes the wheat to decompose
   (B) if they are quickly threshed into hay before warmer weather arrives to decompose them
   (C) for them to be threshed quickly into hay before they decompose when warmer weather arrives
   (D) if the wheat is quickly threshed into hay before it decomposes when warmer weather arrives
   (E) to have it quickly threshed into hay before warmer weather arrives and decomposes the wheat

9. Carbon-14 dating reveals that the bones found in South Africa are nearly 3,000 years <u>as old as any of their supposed</u> Arab ancestors.

   (A) as old as any of there supposed
   (B) older than any of their supposed
   (C) as older as they supposed
   (D) older than any of there supposed
   (E) as older as their supposedly

Questions 10–12 are based on the following passage.

A person is diagnosed with insomnia when he or she has trouble falling asleep or is unable to remain sleeping for normal periods of time. Over one-third of Americans experience occasional insomnia, and chronic insomnia occurs in about 10% of the adult American population. Insomnia can cause
5 a person to be fatigued during the day, alter a person's mood, and affect concentration. Although insomnia can occur in people of all ages, insomnia is most common among women and older adults. Although most people believe that insomnia is caused by stress, many medical problems can disrupt sleep and produce symptoms of insomnia.

10 Sleep-related breathing disorders, such as sleep apnea, can cause insomnia by repeatedly interrupting breathing during the night. Pauses in breathing might last only a few seconds and are usually not remembered. However, these brief pauses are disruptive and can cause non-restorative sleep. Conditions like sleep apnea are most common in men, people who
15 snore, overweight people, and the elderly. A person might have a sleep-related breathing disorder if wheezing, grunts, snorts, or other abnormal sounds interrupt his or her breathing.

In addition to breathing disorders, brief muscle contractions can cause involuntary leg movements. These small jerks usually last for only a few
20 seconds. However, episodes of this behavior can occur repeatedly throughout the night. Normally, the sleeper is unaware of this limb movement. Even so, these jerks can interrupt a person's sleep hundreds of times each night. These jerky limb movements can increase in severity and frequency as a person gets older.

25 Acid reflux or heartburn can also cause symptoms of insomnia. The backup of the stomach contents into the esophagus is uncomfortable and can awaken a person from an otherwise sound sleep. Acid reflux causes pain or tightness in the chest. Reflux can usually be controlled during the daytime by swallowing and sitting in an upright position. Severe cases of acid reflux
30 require medication. During the night, people suffering from acid reflux do not swallow as frequently and their reclined position causes more reflux to occur. A person suffering from acid reflux will often wake up to cough or choke the painful reflux away.

10. The primary focus of the passage is on which of the following?

(A) Comparing the symptoms of sleep apnea with acid reflux

(B) Describing medical conditions that can lead to insomnia

(C) Evaluating the effects of insomnia on overweight people

(D) Explaining how a person can overcome insomnia

(E) Analyzing medical research that suggests insomnia is most common in women and the elderly

11. The author states, "Although most people believe that insomnia is caused by stress, many medical problems can disrupt sleep and produce symptoms of insomnia" (lines 7–9) most likely in order to

    (A) show that the focus of the passage is on medical conditions that cause insomnia

    (B) introduce a controversial belief that insomnia is never caused by stress or anxiety

    (C) explain how medical problems can cause symptoms of insomnia

    (D) introduce scientific research that suggests insomnia is mostly caused by medical conditions

    (E) analyze why insomnia affects mostly women and the elderly

12. According to the passage, conditions that cause insomnia

    (A) are often related to life threatening illnesses or diseases

    (B) can be prevented or treated only with medication

    (C) may not be known to the person suffering from insomnia

    (D) are usually somehow related to stress and anxiety

    (E) are all known to cause great discomfort to the sleeper

13. Dr. Morison's research among Asian children in California indicates that the more the children use both their native language and English, their academic benefit is greater in skills underlying writing ability and logic problems.

    (A) their academic benefit is greater in skills underlying writing ability and logic problems

    (B) their academic benefit is the greater in skills underlying writing ability and logic problems

    (C) the greater is their academic benefit in skills underlying writing ability and logic problems

    (D) in skills underlying writing ability and logic problems, their academic benefit is the greater

    (E) in skills underlying writing ability and logic problems, the greater academic benefit is theirs

14. On the basis of a decrease in the driver's education age population, many driving schools now expect increasingly smaller beginner classes each year. Surprised by the 30% increase in interest over the previous year, however, administrators at Ace Driving School now plan to hire more instructors for all programs taken by beginning drivers.

Which of the following statements about Ace Driving School's current qualified applicants, if true, would strongly suggest that the administrator's plan is flawed?

   (A) A substantially higher percentage than usual plan to study for chauffeur's licenses after completing driver's education.

   (B) According to the information collected about the potential students, their level of knowledge about watercraft is unusually high.

   (C) According to the potential students, none of them drove motorcycles in foreign countries.

   (D) A substantially lower than usual percentage rate Ace Driving School as their first choice among the driving schools that they are investigating.

   (E) A substantially lower percentage than usual indicated that they will not own vehicles immediately after completing their driver's education.

15. A medical expert discovered that people who have low levels of white blood cells tend to score lower on tests of mental illness (indicating a greater chance of becoming mentally ill) than do people with normal levels of white blood cells. The medical expert concluded from this information that white blood cells protect against mental ailments as well as against infection.

The medical expert's conclusion depends on which of the following assumptions?

   (A) High levels of white blood cells protect against mental illness better than normal levels of white blood cells.

   (B) Mental illness is similar to infection in its effects on the human body.

   (C) People with high levels of white blood cells cannot develop infections.

   (D) Mental illness does not cause people's level of white blood cells to decrease.

   (E) Psychological treatment of mental illness is not as effective as drug therapy.

16. Car manufacturers: Newly developed safety features, although not fully tested to discover malfunctions, must be installed immediately in all vehicles. These safety features enable drivers to survive crashes.

Car Dealers: Drivers will not drive vehicles with safety features that are not fully tested. Malfunctioning safety features could distract drivers, causing crashes.

The dealers' objection is most strengthened if which of the following is true?

(A) It is always possible for safety features to malfunction.

(B) Air bags, although not fully tested when first put into use, have achieved excellent performance and safety records.

(C) Although safety features will enable drivers to avoid some crashes, the likely malfunction of the not fully tested safety features will cause even more crashes.

(D) Many vehicle collisions are caused in part by distracted drivers.

(E) Safety features, at this stage of development, appear to have worked better in commercial vehicles than in military vehicles during tests conducted over a 3-month period.

17. Lacking information about electricity use, families tend to overestimate the amount of energy used by <u>equipment, such as computers, that are noticeable and must be turned on and off and underestimate that</u> used by inconspicuous equipment, such as air purifiers.

(A) equipment, such as computers, that are noticeable and must be turned on and off and underestimate that

(B) equipment, such as computers, that are noticeable and must be turned on and off and underestimate when

(C) equipment, such as computers, that is noticeable and must be turned on and off and underestimate it when the amount

(D) noticeable equipment, such as computers, that must be turned on and off, and underestimate the amount

(E) noticeable equipment, such as computers, that must be turned on and off and underestimate it when

18. Zoologists at the Arborland Zoo have discovered a distinct animal mutation, one <u>that they believe is</u> a type previously unknown to science.

(A) that they believe is

(B) that they believe to be

(C) they believe that it is

(D) they believe that is

(E) they believe to be of

Questions 19–22 are based on the following passage.

It is widely accepted that William Faulkner (1897–1962) perfected revolutionary literary devices such as stream of consciousness, multiple narrations, and time shifts within a narrative. Faulkner is known for producing literary works filled with emotional turmoil and unflinching hon-
5   esty. It has also been argued that Faulkner's works are some of the best representations of Southern Gothic literature.

Faulkner's Deep South roots greatly influenced his writing. Faulkner's remarkable understanding of race relations and his clever satire of Southern characters draws on his own memories of growing up in
10   Missisippi. Faulkner set many of his short stories and novels in the fictional Yoknapatawpha County. Faulkner acknowledges that Yoknapatawpha was modeled after his own memories of Lafayette County, Mississippi.

Faulkner came from a very old and relatively prominent Southern
15   family. He grew up surrounded by traditional folklore, family stories, accounts from the Civil War, and lectures about being a Southern gentleman. In Faulkner's works, he examines how traditional values and beliefs affected Southern society after the Civil War. Faulkner was particularly concerned with the rampant racism and abuse that African
20   Americans suffered in the South. Although Faulkner's novels do not shy away from describing the brutality and anguish that life can bring, his works are filled with profound compassion and humor. Faulkner refused to balk at painful or controversial issues and he was intrigued with understanding human freedom. Faulkner's work explores, condemns,
25   and analyzes obstructions to human freedom and happiness by examining racism, shame, fear, false pride, and abstract ideals. Much of Faulkner's analysis is accomplished through the application of brilliant symbolism and exquisite dialogue.

Although Faulkner was raised in the rural Deep South, he became
30   acquainted with the world by joining the Royal Air Force. During his time as a fighter pilot, he became deeply influenced by what he saw during his travels to major American and European cities. Faulkner was also fascinated by the modernist influences that were changing art, literature, theater, and music. For a few years, Faulkner even lived in the famous
35   French Quarter of New Orleans and became friends with other aspiring writers and artists.

19. The passage is primarily concerned with which of the following?

(A) Evaluating criticisms of Faulkner's novels and writing style

(B) Examining the history of Southern Gothic literature

(C) Discussing various literary techniques and discovering their origins

(D) Criticizing racism and abstract ideals for being obstructions to freedom

(E) Analyzing Faulkner's style, work, and inspiration

20. The author implies which of the following in the passage?

  (A) Faulkner decided to become a writer after his stay in the French Quarter.

  (B) Faulkner's childhood in the Deep South was not the only thing that influenced him.

  (C) Faulkner uses compassion and humor to disguise the brutal realities he portrays in his work.

  (D) Faulkner also became a skilled artist and musician in the modernist tradition.

  (E) Faulkner's experiences with being a victim of racism greatly inspired his writing.

21. Which of the following best describes the relation of the first paragraph to the passage as a whole?

  (A) It makes a broad observation to be illustrated and exemplified.

  (B) It outlines an argument to be analyzed by the author.

  (C) It poses a question to be answered in the passage.

  (D) It provides general information that the rest of the passage builds on.

  (E) It introduces controversial information and facts to be reconciled.

22. The inspirations, events, people, and places that influenced Faulkner's work are most similar to which of the following?

  (A) An artist having muses from nature, popular culture, architecture, and literature

  (B) A musician being able to reconstruct ancient melodies using modern influences

  (C) An actor having different personas when playing diverse roles

  (D) A painter intentionally mixing different colors of paint in order to create the perfect shade

  (E) A writer depending on an editor to help formulate his ideas and structure

23. Most consumers often do not use the fitness equipment they purchase. For instance, 4% of the families in the United States own treadmills, but only 46% of the treadmill owners run or walk on their treadmills more than once a month, and only 19% of the treadmill owners run or walk on their treadmills more than once a week.

  Which of the following, if true, casts most doubt on the claim that most consumers get little use out of the fitness equipment they purchase?

(A) People who use treadmills are most vulnerable to joint injuries the first year in which they use the treadmill.

(B) People who own treadmills often exaggerate the regularity with which they use their treadmills in surveys designed to obtain such data.

(C) Many consumers purchase treadmills to use for other purposes besides running or walking.

(D) Consumers who purchase treadmills often purchase other fitness equipment as well.

(E) Consumers who purchase treadmills are usually not in better shape than consumers who purchase stationary bicycles.

24. Three decades after the Rogue River Dam was built, none of the six frog species native to the Rogue River was still reproducing adequately in the river below the dam. Since the dam reduced the average water temperature in the river below the dam from 60° to 17°, wildlife experts argue that warm water temperatures are needed to prompt the native frog species to reproduce.

Which of the following statements, if true, would most strengthen the experts' argument?

(A) The six native frog species were able to continue reproducing in parts of the river above the dam where the average temperature of the water was around 60°.

(B) Before the dam was built, the Rogue River often overflowed and brought critical nutrients from the banks that helped facilitate frog reproduction.

(C) The highest recorded temperature of the Rogue River before the dam was built was 72°, whereas the highest recorded temperature of the river after the dam was built was 33°.

(D) Nonnative species of frog, introduced after the dam was built, have begun competing with the native frog species for insects.

(E) All of the frog species native to the Rogue River are also native to other rivers in South America.

25. However much Korean leaders may argue that there is too much pollution in the cities and that the government does not enforce environmental regulations, it is not easy to find widespread support for environmental reforms.

(A) However much Korean leaders may argue that

(B) Despite the argument among Korean leaders to the fact

(C) Although Korean leaders argue

(D) Even though Korean leaders may present arguments

(E) There is arguments among Korean leaders that

26. <u>Based on the account of various ancient anthropologists</u>, modern scientists have presented a vague report of the activities of an all-female army that, perhaps, included members who were larger than the average modern female.

    (A) Based on the account of various ancient anthropologists

    (B) Basing it on various ancient anthropologists' accounts

    (C) With accounts of various ancient anthropologists used for a basis

    (D) By the accounts of various ancient anthropologists

    (E) Using accounts of various ancient anthropologists

27. Business representatives report that soaring <u>rates of medical insurance have risen to compel</u> cutbacks in hiring and advertising.

    (A) rates of medical insurance have risen to compel

    (B) rates of medical insurance are forced for

    (C) medical insurance rates are forcing

    (D) rises in medical insurance rates are forcing

    (E) medical insurance rates are rising forcing

28. Unlike a normal home loan, which requires a 10%–20% down payment, <u>the interest-only loan buyer is not required to make</u> an initial down payment on their home.

    (A) the interest-only loan buyer is not required to make

    (B) with interest-only loaning there is not the requirement of

    (C) interest-only loaners are not required to make

    (D) for interest-only buyers there is no requirement of

    (E) an interest-only loan does not require buyers to make

Questions 29–32 are based on the following passage.

    During warm summer nights, brilliant flashes of lightning might periodically appear without any accompanying rainfall or thunder. This phenomenon is referred to as *heat lightning*. Folk weather mythology maintains that heat lightning is merely very hot air expanding until it creates
5   large sparks. Many trustworthy professionals will even say that heat lightning does not exist. This assertion is not completely accurate.

    The term *heat* in heat lightning does not have to do with the temperature of the lightning itself. The term *heat lightning* most likely became popular because this form of lightning is associated with air mass thunderstorms in warm weather. During hot and humid weather, brief storms
10   can scatter across large regions. These storms often travel long distances and are known for bringing cooler temperatures and refreshing winds. Because these scattered thunderstorms do not produce a heavy cloud cover, storm watchers can often see storms below the horizon. During

15 some thunderstorms, the light from lightning bolts can be seen as far as 100 miles away depending on the height of the bolt, the clarity of the air, and the elevation of the viewer. In comparison, thunder can usually only be heard from 5–15 miles away.

20 Heat lightning is not a special type of lightning. Instead, heat lightning is merely ordinary thunderstorm lightning that appears too far away from the observer for any thunder to be heard. The movement of sound in the atmosphere depends on the atmospheric properties of the air. Temperature and density can both be factors determining how far away thunder can be heard. Both temperature and density change with
25 altitude. The loud booms that thunder creates are refracted through the lower levels of the atmosphere. This refraction creates spaces through which the sound of thunder does not disseminate. The sound of thunder usually reflects off the earth's surface. The grumbling noises that can be heard are mostly due to these sound reflections. The earth's shape also
30 contributes to people being unable to hear thunder. Although harmless when seen from a distance, heat lightning can be a warning that a storm is approaching.

29. The primary function of the passage as a whole is to

(A) discuss the failings of folk weather mythology and modern meteorological techniques

(B) identify the characteristics of heat lightning and thunder

(C) examine laws of science relating to sound and speed

(D) correct common misconceptions about thunder and storms

(E) explain how and why a certain phenomenon occurs

30. The passage most clearly implies which of the following about heat lightning?

(A) Heat lightning is caused by hot air expanding until it creates sparks.

(B) Heat lightning affects the temperatures of the surrounding air.

(C) Characteristics of thunder make heat lightning appear different from thunderstorm lightning.

(D) Heat lightning occurs only during long periods of hot and humid weather.

(E) Temperature and density affect the intensity of heat lightning.

31. Which of the following best describes the structure of the passage?

(A) Two theories about heat lightning are presented and the shortcomings of both are identified.

(B) A scientific account disproves two theories presented in the beginning of the passage.

(C) An argument is presented and counter arguments are mentioned.

(D) A hypothesis about heat lightning is proven by citing specific scientific research.

(E) A warning about the dangers of lightning is presented by discounting other theories.

32. The function of the first paragraph is to

(A) introduce common misconceptions about heat lightning

(B) introduce arguments that are systematically disproved through scientific experiments

(C) argue against using folk weather mythology to describe weather phenomena

(D) debate whether weather professionals are correct in their assessment about heat lightning

(E) discuss the effects that warm weather can have on lightning and thunder

33. Ancient Mayan burial sites dating back thousands of years indicate that the residents of Mexico at that time <u>were part of a widespread society of craft-making people</u>.

(A) were part of a widespread society of craft-making people

(B) had been part of a widespread society of people who were craft making

(C) were people who were part of a widespread society that was craft making

(D) had been craft-making people of a widespread society

(E) were a part of a craft-making people in a widespread society

34. In addition to having less sugar than soda pop does, <u>the nutrients in fruit juice are higher quality than that in soda pop</u>, with more of the natural fibers vital to the human diet.

(A) the nutrients in fruit juice are higher quality than that in soda pop

(B) fruit juice contains a higher nutrient level

(C) the nutrients in fruit juice is higher in quality than it is in soda pop

(D) fruit juice nutrients is higher in quality than in soda pop

(E) fruit juice has a higher nutrients in quality

35. An array of financial incentives has led to a boom in the real estate market; <u>so copious has capital been for residential real estate that</u> builders regularly scour the city for areas in which to start construction.

    (A) so copious has capital been for residential real estate that
    (B) capital has been so copious for residential real estate, so that
    (C) the copious of capital for residential real estate has been so
    (D) such has the copious of capital been for residential real estate that
    (E) such has been the copiousness of capital for residential real estate that

36. It is true that it is against the law to sell alcohol to minors. But if my store does not do so, stores on other blocks will.

    Which of the following is most like the argument above in its logical structure?

    (A) It is true that it is against the school's policy to negotiate with picketers. But if the school wants to prevent lost class time, they must negotiate in some cases.
    (B) It is true that it is illegal to drop out of school before the age of sixteen. But there is a long tradition in the United States of religious objections to attending school after eighth grade.
    (C) It is true that it is illegal for professional athletes to bet on professional sporting events. But if the evidence is examined carefully, it will clearly be seen that the accused athlete was not placing wagers.
    (D) It is true that it is against the law to steal automobiles. But someone else certainly would have stolen the automobile if the defendant had not done so first.
    (E) It is true that company policy forbids supervisors from dating employees. But there have been many supervisors who have disobeyed this policy.

37. In recent years, many carpenters have been earning acclaim as artists. But since woodwork should be functional, carpenters must build their pieces with an eye to the pragmatic utility of their creations. For this reason, carpentry should not be considered an art.

    Which of the following is an assumption that supports the conclusion drawn above?

    (A) Some woodwork is placed in museums, where it will not be used by consumers.
    (B) Some carpenters are more concerned than others with the degree of utility in the creations they produce.
    (C) Carpenters should focus more on making their creations practical and useful.
    (D) A piece should not be considered a work of art if the creator pays attention to the object's pragmatic utility.
    (E) Carpenters are not concerned with making a profit from their work.

38. The recent rise in the value of the British pound was triggered by a prediction of rapid economic growth in the coming quarter. But the prediction would not have affected the value of the pound had it not been for the continuing strength of the European Union. Therefore, the European Union must continue to be remain strong to prevent any future declines in the value of the pound.

Which of the following, if true, would most seriously weaken the conclusion about how to prevent declines in the value of the pound?

(A) The British government has been a key player in helping strengthen the European Union.

(B) The European Union has caused great economic growth throughout Europe.

(C) The value of the pound increased several times in the year prior to recent predictions of rapid economic growth.

(D) Before the European Union was formed, predictions of slower economic growth often caused declines in the pound's value.

(E) Without the European Union, economic growth would stall in France and Spain.

39. Normally, decision making by doctors that is based on medical protocol has been considered preferable to instinctive decision making. However, a recent study in a top medical journal found that the most highly regarded doctors use instinct considerably more than less highly regarded doctors. This study confirms the unconventional view that instinct is actually more effective than reasoning based on traditional medical procedure.

The conclusion above is based on which of the following assumptions?

(A) Decisions based on medical protocol are unsuitable for making many real-life medical decisions.

(B) Highly regarded doctors have the ability to use either instinct or medical protocol to make decisions.

(C) The medical decisions made by less highly regarded doctors can be made as easily by using medical protocol as by using instinct.

(D) Highly regarded doctors use instinct in making the majority of their medical decisions.

(E) Highly regarded doctors are better at decision making than less highly regarded doctors.

40. A government study reveals that the <u>numbers of men not employed outside of the home grew by more than a 10% increase</u> in the past decade.

(A) the numbers of men not employed outside of the home grew by more than a 10% increase

(B) numbers of men not employed outside the home grew more than 10%

(C) numbers of men not employed outside the home were raised by more than 10%

(D) number of men not employed outside the home increased by more than 10%

(E) number of men not employed outside the home was raised by more than a 10% increase

41. The most important decision for most residents living in a neighborhood undergoing <u>being rezoned for commercial real estate is if to sign</u> a no-sell pledge with the other residents.

(A) being rezoned for commercial real estate is if to sign

(B) being rezoned for commercial real estate is whether they should be signing

(C) being rezoned for commercial real estate is whether or not they sign

(D) rezoning for commercial real estate is if to sign

(E) rezoning for commercial real estate is whether to sign

Practice Test 1 Answer Key and Explanations

Analysis of an Argument and Analysis of an Issue

Because grading the essay is subjective, we've chosen not to include any "graded" essays here. Your best bet is to have someone you trust, such as your personal tutor, read your essays and give you an honest critique. Make the grading criteria mentioned in Chapter 1 available to whomever grades your essays. If you plan on grading your own essays, review the grading criteria and be as honest as possible regarding the structure, development, organization, technique, and appropriateness of your writing. Focus on your weak areas and continue to practice in order to improve your writing skills.

Quantitative

1. **The correct answer is C.** Because Jennifer was 23 years old 7 years ago, her age is now 23 + 7, or 30. x years ago, Jennifer was x years younger than she is now, so her age was $30 - x$.

2. **The correct answer is B.** To solve, first calculate the production rate. The production rate of each machine is $\frac{540}{12}$ = 45 containers per minute. Therefore, the production rate for 20 machines is 45(20), or 900 containers per minute. Multiplying the production rate for 20 machines (900) by the number of minutes gives (8): 900(8) = 7,200.

3. **The correct answer is D**. The area of a rectangle is found by multiplying the length by the width. The area of the rectangular portion of the park is $40x = 1,360$ feet if x is the unknown dimension. Solve for x:

➤ $x = 1,360 \div 40$

➤ $x = 34$

Now you know the length and the width: 40 and 34. The amount of the fencing needed, then, is $34 + 40 + 34$, or 108 feet.

4. **The correct answer is A**. Statement (1) alone is sufficient because if 90% of the male voters, voted for O'Donnell, then 100% − 90%, or 10% of the male voters voted for Johnson. Statement (2) alone is not sufficient because it gives no information about the male voters.

5. **The correct answer is E**. Statement (1) alone is not sufficient because it does not say how many gallons of gasoline were purchased or how many miles were driven. Statement (2) alone is also not sufficient because it does not specify how much money was spent on gasoline. Because you do not know the total amount spent on gasoline or the number of gallons bought, the two statements together are not sufficient.

6. **The correct answer is C**. If a product xy is divisible by the prime number 3, then either x or y is divisible by 3. Statement (1) alone is not sufficient because it does not determine whether x is divisible by 3. Statement (2) alone is not sufficient because no information is given about x. The two statements together are sufficient. If xy is divisible by 3 and y is not divisible by 3, you know that x is divisible by 3.

7. **The correct answer is E**. The sum of the 4 original numbers must be 4(9), or 36. When one number is discarded, the sum of the remaining 3 numbers must be 3(6), or 18. Therefore, the discarded number is 36 − 18, or 18.

8. **The correct answer is A**. To solve, first calculate the total sales during each week. The total sales revenue from the skis during the first week was 10(95), or $950.00. During the second week, total sales revenue was 15(75.50), or $1,132.50. Now, find the difference between week 2 and week 1: $1,132.50 − $950.00 = $182.50.

9. **The correct answer is C**. To solve, set the number of members to x. If x is the number of members in the sorority, at least $12x$ dollars was collected. Therefore, $12x$ must be less than or equal to $699.00. Solve for x:

➤ $12x = 699$

➤ $\dfrac{699}{12} = 58\,\dfrac{1}{4}$

Because x must be a whole number, (you can't have $\dfrac{1}{4}$ of a sorority member!) the greatest possible value for x is 58.

10. **The correct answer is B.** To solve, first recognize that $\dfrac{7}{4}$ represents the ratio 7:4. Statement (1) alone is not sufficient because s and t could be any numbers in the ratio 7:4. Statement (2) alone is sufficient because the equation in the question and the equation in statement (2) form two equations with two unknowns, which can be solved.

11. **The correct answer is C.** To solve, pick values for the variables. If $rw > 0$, both v and w could equal either 1 or -1. If $wx < 0$, either w or x could equal -1, if the other equaled 1. Statement (1) alone is not sufficient because both sets of the values $v = 1$, $w = 1$, $x = -1$, $w = -1$, $v = -1$, and $x = 1$ are consistent with the statement. Statement (2) alone is not sufficient because it gives no information about x. The two statements together are sufficient. Since $vw > 0$ and $v > 0$, w must be greater than 0; since $wx < 0$ and w is greater than 0, x must be less than 0.

12. **The correct answer is A.** To solve, let k stand for Kevin's age now. Statement (1) indicates that $k = 2(k - 4)$, so $k = 8$. Statement (1) alone is sufficient. Letting l represent Lynn's age now, statement (2) implies that $l = 3(k - 4)$. This does not determine Kevin's age.

13. **The correct answer is E.** To solve, let p stand for the number of brand P candies Diana purchased. Because she purchased a total of 12 boxes of candy, the number of brand Q candies she purchased was $12 - p$. Set up an equation for the total cost of the candy:

➤ $4p + 2.5(12 - p) = 42$

➤ $4p + 30 - 2.5p = 42$

➤ $1.5p = 12$

➤ $p = 8$

14. **The correct answer is E.** If the length and the width of the garage floor are l and w, respectively, the new length and width are $1.3l$ and $1.3w$. Solve for the percent increase: $(1.3l)(1.3w) = 1.69lw$. The percent increase in area is 69%, because 1.69 is .69 greater than 1.

15. **The correct answer is E.** The easiest way to solve this problem is to try the answer choices:

➤ **A**: you know that 2 + 3 = 5, and both 2 and 3 are prime numbers. Eliminate this choice.

➤ **B**: you know that 5 + 3 = 8, and both 5 and 3 are prime numbers. Eliminate this choice.

➤ **C**: you know that 11 + 3 = 14, and both 11 and 3 are prime numbers. Eliminate this choice.

➤ **D**: you know that 13 + 3 = 16, and both 13 and 3 are prime numbers. Eliminate this choice.

➤ **E**: you know that 2 + 25 = 27, but 25 is not a prime number. This is the correct answer choice.

16. **The correct answer is D.** Because 7.4% of the women in the work force were unemployed in April, the number of unemployed women could be found if the total number of women in the work force was known. Let w be the total number of women in the work force. Statement (1) indicates that $(7.4\%)w = 4.42$ million. The value of w can be found by solving for w in this equation. Statement (2) indicates that $(7.4\% - 7.1\%)w = 240,000$. The value of w can also be found by using statement (2) alone.

17. **The correct answer is E.** Both statements together are not sufficient to answer the question because statements (1) and (2) could both have either 1 *or* 2 numbers that are greater than 60 and still satisfy the conditions in both statements (1) and (2).

18. **The correct answer is B.** Statement (1) alone is not sufficient because you are told only what time the printer began filling the order. From statement (2) you can conclude that $\frac{5}{6} - \frac{1}{2}$, or $\frac{1}{3}$ of the order was filled in 40 minutes. At this pace, the entire order would be filled in 120 minutes. If half the order would be filled by 1:30 p.m., the entire order was filled by 2:30 p.m. Statement (2) alone is sufficient.

19. **The correct answer is A.** To solve, first calculate the number of union workers. The number of union workers is $\frac{1}{4}(2,400)$, or 600.

Next, reduce this number by $\frac{1}{4}$: $\frac{1}{4}$ (600) = 150, and 600 − 150 = 450. The total number of employees would then be 2,400 − 150, or 2,250. Therefore, the new percentage of total employees who are union members is $\frac{450}{2250}$, or .20, which is the decimal equivalent of 20%.

20. **The correct answer is D**. Numbers are reciprocal to each other if (and only if) the product of those two numbers is 1:

➤ $4 \times \frac{1}{4} = \frac{4}{4}$ or 1; eliminate answer choices B and E.

➤ $\frac{1}{15} \times -\frac{1}{15} = \frac{1}{225}$, which does not equal 1; eliminate answer choice C.

➤ $\sqrt{3} \times \frac{\sqrt{3}}{3} = \frac{3}{3}$, or 1. Therefore, answer choice D must be correct.

21. **The correct answer is A.** The average is equal to the total cost divided by the total number of folders. The total number of folders is $x + y$, and their total cost is $4x + 7y$ dollars. The average cost per folder is $\frac{4x + 7y}{x + y}$

22. **The correct answer is B**. Because you know that $s + m = p$, you also know that $m = p - s$. Statement (1) alone is not sufficient because you do not have any information about p. Statement (2) alone is sufficient because you can solve the equation for m.

23. **The correct answer is C**. Statement (1) alone is not sufficient because the total number of male and female residents born in Town C is unknown. Statement (2) alone is not sufficient because no information about the female residents born in Town C is given. From statements (1) and (2) together, you are able to determine the percent of residents born in Town C, but neither statement alone is sufficient.

24. **The correct answer is C**. To solve, first add the fractions (find the LCD):

➤ $\frac{1}{2} + \frac{1}{4} + \frac{1}{5} =$

The LCD is 20, because 2, 4, and 5 all divide evenly into 20, as shown here:

$\frac{1}{2} = \frac{10}{20}$; $\frac{1}{4} = \frac{5}{20}$; $\frac{1}{5} = \frac{4}{20}$

➤ $\frac{10}{20} + \frac{5}{20} + \frac{4}{20} = \frac{19}{20}$

Therefore, you know that $\frac{19}{20}$ of the inherited money was invested in gold, stocks, and government bonds. If t is the total amount inherited, you know that $(\frac{1}{20})t = \$20,000$, and $t = \$400,000$.

25. **The correct answer is D**. To solve, calculate the total charge for both Debbi and Tom. Debbi's total charge was $22.00 + 0.10x$ and Tom's total charge was $28.00 + 0.05x$. Because you know these quantities are the same, $22.00 + 0.10x = 28.00 + 0.05x$. Solve for x:

➤ $22 + .10x = 28 + .05x$

➤ $.05x = 6$

➤ $x = 120$

26. **The correct answer is E**. Statement (1) alone is not sufficient because $r = 4$ cannot be written as the sum of two different prime numbers. However, $r = 5$ can. Statement (2) alone is not sufficient because some odd integers can be written as the sum of two different prime numbers and others cannot. The two statements together are also not sufficient for these same reasons.

27. **The correct answer is E**. Statement (1) alone is not sufficient because it gives only the value of c. Statement (2) alone is not sufficient because the value of both c and d could be 1 *or* –1. The two statements together are not sufficient because if $c = 6$, d could be either 6 or –6.

28. **The correct answer is E**. Statement (1) alone is not sufficient because the amount of the gross revenues during the first week is unknown. Statement (2) alone is not sufficient because no information is given about the gross revenues in the second week. Statements (1) and (2) together are not sufficient because you need information about the gross revenues of the first or third week to solve the problem.

29. **The correct answer is B**. To solve, calculate the production rates for each worker. Machine C produces $\frac{150}{50}$, or 3 doll parts per second and Machine D produces $\frac{160}{40}$, or 4 doll parts per second. Working simultaneously, they produce 7 doll parts per second. Therefore, it would take them $\frac{210}{7}$, or 30 seconds working together to produce 210 doll parts.

30. The correct answer is E. To solve, simply reduce the fraction, as
follows:

$\frac{5.005}{4.004} = 5(1.001) \div 4(1.001) = \frac{5}{4}$, which is equal to 1.25.

31. The correct answer is A. To solve, first convert $\frac{1}{4}$ to .25, its decimal
equivalent:

➤$(\frac{1}{4})^4 = (.25)^4$

Raising .25 to the fourth power is the same as multiplying .25 by itself
four times.

➤$(.25)(.25)(.25)(.25) = 0.0039062$

32. The correct answer is D. This question can be answered if you
know the value of r. According to statement (1), $14 = 0.04r$. Using this
equation, you can solve for r. Therefore, statement (1) alone is sufficient. Statement (2) alone is also sufficient because you can use the
equation given in statement (2) to solve for r: $r(\frac{2}{3}) = 200$.

33. The correct answer is A. From statement (1), you can conclude that
15 videocassettes represents half of the total videocassettes that Bob
has. If you put this information into an equation and let x be the total
number of videocassettes that Bob has, you know that $x - 15 = \frac{1}{2x}$.
You can solve this equation for x; therefore, statement (1) alone is sufficient. Statement (2) alone is not sufficient because you are told only
the ratio of action videocassettes to horror videocassettes.

34. The correct answer is C. To solve, first calculate the total cost of
lemonade. The total cost of the 200 gallons of lemonade is $9.10(200),
or $1,820. The time required to drink the lemonade at a rate of
$70.00 worth of lemonade per hour is $\frac{1820}{70}$, or 26 hours.

35. **The correct answer is C.** To solve, let *s* be the amount of money that Shirley actually has. Then, set up an equation for 2*s* and solve for *s*, as follows:

➤ $2s = 3(.94) + 2(1.30)$

➤ $2s = 2.82 + 2.60$

➤ $2s = 5.42$

➤ $s = 2.71$

36. **The correct answer is E.** The fax machine processes documents at the rate of 2 documents in $\frac{1}{4}$ second, which is equivalent to 8 documents per second. Because 4 minutes equals 240 seconds (4 × 60), the fax machine processes 240 × 8, or 1,920 documents in 4 minutes.

37. **The correct answer is C.** The amount of money raised will be the total from fundraising and individual donations. Statement (1) alone is not sufficient because it gives only information about fundraising. Statement (2) alone is not sufficient because it gives only the amount of money earned from donations. However, from statements (1) and (2), you can calculate the total amount of money earned.

Verbal

1. **The best answer is D.** The passage discusses how the cotton gin changed the economy of the South. For instance, the passage states, "Farmers who produced other crops were displaced as cotton plantations were formed. Cotton was so profitable that many farmers stopped planting food crops. This led to a sharp decrease in food supplies." In addition, the passage discusses how the cotton gin made the Southern economy rely heavily on slave labor. Answer choice A is incorrect because it is beyond the scope of the passage. The passage is about the cotton gin, not about slavery. Although the passage mentions that the *charka* was an invention similar to the cotton gin, the primary focus of the passage is not on comparing the two machines; therefore, answer choice B is incorrect. Answer choices C and E are incorrect, because the passage focuses neither on contradicting historians nor on criticizing farmers.

2. The best answer is B. The passage states, "The cotton gin also played a devastating role in causing the continuance of slavery in America. Prior to the invention of the cotton gin, slavery had become unpopular in America." Answer choice D may have appeared to be correct because the passage states that food crop production decreased. However, this does not suggest that the production of other textile crops ceased. Likewise, the other answer choices are not supported by the passage.

3. The best answer is C. The passage states, "Although the cotton gin is considered to be one of the most important inventions in American history, the cotton gin also played a devastating role in causing the continuance of slavery in America." The rest of the paragraph discusses why the cotton gin had this effect. Answer choice E may have appeared to be correct. However, there is no evidence presented in the passage to support the assertion made in answer choice E; it is beyond the scope of the passage. Likewise, the other answer choices are not supported by the passage.

4. The best answer is A. If the number of men who began to drink alcohol is greater than the number of men who quit drinking alcohol, you would expect an increase in the number of adults who drink alcohol. Answer choices B, C, D, and E would all explain why the number of adults who drink alcohol has decreased while the sale of alcohol has increased.

5. The best answer is A. Answer choice A potentially contradicts the conclusion by adding a premise that ranks the grains in an order that suggests the conclusion drawn in the passage is false. All of the other answer choices, when added to the premises in the passage, help the logical progression toward the conclusion.

6. The best answer is D. The phrase "a traumatic incident that occurred when they were adolescents" uses the relative clause "that occurred" to modify "a traumatic incident" and uses "they were" to refer to adult men and women. Answer choice A is incorrect because it erroneously introduces the phrase "when an adolescent" with "occurring." This makes "traumatic incident" the grammatical referent of "when an adolescent." In addition, the singular "adolescent" does not correctly agree with the plural "adult men and women" mentioned in the passage. Answer choice B is incorrect for similar reasons. Answer choice C is incorrect because it introduces the term "adolescent" with the indefinite article "a" instead of the indefinite article "an." Answer choice E is wordy and awkward and incorrectly includes the helping verb "has."

7. **The best answer is C**. Answer choice C correctly describes the rough equivalence between the area of Maine and the area overseen by the ranch-management companies. Answer choice B may have appeared to be correct. However, answer choice B uses "have," which does not agree with the singular subject "number." Likewise, answer choice A is incorrect. Answer choices D and E are not the best choices because they include the word "up," which is unnecessary.

8. **The best answer is A**. Answer choice A most clearly demonstrates the parallel infinitives. Answer choice A also demonstrates the cause-and-effect relationship between the arrival of warm weather and the decomposition of the wheat. Answer choices B and C are incorrect because the pronouns "they" and "them" are ambiguous. Answer choice D is awkward and incorrectly uses the conjunction "if" instead of the preposition "for." Answer choice E may have appeared to be correct because it begins with an infinitive. However, the singular pronoun "it" does not agree with the plural noun "crops."

9. **The best answer is B**. Answer choice B uses "older than" to make it clear that the age of the South African bones is greater than the age of their supposed Arab ancestors. The adverbial phrase "as old" incorrectly suggests that the ages are the same, so answer choice A should be eliminated. Likewise, answer choices C and E are incorrect, because the phrase "as older" is not appropriate. Answer choice D may have appeared to be correct. However, the word "there" indicates a location; the correct word is the possessive pronoun "their," as used in answer choice B.

10. **The best answer is B**. The passage discusses several medical conditions that either cause or contribute to sleeplessness or non-restorative sleep. Answer choices A, C, and D are too specific and beyond the scope of the passage. Answer choice E may have appeared to be correct because the passage does state that insomnia is most common in women and the elderly. However, the passage does not analyze any research that suggests this.

11. **The best answer is A**. The author tries to provide evidence that disproves the myth that insomnia is caused only by stress or psychological disorders. The passage provides information on three conditions that cause insomnia and do not relate to stress. Answer choice B may have appeared to be correct. However, the author does not state that stress or similar psychological disorders never cause insomnia. Likewise, the other answer choices are beyond the scope of the passage and are, therefore, not supported by details in the passage.

12. **The best answer is C**. The passage states, "Normally, the sleeper is unaware of this limb movement." In addition, the passage states, "Pauses in breathing might last only a few seconds and are usually not remembered." These statements imply that sleep interruptions are not remembered and the person suffering from these conditions may not know what occurs during the night. Answer choice E may have appeared to be correct. However, the passage only states that acid reflux may cause pain during sleep. The passage actually suggests that people suffering from sleep apnea or involuntary limb movement usually do not even remember being affected by their condition. Likewise, the other answer choices are not supported by the passage.

13. **The best answer is C**. Answer choice C correctly completes the sentence by using a parallel phrase. All of the other answer choices are awkward and contain faulty parallelism.

14. **The best answer is D**. If a considerable percentage of the students who expressed interest in Ace Driving School end up attending their first choice driving school, Ace Driving School may not have a larger number of beginning drivers and would not need the additional instructors. None of the other answer choices are relevant or determine the number of beginning drivers who will attend Ace Driving School.

15. **The best answer is D**. The medical expert concludes that normal levels of white blood cells can protect against mental ailments and infections. If, contrary to D, mental illness does cause people's level of white blood cells to decrease, the medical expert's conclusion is invalid. Answer choice B may have appeared to be correct. However, the medical expert's conclusion does not depend on mental illness having the same effects on the human body as do infections. Likewise, the remaining answer choices do not include necessary assumptions.

16. **The best answer is C**. Answer choice C is correct because it confirms that what drivers fear will happen is likely to happen. The other answer choices are incorrect because the dealers' objection can be strengthened only by an unfavorable outcome of using the new safety features. These answer choices are either irrelevant or support the arguments of the car manufacturers.

17. **The best answer is D**. Answer choice D correctly parallels the "amount of energy used by" with "that used by." "That" is substituted for "amount." Answer choice A is wordy and awkward and should be eliminated. Answer choice B may have appeared to be correct. However, answer choice B incorrectly uses the plural verb "are" with

the singular noun "equipment." In addition, the word "when" is inappropriate in this sentence. Answer choices C and E are incorrect because they include the ambiguous pronoun "it."

18. **The best answer is E.** Answer choice E is correct because the word "that" should be omitted; "one" is adequate to introduce the modifier. The remaining answer choices include the unnecessary pronoun "that."

19. **The best answer is E.** The passage is mostly concerned with discussing different aspects of Faulkner's life that influenced his writing. In addition, the passage discusses Faulkner's writing style and the subject matter of his work. Answer choices A, B, and C are either too narrow or too broad and are beyond the scope of the passage. Answer choice D may have appeared to be correct because the passage does state that Faulkner believed that racism and abstract ideals were detrimental to human freedom and happiness. However, the author does not use this passage as a way to criticize racism or abstract ideals.

20. **The best answer is B.** The passage states, "Although Faulkner was raised in the rural Deep South, he became acquainted with the world by joining the Royal Air Force. During his time as a fighter pilot, he became deeply influenced by what he saw during his travels to major American and European cities. Faulkner was also fascinated by the modernist influences that were changing art, literature, theater, and music." Answer choice C may have appeared to be correct. However, the passage actually states, "Although Faulkner's novels do not shy away from describing the brutality and anguish that life can bring, his works are filled with profound compassion and humor." This does not imply that Faulkner disguised brutality with compassion or humor. Likewise, the other answer choices are not supported by details in the passage.

21. **The best answer is D.** The first paragraph gives general background information on Faulkner that the passage later discusses in greater detail. For instance, the passage states, "Faulkner is known for producing literary works filled with emotional turmoil and unflinching honesty." Later in the passage, the author reveals that Faulkner wrote about controversial issues and life's brutality. Answer choice B may have appeared to be correct because the author does mention that some people regard Faulkner's work as the most representative of Southern Gothic literature. However, the author does not try to argue against or defend this point. Likewise, the other answer choices are not supported by the passage.

22. **The best answer is A**. The passage reveals that Faulkner received inspiration and was influenced by many different events, things, locations, and interests. Answer choice D may have appeared to be correct. However, there is no evidence that Faulkner intentionally chose to combine his inspirations or influences to create his work. Likewise, the other answer choices are not supported by the passage.

23. **The best answer is C**. Answer choice C is correct because it contradicts the claim that people are not getting a lot of use out of their treadmills simply because they are not running or walking on them. It indicates that consumers use their exercise equipment for things *other than* running or walking. Answer choice A is incorrect because it supports the claim that most consumers get little use out of the fitness equipment they purchase; this offers a potential reason for consumers not to use the treadmill. Answer choice B is incorrect because it indicates that researchers believe that consumers use the treadmill *more often* than they actually do. The information contained in answer choices D and E does not indicate how much or how little consumers use the exercise equipment that they purchase.

24. **The best answer is A**. For the wildlife experts' argument to be correct, the frogs would have to still be reproducing in areas of the river that maintain the 60° temperature. Answer choice A confirms that the frogs are able to continue reproducing in areas of the river that have an average temperature of 60°. Answer choice D may have appeared to be correct. However, this explanation does not support the wildlife experts' argument that water temperatures are responsible for the decline in native frog populations. Likewise, the remaining answer choices do not contain information that would strengthen or support the argument.

25. **The best answer is A**. The sentence as it is written is clear and concise. Answer choices B, C, and D omit the word "that" after "argue." "That" is needed to create parallel structure. Answer choice E is incorrect because "is" does not agree with the plural noun "arguments."

26. **The best answer is E**. Answer choice E is the correct choice because it correctly uses "using" to introduce the modifier describing how the modern scientists obtained the information for their account. The remaining answer choices are awkward or unclear.

27. **The best answer is C**. The sentence as it is written is redundant; it is not necessary to say that the "soaring rates" have "risen." Likewise, answer choice E is incorrect. Answer choice B is awkward and does

not effectively convey the intended meaning of the sentence. Answer choice D is incorrect because the insurance rates, not the "rises," are soaring.

28. **The best answer is E**. Answer choice E correctly uses parallel construction and draws a coherent comparison between normal home loans and interest-only loans. Answer choice A may have appeared to be correct. However, answer choice A is flawed because it compares an inanimate home loan with an interest-only loan buyer. Answer choice B is awkward and written in the passive voice, so it should be eliminated. Answer choice C is incorrect because the "buyers," not the "loaners" make the down payment. This choice is also very awkward. Eliminate answer choice D because it uses the passive voice.

29. **The best answer is E**. The passage is primarily concerned with discussing how and why heat lightning occurs. For instance, the passage states, "During some thunderstorms, the light from lightning bolts can be seen as far as 100 miles away depending on the height of the bolt, the clarity of the air, and the elevation of the viewer. In comparison, thunder can usually be heard from only 5–15 miles away." Answer choice A may have appeared to be correct because the passage contradicts the beliefs about heat lightning from folk weather mythology and weather professionals. However, this is not the primary purpose of this passage. Likewise, the remaining answer choices are beyond the scope of the passage.

30. **The best answer is C**. The passage states, "Heat lightning is not a special type of lightning. Instead, heat lightning is merely ordinary thunderstorm lightning that appears too far away from the observer for any thunder to be heard." Answer choice E may have appeared to be correct. However, the passage actually states, "Temperature and density can both be factors determining how far away *thunder* can be heard." Likewise, the other answer choices are not supported by the passage.

31. **The best answer is B**. The passage disproves the theories presented by folk weather mythology and weather professionals and presents scientific information about how and why heat lightning occurs. Answer choices A, C, and E are beyond the scope of the passage. Answer choice D may have appeared to be correct. However, there is no specific scientific research presented. Instead, general scientific knowledge is used to explain how and why heat lightning occurs.

32. **The best answer is A**. The first paragraph discusses the erroneous beliefs of folk weather mythology and the views of weather

professionals. Answer choice B may have appeared to be correct. However, no scientific experiments were cited to disprove the arguments presented in the first paragraph. Answer choices C and D are incorrect because there is no argument or debate presented in the first paragraph. Answer choice E is too broad and does not reflect the purpose of the first paragraph.

33. **The best answer is A**. Answer choice A is correct because it uses the simple past tense to create a concise statement. Answer choices B and C are wordy and awkward, and answer choice D uses the incorrect tense of the verb "to be." Answer choice E may have appeared to be correct. However, answer choice E contains inconsistent tenses and lacks succinctness.

34. **The best answer is B**. Answer choice B correctly compares "fruit juice" and "soda pop" by placing "fruit pop" directly after the initial clause. Answer choices A and C incorrectly compare "soda pop" to "nutrients." Answer choices D and E include the correct placement of "fruit juice," but they are awkward and contain grammatical errors.

35. **The best answer is A**. Answer choice A is correct because it correctly and concisely demonstrates the relationship between the copious capital and the builders' actions. Answer choice B may have appeared to be correct. However, the "so" that appears before "that" is both unnecessary and grammatically incorrect. Likewise, answer choices C, D, and E are awkward and contain numerous grammatical errors.

36. **The best answer is D**. Answer choice D is correct because it contains the argument present in the original passage. The original passage argues that even though something is illegal or wrong, it is justified because others would also do the same illegal action. Answer choice E may have appeared to be correct. However, answer choice E argues that the illegal or wrong activity has already taken place. The remaining answer choices do not contain the same structure as the original argument.

37. **The best answer is D**. If it is true that a piece is *not* a work of art if the creator considered pragmatic utility when making it, the conclusion drawn is supported. Answer choice A may have appeared to be correct. However, the argument does not define art as something that is shown in museums. Therefore, it is irrelevant that some woodwork is placed in museums. Likewise, the remaining answer choices contain assumptions that are either irrelevant or do not support the conclusion.

38. **The best answer is D**. Answer choice D weakens the conclusion because it maintains that predictions of slower growth *did* cause a decline in the value of the pound before the European Union was formed. Answer choice E may have appeared to be correct. However, the passage is concerned with the economic growth of England and not other countries in the European Union. Likewise, the remaining answer choices are either irrelevant or do not weaken the conclusion.

39. **The best answer is E**. If highly regarded doctors were not better at decision making than less highly regarded doctors, the fact that highly regarded doctors use instinct to make their decisions does not support the idea that instinct is better than medical protocol for decision making. Answer choice B may have appeared to be correct. However, it is not necessary to assume that highly regarded doctors can use instinct or medical protocol for making decisions in order to have a logical and convincing argument. Likewise, the remaining answer choices contain assumptions that are either irrelevant or do not support the conclusion.

40. **The best answer is D**. Answer choice D effectively demonstrates the comparison between the larger percent of men who are not currently employed outside the home with the percent of men who were not employed outside the home in the last decade. Answer choice A is incorrect because it is not appropriate to say that something "grew by" an "increase." Answer choices B and C are incorrect because they use the plural noun "numbers." Answer choice E may have appeared to be correct. However, it is superfluous to use both "raised by" and "increase."

41. **The best answer is E**. Answer choice E is the best choice because it completes "whether" with an infinitive "to sign." This serves as the noun equivalent of "most important decision." In addition, answer choice E uses "rezoning" to complete grammatically the phrase begun by "undergoing." Answer choices A, B, and C are incorrect because they include the word "being," which is unnecessary in this sentence. Answer choice D may have appeared to be correct. However, the use of "if" instead of "whether" slightly changes the intended meaning of the original sentence.

GMAT Practice Test 2

This practice GMAT consists of 78 multiple-choice questions and 2 essay tasks, divided into four sections. Please allow approximately 3 hours and 30 minutes to complete the practice test. Each of the test sections should be taken in the time indicated at the beginning of the sections, and in the order in which they appear on this test. There are several different types of questions within each section. Answer each question in order before you move on to the next question. You will not be able to skip around and come back to any questions on the actual computer-adaptive GMAT. Make sure that you read and understand all directions before you begin. To achieve the best results, time yourself strictly on each section. Use the Answer Sheet at the end of the chapter to mark your answers.

We suggest that you make this practice test as much like the real test as possible. Find a quiet location, free from distractions, and make sure that you have pencils and a timepiece. You should read the chapters for each specific section of the GMAT prior to taking this practice test.

Your score on the actual GMAT depends on many factors, including your level of preparedness and your fatigue level on test day.

SECTION 1

30 Minutes

1 Question

Analysis of an Argument

Directions: This section asks you to analyze and critique an argument that is presented. This section is NOT asking you to respond with your perspective on the topic.

Before you begin to write, you should organize your thoughts and plan out your response. Make sure to develop your points fully, but save some time to read over your response and make any necessary revisions.

Your response will be evaluated on your ability to express your ideas clearly, to support your reasoning appropriately, and to apply the standards of written English.

> "Many commuters who invested in hybrid cars feel that it would be too expensive to turn back to traditional internal-combustion engines. But studies of drivers who switched to hybrid cars last year indicate that their cost-per-mile is up. Hence, the purchase of hybrid cars, which constitutes a relatively minor investment compared to the losses that would result from continued higher costs-per-mile, cannot justify persisting on an unwise course. In addition, the choice to drive a hybrid car *is* financially unwise, given that it was motivated by environmental rather than economic concerns."

SECTION 2

30 Minutes

1 Question

Analysis of an Issue

Directions: This section asks you to analyze an issue and offer your perspective on it. There is no correct answer, so consider all of the possible viewpoints as you develop your own.

Before you begin to write, you should organize your thoughts and plan out your response. Make sure to develop your points fully, but save some time to read over and revise your response.

Your response will be evaluated on your ability to express your ideas clearly, to support your reasoning appropriately, and to apply the standards of written English.

"If parents want their children to succeed in life, parents should trust their children and give them as much freedom as possible. Any parent who tries to control a child's behavior through a strict system of rewards and punishments will soon find that such controls have a negative impact on the child's attitude and, consequently, on the child's success."

SECTION 3

75 Minutes

37 Questions

Quantitative

This section consists of two different types of questions. To answer the questions, select the best answer from the answer choices given.

The *Problem-Solving* questions require you to solve the problem and select the best answer choice.

Numbers: All of the numbers used are real numbers.

Figures: A figure given for a question provides information that can be used to solve the problem. Figures are drawn to scale, as accurately as possible, unless it is stated otherwise. A line that appears straight should be considered a straight line. All figures given in this section lie in a plane unless it is stated otherwise.

Each *Data Sufficiency* problem contains a question followed by two statements, (1) and (2). You are asked to determine whether the statements are sufficient to answer the question. You will need to use the information given in the statements along with your knowledge of general mathematics and other common facts (such as the number of minutes in an hour or the number of days in a year) to determine whether

A Statement (1) ALONE is sufficient, but statement (2) alone is not sufficient to answer the question.

B Statement (2) ALONE is sufficient, but statement (1) alone is not sufficient to answer the question.

C BOTH statements (1) and (2) TOGETHER are sufficient to answer the question asked; but NEITHER statement ALONE is sufficient.

D EACH statement ALONE is sufficient to answer the question.

E Statements (1) and (2) TOGETHER are NOT sufficient to answer the question, and additional information specific to the problem is needed.

In any Data Sufficiency problem that asks for the value of an unknown quantity, the statements are sufficient to answer the question only when you can determine exactly one value.

1. At a certain birthday party, each of the children was served either a single scoop or a double scoop of sherbet. How many children were served a double scoop of sherbet?

    (1) At the party, 70% of the children were served a double scoop of sherbet.

    (2) A total of 140 scoops of sherbet were served to all the children at the birthday party.

2. Jill wants to put up fencing around three sides of her rectangular yard and leave a side of 30 feet unfenced. If the yard has an area of 720 square feet, how many feet of fencing does she need?

    (A) 24
    (B) 48
    (C) 78
    (D) 150
    (E) 690

3. By what percent was the price of a certain book increased?

    (1) The price of the book was increased by $0.30.

    (2) The price of the book after the increase was $5.75.

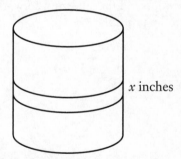

x inches

4. A circular container has a band imprinted around its circumference, as shown above. What is the surface area of this imprinted band?

    (1) $x = 1$

    (2) The height of the container is 2 inches.

5. Which of the following is greater than $\frac{3}{5}$?

    (A) $\frac{1}{5}$

    (B) $\frac{1}{3}$

    (C) $\frac{2}{6}$

    (D) $\frac{4}{9}$

    (E) $\frac{3}{4}$

6. A rope 55 feet long is cut into two pieces. If one piece is 23 feet longer than the other, what is the length, in feet, of the shorter piece?

    (A) 2

    (B) 16

    (C) 23

    (D) 32

    (E) 51

7. The amounts of time that three students worked on a group project are in the ratio of 2 to 3 to 5. If they worked a combined total of 125 hours, how many hours did the student who worked the least number of hours spend on the project?

    (A) 12.5

    (B) 25

    (C) 40

    (D) 62.5

    (E) 110

8. Is it true that $c > d$?

    (1) $3c > 3d$

    (2) $c + e > d + e$

9. If $a + 6b = 21$ and $a = -2b$, then $b =$

    (A) -4

    (B) 4

    (C) 8

    (D) 12

    (E) 20

10. A completely blended cake mix includes only flour and sugar. What is the ratio of the number of grams of flour to the number of grams of sugar in the cake mix?

(1) Exactly 8.5 grams of flour are contained in 10 grams of the cake mix.

(2) Exactly 4.5 grams of sugar are contained in 30 grams of the cake mix.

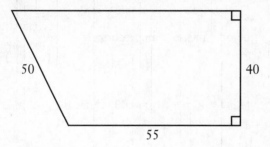

11. What is the perimeter of the figure above?

(A) 145

(B) 180

(C) 200

(D) 230

(E) 255

12. Carrie works x floors above the ground floor of a high-rise building. It takes her 42 seconds per floor to walk down the steps and 2 seconds per floor to ride the elevator. If it takes Carrie the same amount of time to walk down the steps to the ground floor as to wait for the elevator for 4 minutes and ride down, what is the value of x?

(A) 6

(B) 10

(C) 12

(D) 20

(E) 60

13. What is the value of $|a|$?

(1) $a = -|a|$

(2) $a^2 = 4$

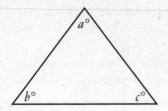

14. What is the value of $c°$ in the triangle above?

    (1) $a + b = 120°$

    (2) $b + c = 102°$

15. A certain tax rate is \$9.40 per \$1,000.00. What is this rate, expressed as a percent?

    (A) 94%

    (B) 9.4%

    (C) .94%

    (D) .094%

    (E) .0094%

16. Which of the following CANNOT yield an integer when divided by 6?

    (A) The quotient of two even integers

    (B) An integer less than 6

    (C) The sum of an odd and an even integer

    (D) A negative integer

    (E) The product of two prime integers

17. A certain café sells cappuccino in 12-ounce mugs and 20-ounce mugs, and all mugs of the same size sell for the same price per mug regardless of the number of mugs purchased. What is the price of a 20-ounce mug of cappuccino in this café?

    (1) The total price of a 12-ounce mug and a 20-ounce mug is \$5.30.

    (2) The total price of two 12-ounce mugs and one 20-ounce mug is \$7.40.

18. If a and b are consecutive positive integers, is a greater than b?

    (1) $a - 1$ and $b + 1$ are consecutive positive integers.

    (2) a is an odd integer.

19. Jenna and Kristen were among a group of people who sold coupon books to raise money for leukemia research. If Jenna and Kristen together sold a total of 200 coupon books, how many of the coupon books did Jenna sell?

    (1) Kristen sold $\frac{1}{3}$ as many coupon books as Jenna did.

    (2) Kristen sold 5% of all the coupon books sold to raise money for leukemia research.

20. $\dfrac{\frac{1}{4} + \frac{1}{3}}{\frac{1}{2}}$

    (A) $\dfrac{1}{6}$

    (B) $\dfrac{1}{3}$

    (C) $\dfrac{2}{3}$

    (D) $\dfrac{6}{7}$

    (E) $\dfrac{7}{6}$

21. Is the integer x even?

    (1) x is divisible by 2.
    (2) x is divisible by 6.

22. How many minutes does it take to travel 130 kilometers at 600 kilometers per hour?

    (A) 10
    (B) 13
    (C) 46
    (D) 60
    (E) 78

23. Twenty percent of the computer technicians have passed the certification test. Among the technicians who have not passed the test, 21 have taken a preparatory course and 15 have not taken the course. How many computer technicians are there?

    (A) 9
    (B) 20
    (C) 36
    (D) 45
    (E) 80

$$4.6\blacklozenge\oplus8$$

24. If ♦ and ⊕ each represent single digits in the decimal above, what digit does ♦ represent?

    (1) When the decimal is rounded to the nearest tenth, 4.6 is the result.

    (2) When the decimal is rounded to the nearest hundredth, 4.63 is the result.

25. If $(x - 1)^2 = 1,600$, which of the following could be the value of $x - 7$?

    (A) 9

    (B) 32

    (C) 34

    (D) 41

    (E) 48

26. What percent of 45 is 9?

    (A) 5%

    (B) 20%

    (C) 40.5%

    (D) 45.9%

    (E) 80%

27. If a soccer team scores an average (arithmetic mean) of x goals per game for y games and then scores z goals in its next game, what it is the team's average score for the $y + 1$ games?

    (A) $\dfrac{xy+z}{y+1}$

    (B) $\dfrac{x}{y+z}$

    (C) $xyz(y + 1)$

    (D) $y + 1(xy + z)$

    (E) $y + 1 \dfrac{(xy)}{z}$

28. A certain party currently has how many guests?

    (1) If 3 additional guests arrive at the party and all of the present guests remain, there will be at least 20 people at the party.

    (2) If no additional guests arrive and 3 of the present guests depart, there will be fewer than 15 people at the party.

29. If $a = -2$, what is the value of $-4a^2$?

    (A) -16

    (B) -8

    (C) 4

    (D) 8

    (E) 16

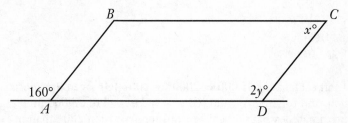

30. In the figure above, if $ABCD$ is a parallelogram, then $x + y =$

    (A) $20°$

    (B) $40°$

    (C) $60°$

    (D) $100°$

    (E) $180°$

31. $\sqrt{997}$ is between

    (A) 28 and 29

    (B) 29 and 30

    (C) 30 and 31

    (D) 31 and 32

    (E) 32 and 33

32. If n is equal to one of the numbers $\frac{1}{5}$, $\frac{3}{8}$, or $\frac{6}{7}$, what is the value of n?

    (1) $\frac{1}{5} < n < \frac{1}{2}$

    (2) $n < \frac{9}{10}$

33. The ratio of two quantities is 2 to 5. If each of the quantities is decreased by 3, what is the ratio of these new quantities?

    (A) 1 to 4

    (B) 1 to 3

    (C) 1 to 2

    (D) 3 to 4

    (E) It cannot be determined from the information given.

34. If 7 and 13 are the lengths of two sides of a triangle, which of the following could be the length of the third side?

    I. 6

    II. 17

    III. 21

    (A) I only

    (B) II only

    (C) I and II only

    (D) II and III only

    (E) I, II, and III

35. Jenny and Jeff each saved $5,000 in 2000. In 2001 Jeff saved 9% more than in 2000, and together he and Jenny saved a total of $8,000 in 2001. Approximately what percent less did Jenny save in 2001 than in 2000?

    (A) 9%

    (B) 25%

    (C) 49%

    (D) 51%

    (E) 63%

36. If m, n, and o are integers, is $m - n + o$ greater than $m + n - o$?

    (1) n is a negative integer.

    (2) o is positive integer.

37. How many miles long is the route from Long Lake to Grand Bay?

    (1) It will take 1 hour less time to travel the entire distance at an average of 45 miles per hours than at an average rate of 40 miles per hour.

    (2) It will take 9 hours to travel the first half of the total distance at an average rate of 20 miles per hour.

SECTION 4

75 Minutes

41 Questions

Verbal

This section consists of three different types of questions. To answer the questions, select the best answer from the answer choices given.

The *Sentence Correction* questions contain a sentence that is either partially or completely underlined. Following the sentence are five answer choices, each giving you five different ways to phrase the underlined portion of the sentence. Answer choice A repeats the original sentence; choose answer choice A if you do not want to change the underlined portion at all. The remaining answer choices are all different.

Your answer choices will depend on the standards of written English; especially sentence construction, grammar, and word choice. The questions test your ability to express an idea clearly, simply, and correctly, without being awkward or redundant, while obeying all grammar rules.

Each *Reading Comprehension* question is based on the content of the accompanying passage. Read the passage and choose the best answer from each of the questions that follow. The correct answers will refer to information that is stated or implied in the passage.

To answer the *Critical Reasoning* questions, read the question and any accompanying information, and then select the best answer choice from those given.

1. Regarded as one of the most important of America's 20th century novelists, John Steinbeck has written over 30 novels and novellas; his works—translated into over 30 languages—are discussed by literary critics more often <u>than any</u> 20th century American author.

   (A) than any
   (B) than any other
   (C) than are any
   (D) than those of any other
   (E) as are those of any

2. In a recent survey, 51% of the public favored <u>laws as strong or stronger than</u> the present laws protecting the environment.

   (A) laws as strong or stronger than

   (B) laws that are stronger; or at least so strong as,

   (C) at least as strong laws as is

   (D) laws as strong or stronger than is

   (E) laws at least as strong as

Questions 3–6 are based on the following passage.

Phobias are anxiety disorders that affect a significant portion of the American population. Some experts believe that nearly 25% of Americans live with irrational fears that prevent them from doing everyday activities. Phobias, like other anxiety disorders, can greatly affect a
5   person's quality of life. A *phobia* can be defined as an unrelenting, anomalous, and unfounded fear of an object or situation. Phobias are normally developed from a past negative experience or encounter.

There are three distinct classes of phobias. All phobias are classified as being a form of either agoraphobia, social phobia, or specific phobia.
10   Agoraphobics have an intense fear of being in a situation where immediate escape is not possible. Agoraphobia is the most disabling type of phobia, and treatment is complicated because there are so many associated fears.

Social phobias are fears related to people or social situations. Social
15   phobias can greatly interfere with work responsibilities and personal relationships.

Specific phobia is a general category for any phobia other than agoraphobia and social phobia. There are four categories of specific phobias: situational phobias, fear of natural environments, animal phobias, and
20   medical-related phobias. Over 350 different phobias are included in these four categories. Observers can often notice symptoms of a person experiencing intense fear. In many cases, a person facing a phobia will show signs of panic, trepidation, and terror. He or she may also exhibit physical signs including rapid heartbeat, shortness of breath, and trembling.

25   Hollywood producers have brought attention to phobias through their films. For instance, Jack Nicholson played a writer with an obsessive-compulsive disorder in *As Good as It Gets*. In the film, Nicholson portrayed a character who was afraid of germs, public places, and open spaces. Although this movie took a comedic approach in showing how
30   people with phobias deal with their excessive fears, the film accurately portrayed how everyday life can be complicated by a phobia.

In order to treat their illnesses, people suffering from extreme phobias are often forced to meet with behavioral specialists. These specialists believe that the exaggerated fear experienced is an acquired reflex to
35 nondangerous stimuli. For example, a normal fear resulting from a dangerous stimulus, such as being bitten by a dog, can turn into an irrational fear of all animals. Behavioral specialists attempt to combat irrational fears through repeated exposure to the fearful stimulus. For instance, a person afraid of dogs might be introduced first to a small, nonthreaten-
40 ing dog, and then be repeatedly exposed to larger dogs in controlled situations until the fear eventually disappears.

Joseph Wolpe, a well-known behavioral specialist, developed a method designed to help patients suffering from phobias. His method, system desensitization, is a complex process that involves three important steps.
45 First, patients are taught to relax their bodies and minds. Next, the patient and behavioral specialist establish an anxiety hierarchy of the fear-inducing stimuli. Often the patients are asked to rate their fear level based on a scale of 1 to 10. Last, counter conditioning relaxation is used to help patients respond to the stimuli in order of their severity. System
50 desensitization is most frequently used in cases of severe phobias. It is the most popular treatment option when helping people suffering from social phobias. Even though Wolpe's method is used frequently, certain aspects of the method are controversial and are not accepted by all members of the psychological community.

3. Which of the following would most logically be the topic of a paragraph immediately following the end of the passage?

    (A) A discussion about the allegedly contentious aspects of the method mentioned previously

    (B) An in-depth biographical sketch of Joseph Wolpe's life and work in psychology

    (C) An examination of brain activity that contributes to phobias and irrational fears

    (D) An impassioned argument made by the author in favor of using Joseph Wolpe's method to treat phobias

    (E) A debate about pioneering research that advocates using medication to eliminate phobias

4. It can be inferred from the passage that people with phobias are likely to

    (A) experience little fear during behavioral therapy

    (B) overcome phobias only when undergoing system desensitization

    (C) determine the precise event or encounter that caused their phobias

    (D) seek alternative methods of treatment

    (E) show signs of distress only when observers are present to witness their fears

5. The author's attitude toward Joseph Wolpe's method is best described as

   (A) apathetic

   (B) impartial

   (C) diffident

   (D) antagonistic

   (E) sycophantic

6. According to the passage, all of the following would be classified as specific phobias EXCEPT:

   (A) fear of insects

   (B) fear of the dark

   (C) fear of clowns

   (D) fear of vaccinations

   (E) fear of strangers

7. Researchers have recently discovered that computer keyboards can become contaminated with bacteria that cause skin infections and more serious ailments such as pneumonia. They found that contamination usually occurs after keyboards have been used for three to four weeks. For that reason, people should disinfect their computer keyboards at least once a month.

Which of the following, if true, would most weaken the conclusion above?

   (A) The researchers could not discover why keyboard contamination usually occurred only after three to four weeks of use.

   (B) The researchers failed to investigate contamination of keyboards by viruses, yeasts, and other pathogenic organisms.

   (C) The researchers found that among people who used keyboards contaminated with bacteria that cause skin infections and pneumonia, the incidence of these diseases was no higher than among people who used uncontaminated keyboards.

   (D) The researchers found that people who disinfected their keyboards thoroughly after each use were just as likely to have contaminated keyboards as were people who disinfected their keyboards only once every three to four weeks.

   (E) The researchers found that, after six to eight weeks of use, more bacteria existed on computer keyboards than after three to four weeks of use.

8. Which of the following best completes the next paragraph?

In a recent investigation of college applicants, 30% confessed to being at least slightly dishonest when filling out their applications. However, the study may have underestimated the percentage of college applicants who lie on their applications, because _____.

(A) some normally honest people participating in the study might have claimed to be dishonest

(B) some of the people participating in the study who claimed to be only slightly dishonest are likely very dishonest

(C) some dishonest people participating in the study may have claimed to be honest when questioned by the study's investigators

(D) some people who are not college applicants are probably slightly dishonest as well

(E) some people who claimed to be dishonest during the study may have been answering honestly

9. Scientists believe that, unlike most of the 2,500 female mosquito species, one particular female species in the Florida Keys is restricted to a nectar diet, <u>but not a blood meal, and it lays</u> eggs in the soil, rather than in standing water.

(A) but not a blood meal, and it lays

(B) instead of a blood meal, and laying

(C) not a blood meal, and is laying

(D) rather than a blood meal, and lays

(E) but not a blood meal, laying

10. Over 800 endangered species in Colorado, such as the whooping crane, have survived a close brush with <u>extinction; their numbers are now several times greater than</u> before the establishment of the Non-Game and Endangered Wildlife Program.

(A) extinction; their numbers are now several times greater than

(B) extinction; their numbers are now several times more than

(C) extinction, its numbers now several times what they were

(D) extinction, now with several more the numbers they had

(E) extinction, now with numbers several times greater than

11. The speed at which the Earth and other planets, such as Mars, Saturn, and Pluto, <u>revolves are determined from</u> eccentricity and distance.

(A) revolves are determined from

(B) revolves are determined because of

(C) revolve was determined through

(D) revolves is determined by

(E) revolve is determined as a result of

12. The cost of manufacturing automobiles in State M is 20% less than the cost of manufacturing automobiles in State O. Even after transportation costs and interstate taxes, it is still more profitable for automobile companies to ship automobiles from State M to State O than to manufacture automobiles in State O.

The statements above, if true, best support which of the following assertions?

(A) The interstate taxes on automobiles shipped from State M to State O are less than 20% of the cost of manufacturing the automobiles in State O.

(B) It takes 20% fewer man-hours to manufacture an automobile in State M than in State O.

(C) The interstate taxes on automobiles shipped from State M to State O are more than 20% of the cost of manufacturing automobiles in State O.

(D) Shipping automobiles from State M to State O will eradicate 20% of the manufacturing jobs in State O.

(E) Labor costs in State M are 20% less than those in State O.

Questions 13–15 are based on the following passage.

Federalism has evolved dramatically since its roots in the writings of Johannes Althusius (1557–1630). Essentially, proponents of federalism believe that governing authority should be divided into a central governing body and one or more subunits. Federalism differs from the
5 governments of entities that have a single level of government. In a federalist state, power is constitutionally divided between two or more territorial levels of government. The different levels of government have some absolute authority and yet can act independently in certain areas of governing. For instance, Americans have political obligations to both
10 their state and federal governments. In America, the 50 states have designated powers and control over their territories. In other federal societies, the powers and authority granted to the subunits and central body vary greatly. Normally, the center is responsible for defending its subunits and creating a national foreign policy. Both of these tasks would
15 be difficult for the individual subunits to manage alone. This does not imply that subunits have no role in deciding how the center will manage their foreign affairs. In most federalist states, representatives or the citizens themselves vote in legislative bodies that make some decisions for all of the subunits.

20 Proponents of federalism have promoted the idea that federalism protects liberty and freedom. It is certainly true that states can avert foreign threats and prevent war by joining together and becoming powerful enough to discourage enemies from attacking them. In addition, federalism can prevent conflict and aggression among the states themselves.

25   A good example of this occurred in the 19th century in the American South. The Confederate States of America joined together to form a federation to protect themselves from the United States of America. It is clear that no single Southern state would have been able to ward off the Northern armies. However, all the Southern states joined together were
30   a daunting enemy, despite the fact that the United States of America eventually prevailed. In addition, federalism allows formerly sovereign governments of small states to have influence as a subunit. For instance, a newly colonized nation may be allowed to remain partially independent in a federal state. As a subunit, even a small state can gain limited
35   autonomy by having a voice in the central government.

Federalism does more than protect freedoms and democracy. Federalism can also promote economic prosperity. Normally, federal states have freer trade amongst themselves than they would have as completely independent states. Small states can band together and create
40   larger and more prosperous economies by sharing and trading natural resources. Federalist states can also use their unity to bargain with otherwise larger and more powerful nations.

Federalism also protects minorities and individuals against injustice from their local governing bodies. The center checks the power of its
45   subunits and intervenes when necessary. Generally, the center protects all its citizens from any subunit injustice. In turn, the subunits can band together to protest any injustice done by the central governing body.

Federalism usually allows for more political participation. Citizens are generally called upon to elect and contribute to local and national poli
50   tics. Federalism allows ethnic and cultural minorities to have a voice. Even if these minorities are not powerful enough to influence central government affairs, they are likely to be able to influence their subunit governments. In addition, if territories have markedly different desires and needs, federalism allows local variation in laws and norms. In addi
55   tion, by keeping some power at the local level, the center is not overloaded and is able to run more efficiently. Local leaders and governments are also more likely to be aware of the needs and wants of their populations. Larger centralized governments are usually less aware of what occurs at regional or local levels.

13. The author's primary objective in the passage is to

    (A) defend federalism against attacks from other governing systems

    (B) explain how federalism can benefit states and people in various ways

    (C) establish a link between federalism and economic prosperity

    (D) analyze the effects of federalism on colonized nations

    (E) argue that federalism is the only governing system that protects ethnic and cultural minorities

14. Which of the following does the author suggest may be an effect of federalism?

(A) A small national government will be able to maintain its sovereignty against internal strife or civil war.

(B) Rebellious states will be able to form new nations successfully and become federalist states.

(C) Local laws and norms will be overruled by laws made by the central governing body.

(D) All federalist states will have governing bodies that have nearly identical powers and responsibilities.

(E) A central governing body will be influenced by the voices of subunit representation.

15. The author refers to the Confederate States of America (lines 24–25) primarily in order to

(A) emphasize the superior strength and military power that the Confederate States of America had over the United States of America

(B) show how colonized nations can use federalism to ensure a degree of autonomy

(C) relate details about how the Confederate States of America were able to defend themselves successfully

(D) gain sympathy for the Confederate States of America by defending federalism in general

(E) give an example of a federalist state that used federalism to its advantage

Questions 16–19 are based on the following passage.

Here, there, and everywhere. This is not just the title of a Beatles song, it is, quizzically, a guiding principle of the universe if we take the physics of Werner Heisenberg seriously. Who knew physics could be so poetic? Without employing a plethora of equations, one can say that
5 Heisenberg's "uncertainty principle" from quantum physics means, roughly, that the very attempt to locate a subatomic particle will, paradoxically, prevent one from finding precisely where that particle is. Other well-known scientific minds might disagree with Heisenberg's theory.

For example, Isaac Newton, the inventor of classical physics and cal-
10 culus gave us a reliable set of equations for predicting the motion of objects, just as he also gave us comforting aphorisms such as "A body at rest tends to stay at rest." Albert Einstein, with his theory of relativity, added a little bit of uncertainty, in the style of, "Well, if that body isn't at rest but is moving near the speed of light, it's not going to stay the same
15 weight; in fact, it will get really heavy." The gaining of mass by bodies moving at high speeds is a staple of Einsteinian physics. With

Heisenberg, however, we go beyond the healthy variety and variance that Einstein added to spice up Newton's ideas, and we get a little potential craziness, such as "A body tends to stay at rest…but where is that body if
20 you can't really find it? And how can you even be sure it's at rest if you don't know where it is?" Newton probably would have torn his hair out over it.

In actuality, Heisenberg may not be quite so bad as all that; his theory is based on observations and experiments. Additionally, science has great
25 room for uncertainty anyway, which is why so many experiments are done and why scientists are always ready to revise their hypotheses and theories to fit the facts—not the other way around. In addition, although Heisenberg had doubts about the exact locations of subatomic particles, he would probably not imply that if you looked for one in Miami, it
30 would actually end up in Tupelo, Mississippi. Atoms are very small, after all, so subatomic particles and the associated distances would be correspondingly smaller. The real danger here may be precisely that there are those who would take what is not necessarily a huge amount of uncertainty and blow it out of proportion to justify attacks on science and rea-
35 son. So, Heisenberg has his uses, but he should be taken with a grain of salt, or preferably a whole sack of salt. We can accept his idea of uncertainty without becoming completely uncertain about everything, as some super-skeptics and cynics—or idealistic solipsists who think reality is all in their minds anyway—would have us do. And you don't have to be a
40 proton to be "positive" about that because subatomic particles have a healthy but limited skepticism about exactly where they should be—and it is limited because particles don't tend to wander as far as Tupelo if their parent atom is in Miami—we too can enjoy the same limited skepticism about some of the wilder applications of Heisenberg's fascinating ideas
45 without dismissing his work entirely.

16. According to Einsteinian physics
   (A) relativity is uncertain
   (B) the mass of objects moving at high speeds increases
   (C) objects traveling near the speed of light maintain stable weights
   (D) an object never remains in one place for very long
   (E) the mass of an object is not dependent on its speed

17. According to the passage, which of the following is true about Heisenberg's "uncertainty principle"?
   (A) It should be dismissed entirely.
   (B) It is easily proven.
   (C) It is based on scientific theory.
   (D) It contradicts Einstein's theory of relativity.
   (E) It is the precursor of classical physics.

18. It can be inferred from the passage that

(A) Heisenberg's ideas, although controversial, should not be discounted

(B) few physicists agree with Heisenberg's "uncertainty principle"

(C) skeptics of Heisenberg's theory have recently disproved it

(D) Heisenberg's "uncertainty principle" reveals little about the nature of atoms

(E) Heisenberg was never able to study subatomic particles

19. In the passage, the author is primarily interested in

(A) convincing the reader to agree with Heisenberg

(B) suggesting alternatives to Heisenberg's "uncertainty principle"

(C) emphasizing the importance of rigorous scientific study

(D) exploring the reasons behind Heisenberg's decision to become a physicist

(E) presenting a theory about the study of subatomic particles

20. Insurance Company P is considering creating a new policy to cover services required by children who suffer from ailments that are common among adolescents. Premiums for the potential policy must be inexpensive enough to attract customers. Consequently, Company P is worried that the earnings from the policies would not adequately cover the claims that would be filed.

Which of the following strategies would be most likely to lessen Company P's losses on the new policies?

(A) Attract parents of infants who would be unlikely to file claims for several years.

(B) Insure only children who did not endure any serious diseases as infants.

(C) Insure only those children who are unable to obtain insurance from any other company.

(D) Insure only those children whose families can afford to pay for the medical services.

(E) Include more services in the policy than are included in other less-expensive policies.

21. A program established by a prestigious high school allows families to prepay their children's future tuition at existing rates. The program then pays the tuition yearly for the student when the child enrolls in the high school. Families ought to participate in the program in order to decrease the cost of attending this prestigious school.

Which of the following, if true, is the most compelling reason for families not to participate in this program?

(A) The parents are unsure about what classes their child will take in the prestigious high school.

(B) The yearly cost of tuition at the prestigious high school is anticipated to increase faster than the annual increase in the cost of living.

(C) The prepayment plan would not cover the cost of field trips or uniforms at the prestigious high school.

(D) Next year, the prestigious high school is considering raising its tuition drastically.

(E) The amount of money earned by putting the prepayment funds in a regular account that builds interest will be greater than the total cost of tuition at the prestigious high school.

22. By offering lower prices, outstanding customer service, and the latest merchandise, the sporting goods company <u>has not only captured customers from other sporting goods companies but also forced them</u> to offer competitive prices and a better selection of merchandise.

(A) has not only captured customers from other sporting goods companies but also forced them

(B) has not only captured customers from other sporting goods companies, but it also forced them, the companies,

(C) has not only captured customers from other sporting good companies but also forced these companies

(D) not only has captured customers from other sporting goods companies, but it also has forced them

(E) not only captured customers from other sporting goods companies, but it also has forced them

23. Even though the hiking group entered the forest with far more supplies than <u>they had on their previous hikes</u>, it had provisions for only 10 days.

(A) they had on their previous hikes

(B) their previous hikes had had

(C) they had for any previous hikes

(D) in their previous hikes

(E) for any previous hike

24. Some analysts have been critical of the research studies conducted by the university because the figures <u>far exceeds those that were previously published</u>.

(A) far exceeds those that were previously published

(B) exceeds by far those previously published

(C) far exceeds those previously published

(D) exceed by far those published previous to this

(E) far exceed those previously published

25. Company T purchases free meal vouchers from people who are awarded the vouchers by Restaurant R for eating regularly at Restaurant R. These coupons are sold to people who pay less for the vouchers than they would pay if they purchased the meal directly from Restaurant R. The sale of these vouchers results in lost profits for Restaurant R.

To discourage people from buying and selling the free meal vouchers, it would be best for Restaurant R to restrict the

(A) days that the vouchers can be used

(B) length of time after receipt that the vouchers can be used

(C) number of restaurant locations at which the vouchers can be used

(D) number of vouchers a customer can receive during the year

(E) use of the vouchers to the original recipients or their immediate family

26. To prevent some conflicts of interest, Company F could ban high-level employees from accepting positions at rival companies for two years after the employee leaves Company F. One high-level employee argued that such a ban would be unreasonable because it would prevent high-level employees from earning a living for two years after they left Company F.

The employee's conclusion logically depends on which of the following assumptions?

(A) Company policies should not restrict the behavior of former employees.

(B) Low-level employees do not often take positions at rival companies after they leave Company F.

(C) Most people at the rival companies were previously employed by Company F.

(D) High-level employees that leave Company F are capable of earning a living only if they join a rival company.

(E) High-level employees that leave Company F are currently permitted to work for rival companies for only two years.

27. <u>As well as hydration, water is a source of</u> essential vitamins and minerals.

(A) As well as hydration, water is a source of

(B) Besides hydration, also water is a source of

(C) Besides hydration, water is also a source of

(D) Water is a source not only of hydration, but also of

(E) Water is a source of not only hydration but, as well, of

28. The admissions department reported that over the last five years, the number of applications submitted for the new degree program grew almost <u>as quick as, and in some years even more quick than</u> for other degree programs.

   (A) as quick as, and in some years even more quick than
   (B) as quick as, and in some years even quicker than, those
   (C) as quickly, and in some years, even more quickly than, those
   (D) so quickly, even quicker than what they did
   (E) so quickly, and even quicker than what they had

29. The U.S. Department of Labor has proposed legislation requiring <u>that employers should retain all employee records</u> indefinitely or for at least 10 years after termination of the employee.

   (A) that employers should retain all employee records
   (B) that all employee records be retained by employers
   (C) employers to retain all employee records
   (D) employers' retention of all employee records
   (E) the retaining by employers of all employee records

30. The documentary company has moved away from the ancient trading routes and <u>now it focuses on the analysis of both corporations doing business domestically and of those</u> doing business internationally.

   (A) now it focuses on the analysis of both corporations doing business domestically and of those doing
   (B) now focuses on the analysis of corporations, both those doing business domestically and those doing
   (C) it focuses on the analysis of corporations now, both those doing business domestically and that do
   (D) focuses now on the analysis both of corporations doing business domestically and that are doing
   (E) focuses on the analysis of both corporations doing business domestically and do

31. An environmentalist group in Canada is trying to change the popular image of owls as terrifying creatures. The group argues that owls are feared and mistreated only because they are timid nocturnal animals that are rarely seen during the day.

    Which of the following, if true, would most weaken the environmentalist group's argument?

    (A) Owls are increasingly losing their natural habitats and are therefore becoming more populous in residential areas.

    (B) Owls are the primary consumers of mice and can help make their territory more appealing to humans that are afraid of rodents.

    (C) Raccoons are timid and nocturnal; yet they are not generally feared and mistreated.

    (D) The general public knows more about the behavior of other feared animal species, including snakes, rats, and crocodiles, than they do about the behavior of owls.

    (E) Owls are feared not only in Canada, but also in Australia and Central America.

32. Contemporaries of Susan B. <u>Anthony's maintained that she is</u> America's greatest intellect.

    (A) Anthony's maintained that she is

    (B) Anthony's maintain that she was

    (C) Anthony's have maintained that she was

    (D) Anthony maintained that she was

    (E) Anthony had maintained that she is

33. <u>With rich</u> natural resources, such as gold, diamonds, extensive forests, fisheries, and large oil deposits, the country of Angola has a poverty rate of 67%.

    (A) With rich

    (B) Having rich

    (C) As rich

    (D) Despite being rich in

    (E) Although rich

Questions 34–36 are based on the following passage.

   Geoffrey Chaucer (1340–1400) was one of the most successful and popular poets of the 14th century. Chaucer's most renowned work is unquestionably *The Canterbury Tales*. Chaucer began this masterpiece in the 1380s. Unfortunately, Chaucer died before he was able to complete
5 the collection of stories. Modern versions of *The Canterbury Tales* are the creations of literary scholars who have attempted to make the unfinished masterpiece as coherent as possible.

The Canterbury Tales is known for its vivid characters and fascinating vignettes. Although all of the pilgrims featured in this work are compelling characters, the Wife of Bath has stood out as the most controversial and interesting of them all. Feminists have tirelessly studied the Wife of Bath's story and prologue in order to try to understand the complex character's meaning. Superficially, the Wife of Bath appears to be the ideal representation of a modern feminist. The Wife of Bath rejects sexual constraints and traditional opinions about women. The Wife of Bath even attacks arguments from the Bible dealing with chastity and virginity.

Many feminists believe that a closer examination of the Wife of Bath shows that the character was not precisely as she seems. Despite her bravado, the Wife of Bath was greatly affected by an abusive husband. The Wife of Bath details the physical and emotional abuse that she suffered during her marriage. One graphic incident even led to the Wife of Bath partially losing her hearing after being struck by her husband. It is interesting to note that Chaucer does not attempt to downplay the horror or injustice of this incident in the story.

The story that the Wife of Bath tells is even more puzzling than her prologue. The story is set in the time of King Arthur. The protagonist of the story is a young knight who is accused of rape. A benevolent queen pardons the knight and saves him from being executed. As an alternate punishment, the queen orders the knight to discover what women desire most. The questionable hero, with the help of his fairy wife, realizes that women want autonomy more than anything.

After telling her tale, the Wife of Bath ends by asking that God send women submissive, young, and virile husbands. She also requests that cantankerous and stingy husbands catch the plague. Although these last words are amusing and seemingly lighthearted, it is important to remember the plight of women in the 14th century. Women were at the mercy of their husbands. Wives were considered inferior beings and were treated as property.

Literary scholars have tried to discover what Chaucer's own views of marriage and society were by studying his characters. It can certainly be argued that Chaucer showed some sympathy for the plight of women and attempted to subtly portray the injustices they faced through the Wife of Bath's story and prologue. Chaucer may have disguised the Wife of Bath's vulnerability by portraying her as a lusty, bawdy, and fun-loving female. It is also undeniable that Chaucer's own position as a courtier was strikingly similar to that of a 14th century wife. Chaucer was very dependent on the good will and favors of the aristocratic society in which he lived. Like the Wife of Bath, Chaucer may have viewed society as constraining and unjust.

34. The passage is primarily concerned with

  (A) defending the Wife of Bath's portrayal of the knight accused of rape

  (B) arguing that courtiers and women were treated similarly during the 14th century

  (C) advocating the use of stories to highlight injustice in society

  (D) recommending that readers pay special attention to the Wife of Bath's prologue

  (E) discussing a character's words and motives to ascertain information about an era

35. The first paragraph performs which of the following functions in the passage?

  (A) It familiarizes the reader with cultural and historical occurrences of the 14th century.

  (B) It criticizes modern revivals and arrangements of unfinished literary works.

  (C) It provides the reader with background information on an author and his work.

  (D) It summarizes the plot of the main literary work being discussed.

  (E) It provides an in-depth biographical sketch of an important literary figure.

36. According to the passage, the Wife of Bath's prologue and story suggest that

  (A) women should avoid marriage and relationships with the opposite sex in order to maintain their autonomy

  (B) rapists and other criminals in the 14th century were rarely punished for their misdeeds

  (C) husbands are easily manipulated by conniving and devious wives

  (D) the Wife of Bath may have been more influenced by societal norms than originally believed

  (E) the Wife of Bath is a role model and inspiration for all women

37. Like Jane Austen, Charles Dickens was greatly influenced by the gothic writings of authors such as Ann Radcliffe, often incorporating gloomy atmosphere and melodrama into his own works.

  (A) Like Jane Austen, Charles Dickens was greatly influenced by

  (B) Like Jane Austen, Charles Dickens' influence was greatly from

  (C) As Jane Austen, Charles Dickens was greatly influenced by

  (D) As did Jane Austen, Charles Dickens' influence was greatly from

  (E) Charles Dickens' influence, as Jane Austen's, was

38. According to a recent study by the university, <u>the number of nontraditional students enrolled in degree programs has grown</u> in every semester since 2001.

    (A) the number of nontraditional students enrolled in degree programs has grown

    (B) the number of nontraditional students who are enrolled in degree programs have grown

    (C) there has been growth in the number of nontraditional students enrolled in degree programs

    (D) a growing number of nontraditional students have been enrolling in degree programs

    (E) nontraditional students have been growing in number for enrolling in degree programs

Questions 39–40 are based on the following.

If there are fewer restrictions on the advertising of medical services, more physicians will advertise their services. The physicians who advertise their services usually charge less than physicians who do not advertise. Therefore, if the newspaper eliminates any of its existing rules, such as mandating licensing information, overall consumer medical costs will be lower than if the newspaper maintains its current restrictions.

39. If the statements above are true, which of the following would most likely also be true?

    (A) If the only restrictions on the advertising of medical services were those that apply to the advertising of legal services, most physicians would advertise their services.

    (B) If the restrictions against advertisements that do not specify licensing information are eliminated, more physicians will advertise their services.

    (C) If more physicians advertise their services, some physicians who do not advertise will also be forced to charge less for their services.

    (D) Some physicians who now advertise will not disclose their licensing information if they do not have to specify the licensing information in their advertisements.

    (E) More patients will use medical services if there are fewer restrictions on the advertising of medical services.

40. Which of the following, if true, would most seriously weaken the argument regarding overall consumer medical costs?

(A) Physicians who do not advertise generally provide the same quality of service as physicians who do advertise.

(B) Most physicians who advertise their licensing information do not lower their fees when they begin to advertise.

(C) Most physicians who now specify their licensing information in their advertisements would continue to do so even if this was not a requirement.

(D) The newspaper has eliminated other restrictions on the advertising of medical services.

(E) The newspaper will not likely remove all of the restrictions that apply solely to the advertising of medical services.

41. Adversaries of laws that require motorcyclists to wear helmets argue that, in a free country, people should have the right to take risks as long as they do not hurt others while taking those risks. As a result, these opponents argue that it should be a personal decision whether a motorcyclist wears a helmet.

Which of the following, if true, would most seriously weaken the opponents' argument?

(A) Many new motorcycles automatically come with helmets that can be stored in the trunk of the motorcycle.

(B) Insurance rates for all motorcyclists are higher because the insurance companies have to pay for the increased injuries to motorcyclists not wearing helmets.

(C) In motorcycle accidents, a greater number of riders who do not wear helmets are injured than are riders who do wear helmets.

(D) Ordinary bicycle riders are also required to wear appropriate protection.

(E) The number of motorcycle fatalities is higher in states that do not have compulsory helmet laws.

Practice Test 2 Answer Key and Explanations

Analysis of an Argument and Analysis of an Issue

Because grading the essay is subjective, we've chosen not to include any "graded" essays here. Your best bet is to have someone you trust, such as your personal tutor, read your essays and give you an honest critique. Make the grading criteria mentioned in Chapter 1 available to the person grading your essays. If you plan on grading your own essays, review the grading criteria and be as honest as possible regarding the structure, development, organization, technique, and appropriateness of your writing. Focus on your weak areas and continue to practice in order to improve your writing skills.

Quantitative

1. **The best answer is C.** Statement (1) alone is not sufficient because the total number of children at the birthday party is unknown. Therefore, the answer must be B, C, or E. Statement (2) alone is not sufficient because there is no information indicating how the 140 scoops of sherbet were divided into single-scoop and double-scoop servings. Therefore, B is incorrect. From statement (1), the ratio of the number of children who were served a single scoop of sherbet to the number of children served a double scoop of sherbet can be determined. This information can be used with the information provided in

statement (2) to determine how many children were served a double scoop of sherbet. Therefore, the correct answer is C.

2. **The best answer is C**. The area of a rectangle is $l \times w$. The question indicates that the area of the yard is 720 square feet and the length (l) of one side is 30 feet. Solve for w, as follows:

➤ $720 = 30 \times w$

➤ $w = 24$

Because a rectangle has opposite sides of equal lengths, you can determine the perimeter by adding the lengths of the 3 sides that will be fenced:

➤ $2(24) + 30 = 78$

If you divided the area (720) by the length of the unfenced side (30), you would arrive at answer choice A. If you divided the area (720) by the number of sides in a rectangle (4) and then subtracted the length of the unfenced side (30), you would arrive at answer choice D. If you subtracted the length of the unfenced side (30) from the area (720), you would arrive at answer choice E. These are not the correct calculations to perform.

3. **The best answer is C**. In statement (1), only the increase in price is provided, and both the original and final price is unknown. Therefore, the answer cannot be A or D. In statement (2), only the final price of the book is provided, so the percent increase cannot be determined. Therefore, answer B is incorrect. From statements (1) and (2) together, the amount of the increase in the price of the book is known and the percent of the increase can be discovered. Therefore, the correct answer is C.

4. **The best answer is E**. The surface area of the imprinted band is the product of the circumference of the band and the width of the band. Therefore, in order to calculate the surface area you must know both the circumference and the width. In statement (1) the width of the band is given, but the circumference is unknown. Therefore, A and D are incorrect. In statement (2), the height of the container is provided, which has no relation to the circumference or the width of the imprinted band. Therefore, statement (2) alone is insufficient with or without statement (1), and the correct answer is E.

5. The best answer is E. One way to approach this problem is to change all the fractions into approximate percentages. To do this, divide the numerator by the denominator, as follows:

➤ $\dfrac{3}{5}$ = 60%

➤ Answer choice A: $\dfrac{1}{5}$ = 20%

➤ Answer choice B: $\dfrac{1}{3}$ = approximately 33%

➤ Answer choice C: $\dfrac{2}{6}$ = approximately 33%

➤ Answer choice D: $\dfrac{4}{9}$ = approximately 44%

➤ Answer choice E: $\dfrac{3}{4}$ = 75%

This approach shows that only $\dfrac{3}{4}$ is greater than $\dfrac{3}{5}$.

You can also solve this problem by finding the Least Common Denominator (LCD) of $\dfrac{3}{5}$ and each of the answer choices. For example, $\dfrac{3}{5}$ becomes $\dfrac{12}{20}$ and $\dfrac{3}{4}$ becomes $\dfrac{15}{20}$. Fifteen parts of 20 is greater than 12 parts of 20, so again, answer choice E is correct.

6. The best answer is B. To solve this problem, set up an equation to determine the length of the shorter piece, substituting x for the unknown, shorter length:

➤ $x + (x + 23) = 55$

➤ $2x + 23 = 55$

➤ $2x = 32$

➤ $x = 16$

The problem states that one piece is 23 feet longer than the other piece, which does not necessarily mean that the shorter piece will be 23 feet long, so answer choice A is incorrect. If you subtracted 23 from 55 you would get answer choice D, which is incorrect. This calculation does not account for both lengths of rope. If you divided the original length of the rope (55) by 2, subtracted 23 and rounded up, you would get answer choice E. This is not the correct calculation to perform.

7. **The best answer is B**. To solve, you must compare the smallest portion (2) to the whole (2 + 3 + 5, or 10). Therefore, the student who worked the least number of hours worked $\frac{2}{10}$, or $\frac{1}{5}$ of the total time (125 hours). Determine the number of hours that is equivalent to $\frac{1}{5}$ of the total time, either by dividing 125 by 5 or multiplying 125 by $\frac{1}{5}$, as follows:

➤ $\frac{1}{5}(125) = 25$

If you divided 125 by 10 instead of 5, you would get answer choice A, which is incorrect. It is necessary to make a comparison between part of the ratio and the whole ratio. You could also set up a proportion, as follows:

➤ 10 is to 125, as 2 is to x

➤ $\frac{10}{125} = \frac{2}{x}$

Cross-multiply and solve for x:

➤ $10x = 250$

➤ $x = 25$

8. **The best answer is D**. In statement (1), when both sides of $3c > 3d$ are divided by 3, the result is $c > d$. Therefore, statement (1) alone is sufficient. In statement (2), when e is subtracted from both sides of $c + e > d + e$, the result is $c > d$. Statement (2) is also sufficient alone, so the correct answer is D.

9. **The best answer is C**. To solve this problem, insert $-2b$ for a in the equation and solve for b, as follows:

➤ $a + 6b = 32$

➤ $-2b + 6b = 32$

➤ $4b = 32$

➤ $b = 8$

If you added $2b$ to $6b$ instead of subtracting $2b$ from $6b$, you may have arrived at either answer choice A or B, depending on whether you retained the negative sign.

10. **The best answer is D.** In any amount of the mix, after the amounts of both ingredients are known, their ratio can be determined. Statements (1) and (2) each provide the amount of one ingredient in the total amount of mix, so the amount of each ingredient can be calculated. Therefore, both statements (1) and (2) are sufficient alone and the correct answer is D.

11. **The best answer is D.** To help you visualize the problem, separate the right triangle from the rectangle in the figure, as follows:

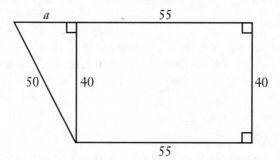

A rectangle has opposite sides of equal lengths, so you can determine the lengths of all the sides in the figure except a. Because you have created a right triangle, you can determine the length of a by using the Pythagorean theorem, as follows:

➤ $a^2 + b^2 = c^2$, where c is the length of the hypotenuse

➤ $a^2 + 40^2 = 50^2$

➤ $a^2 + 1,600 = 2,500$

➤ $a^2 = 900$

➤ $a = 30$

To find the perimeter, add the lengths of each side of the figure:

➤ $2(55) + 50 + 40 + 30 = 230$

12. **The best answer is A.** To solve, set up an equation using the information given in the problem. Set the time it takes Carrie to walk equal to the time it takes Carrie to wait and take the elevator. First, because the other terms are in seconds, convert 4 minutes into seconds:

   ➤ 4 minutes × 60 seconds per minute = 240 seconds

   Set up an equation and solve for x:

   ➤ $42x = 2x + 240$
   ➤ $40x = 240$
   ➤ $x = 6$

13. **The best answer is B.** From statement (1) you can only determine that a is either a negative number or 0, because $|a|$, the absolute value of a, is always either positive or 0. Therefore, statement (1) alone is insufficient, so eliminate answer choice A. From statement (2), you can determine that $a = 2$ or -2. In either case $|a| = 2$. Therefore, the correct answer is B.

14. **The best answer is A.** In any triangle, the sum of the three angles (in this case a, b, and c) equals 180°. Using statement (1), the value 120° can be substituted for $a + b$ in $a + b + c = 180°$ to obtain the value of c. Therefore, statement (1) alone is sufficient. When the equation in statement (2) is combined with $a + b + c = 180°$, only the value of a can be determined. Statement (2) alone is not sufficient and therefore, the correct answer is A.

15. **The best answer is C.** To solve this problem, shift the decimal points to the left. First, change $1,000.00 to $100.00 in order to calculate the tax rate from 100%. Second, because you shifted the decimal place one spot to the left above, you must also shift the decimal one spot to the left in the tax rate. Thus, $9.40 is now $0.94. Now you can see that $0.94 is equivalent to .94% of $100.00. You could also set up a proportion, as follows:

   ➤ 9.4 is to 1,000 as x is to 100

   ➤ $\dfrac{9.4}{1000} = \dfrac{x}{100}$

   Cross-multiply and solve for x:

   ➤ $1,000x = 940$

   ➤ $x = .94$

16. The best answer is C. To solve, plug in some numbers that satisfy the statements in each of the answer choices, as follows (remember to pick numbers that are easy to work with):

➤ Answer choice A: The quotient of 12 divided by 2 is 6, which yields an integer when divided by 6; eliminate answer choice A.

➤ Answer choice B: Whether you choose 5, 4, 3, 2, or 1, the number will not yield an integer when divided by 6. However, integers can also be negative numbers, so if you choose –6, this correctly answers the question. Eliminate answer choice B.

➤ Answer choice C: The sum of any odd and any even integer will never yield a number that is evenly divisible by 6. Answer choice C is correct.

➤ Answer choice D: As you saw in answer choice B, –6 divided by 6 is –1, which is an integer.

➤ Answer choice E: The product of 2 times 3 is 6, which yields an integer when divided by 6; eliminate answer choice E.

17. The best answer is C. Let x and y be the prices of the 12-ounce cappuccino and 20-ounce cappuccino, respectively. According to statement (1), $x + y = \$5.30$. Statement (1) alone is not sufficient because the values of x and y are unknown. According to statement (2), $2x + y = \$7.40$. The value of y is undetermined, so statement (2) alone is insufficient. However, by using both equations from statements (1) and (2), x and y can be determined. Therefore, the correct answer is C.

18. The best answer is A. Consecutive positive integers are integers greater than zero that lie next to each other on the number line. Statement (2) is irrelevant in determining whether a and b are consecutive positive integers. Statement (1) alone is sufficient and therefore, the correct answer is A. Pick numbers for a and b to test statement (1), as follows:

When $a = 2$ and $b = 3$, $a - 1 = 1$, and $b + 1 = 4$; a is *not* greater than b. This answers the question posed, so the information in statement (1) alone is sufficient.

19. The best answer is A. If Jenna sold j coupon books and Kristen sold k coupon books, $j + k = 200$. According to statement (1), $j = \frac{1}{3k}$. The value of k can be determined by solving both equations. From statement (2), the number of coupon books that Kristen sold cannot be determined because the total number of coupon books sold is unknown. Therefore, statement (2) alone is insufficient, but statement (1) alone is sufficient, and the correct answer is A.

20. The best answer is E. To add the terms in the numerator ($\frac{1}{4} + \frac{1}{3}$), you must first convert $\frac{1}{4}$ and $\frac{1}{3}$ into like terms using the Least Common Multiple of 4 and 3, which is 12: $\frac{1}{4} + \frac{1}{3} = \frac{3}{12} + \frac{4}{12}$

Dividing $\frac{7}{12}$ by $\frac{1}{2}$ is the same as multiplying by the reciprocal of $\frac{1}{2}$, which is $\frac{2}{1}$:

➤ $\frac{7}{12} \times \frac{2}{1} = \frac{14}{12}$, which can be reduced to $\frac{7}{6}$.

21. The best answer is D. In statement (1), x is divisible by 2 and only even numbers are divisible by 2. In statement (2) x is divisible by 6 and only even number are divisible by 6. Therefore, both statements alone are sufficient and the correct answer is D.

22. The best answer is B. To solve, you must set up a proportion and solve for x (the number of minutes it takes to travel 130 km at 600 km per hour). Because the question asks for minutes, use 60 minutes in your calculations instead of 1 hour, as follows:

➤ $\frac{600}{60} = \frac{130}{x}$

➤ $600x = 7,800$

➤ $x = 13$

23. **The best answer is D.** According to the question, 20% of the technicians have passed the preparatory course. Therefore, 100% – 20%, or 80% have not passed. You can also infer from the question that 21 + 15, or 36 technicians have not passed the course. If 36 technicians make up 80% of the total technicians, the total number of technicians (or 100%) is equal to x in the following proportion:

➤ $\dfrac{36}{x} = \dfrac{80}{100}$

Cross-multiply and solve for x:

➤ $80x = 3{,}600$

➤ $x = 45$

24. **The best answer is E.** From statement (1) it is clear that the decimal has been rounded up because the tenths digit is 6 in both 4.6♦⊕ 8 and 4.6. Therefore, you know that ♦ must be either 6, 7, 8, or 9. From statement (2) you know that ♦ can represent 3 or 4 depending on the value of ⊕. Statement (2) alone is insufficient and because there is more than one possible value for ♦. Therefore, more information is necessary, so the correct answer is E.

25. **The best answer is C.** To solve this problem, first solve for x, as follows:

➤ $(x - 1)^2 = 1{,}600$

➤ $x - 1 = \sqrt{1600}$

➤ $x - 1 = 40$

➤ $x = 41$

Now, substitute 41 for x in the second equation:

➤ $x - 7 =$

➤ $41 - 7 = 34$

If you substitute the answer choices for x in the first equation, you should see that answer choice A is too small. If you incorrectly subtracted 1 from 40 in the third step, you would get answer choice B. If you solved only the first equation, you would get answer choice D. Remember, the question asked for $x - 7$, not x.

26. **The best answer is B**. Remember that a percent is a fraction in which the denominator is 100. To determine the answer, set up a proportion, as follows:

   ➤ 9 is to 45 as x is to 100

   ➤ $\dfrac{9}{45} = \dfrac{x}{100}$

   Cross-multiply and solve for x:

   ➤ $45x = 900$

   ➤ $x = 20$

27. **The best answer is A**. To answer this question, set up an equation using information in the problem. In this question, the average, or mean, score for the games is calculated by dividing the sum of the goals scored by the number of games ($y + 1$). Determine the sum of all the goals scored:

   ➤ x goals per y games $= xy$ goals
   ➤ z goals in the next game $= z$
   ➤ The sum is $xy + z$

   Now, set up the equation (sum of goals scored ÷ number of games):

   ➤ $\dfrac{xy + z}{y + 1}$

28. **The best answer is C**. Let n be the number of guests at the party. According to statement (1), $n + 3$ is greater than or equal to 20. Therefore, you know that n is greater than or equal to 17. According to statement (2), $(n - 3) < 15$ ($n < 18$). From statements (1) and (2) together, it is clear that the number of guests at the party is 17. Therefore, the correct answer is C because both statements together are sufficient.

29. **The best answer is A**. To solve, simply insert –2 in the equation for a and solve (remember to keep track of the negative signs):

   ➤ $-4a^2$
   ➤ $-4(-2)^2$
   ➤ $-4(4) = -16$

If you did not square –2, you would incorrectly arrive at answer choice B. If you did not square –2 and also forgot the negative sign before –4a^2, you would get answer choice D. If you calculated –2^2 as –4, you would get answer choice E. Remember that a negative number squared yields a positive result.

30. **The best answer is D.** To solve this problem, you should first recognize that the 160° angle is equal to the angle with measure 2y because they are corresponding angles, which are always equal. Therefore, 2y = 160°, and y = 80°. The sum of 2y and x must equal 180°. Therefore, 160° + x = 180°, x = 20°, and x + y = 20° + 80°, or 100°.

31. **The best answer is D.** To answer this question, find a number near 997 for which you know the square root. 30^2 is 900 (or the square root of 900 is 30), which is smaller than 997, so you know that the answer must be greater than 30. Eliminate answer choices A and B. Continue to select numbers above 30, determine the square, and stop when you find which two numbers 997 falls between:

➤30^2 = 900

➤31^2 = (31)(31) = 961

➤32^2 = (32)(32) = 1,024

997 falls between 961 and 1,024, so the $\sqrt{997}$ is between 31 and 32.

32. **The best answer is A.** It is easiest to put the fractions in decimal form in order to figure out this question To do this, divide the numerator by the denominator: ($\frac{1}{5}$ = .20, $\frac{3}{8}$ = .375, $\frac{6}{7}$ =.857). The information in statement (1) can be written as .20 < n < .5. It is clear that n is $\frac{3}{8}$ because this is the only number between .20 and .50. Statement (2) is not helpful because all the values given as options are less than $\frac{9}{10}$. Therefore, the correct answer is A because statement (1) alone is sufficient but statement (2) alone is not.

33. **The best answer is E.** The easiest way to solve this problem is to choose some numbers that satisfy the ratio and try them out. For example, because the ratio is 2:5, try 6:15 or 8:20:

➤ 6:15; decrease each side by 3 to get 3:12, which can be reduced to 1:4.

➤ 8:20; decrease each side by 3 to get 5:17, which cannot be further reduced.

As you can see, because you get a different answer if you use different numbers, there is no way to determine an answer from the information given.

34. **The best answer is B**. According to the Triangle Inequality rule, the length of any side must be less than the sum of the lengths of the other two sides and greater than the difference of the lengths of the other two sides. Therefore, the length of the third side can be no longer than 20 (13 + 7), and no shorter than 6 (13 − 7). The length of the third side can be neither 6 nor 21, but it *could* be 17, so answer choice B is correct.

35. **The best answer is C**. This question takes multiple steps to solve. First, you must compute 9% more than $5,000, to find out how much Jeff saved in 2001, as follows:

➤ $5,000 × 1.09 = $5,450

Next, you need to find how much Jenny saved in 2001, so calculate the difference between the total amount and the amount that Jeff saved, as follows:

➤ $8,000 − $5,450 = $2,550

Now that you know how much Jenny saved in 2001 you must subtract that amount from her 2000 savings:

➤ $5,000 − $2,550 = $2,450

Finally, divide $2,450 by $5,000 to calculate the percentage asked for in the question:

➤ $2,450 ÷ $5,000 = .49, the decimal equivalent of 49%.

36. **The best answer is C**. The inequality $m - n + o > m + n - o$ is equivalent to $o > n$. In statement (1), knowing that n is less than zero is not sufficient because you do not know the value of o. Similarly, knowing that o is a positive number is not sufficient because you do not know the value of n. Therefore, the correct answer is C.

37. The best answer is D. The standard formula needed for this problem is rate × time = distance ($rt = d$) From statement (1) it can be determined that $d = 40t$ and $d = 45(t–1)$ when t is the time it takes to travel the entire distance at 40 miles per hour. These equations can be solved simultaneously to find the value of t and then d. Statement (1) alone is sufficient to solve the problem. However, statement (2) alone is also sufficient because the statement can be expressed as $\frac{d}{2} = 20(9)$. This can be solved for d. Because both statements alone are sufficient to answer the question, the correct answer is D.

Verbal

1. The best answer is D. As it is written, the sentence compares Steinbeck's works to any "20th century American author." This sentence intends to compare Steinbeck's works to the works of other artists; therefore, answer choice D is correct because it uses "those" to refer to "works," clearly indicating what is being compared. Answer choices B and C are incorrect for the same reason that answer choice A is incorrect. Although answer choice E uses "those" in reference to "works," the phrase "as are" is not as sufficient as "than" in indicating comparison.

2. The best answer is E. Answer choice E is the clearest and most concise selection. In addition, answer choice E uses the idiomatic phrase "as strong as." Answer choice A is incorrect because it does not include the second "as." Answer choice B is incorrectly punctuated; a semicolon should be followed by an independent clause. Answer choices C and E are incorrect because they are awkward and include the singular verb "is" to refer to the plural noun "laws."

3. The best answer is A. The last paragraph ends by stating that aspects of Wolpe's method are controversial. An explanation of why the method is controversial would be the most logical way to continue the passage. Answer choices B, C, and E are irrelevant to the topic of discussion in the final paragraph and, therefore, would not make a logical addition. Answer choice D may have appeared to be correct. However, the author remains impartial throughout the passage and also when discussing Wolpe's method. It would not fit the structure or tone of the passage to have the author passionately defend Wolpe's method.

4. **The best answer is D.** The passage indicates that people suffering from phobias often seek help from behavioral specialists whose methods can sometimes be controversial or unusual. This information best supports answer choice D. Based on information in the passage, it is unlikely that people with phobias would experience little fear during behavioral therapy, so answer choice A is incorrect. The passage does not suggest that desensitization is the only way to overcome phobias, so answer choice B is incorrect. Likewise, nothing in the passage indicates that people with phobias show signs of distress only when observers are present, so answer choice E is incorrect. Beware of unequivocal statements that include the word *only*. The passage does not suggest that people with phobias can determine precisely what caused their phobias, so answer choice B is incorrect.

5. **The best answer is B.** The author simply describes Wolpe's method and mentions that some people find aspects of it controversial. The author does not give an opinion about the method or suggest improvements to it. Answer choice A may have appeared to be correct. However, the author describes the method without expressing an opinion about it. Likewise, the other answer choices are not supported by the context of the passage, because they suggest an emotion that is not present.

6. **The best answer is E.** The passage states that specific phobias are "situational phobias, fear of natural environment, animal phobias, and medical-related phobias." A fear of strangers would actually be a social phobia. All the other answer choices would fall into the four categories that make up specific phobias.

7. **The best answer is C.** The underlying assumption in the argument is that disinfecting the keyboard reduces or eliminates any contamination that leads to disease. If the incidence of disease in people who used contaminated keyboards was no higher than the incidence of disease in people who used uncontaminated keyboards, the conclusion would be weakened. Answer choice D may have appeared to be correct, but it deals only with the issue of contamination and ignores the issue of disease. Likewise, the other answer choices are not supported by the paragraph.

8. **The best answer is C.** If applicants who are actually dishonest claimed to be honest during the study, the study's results would show that the percentage of dishonest applicants was smaller than it actually is. Answer choice A would result in a higher estimate of dishonest applicants, so it does not best complete the paragraph. Answer choice

B may have appeared to be correct. However, the study is not testing the degree of dishonesty among the applicants. The study is trying to find out the percentage of applicants who are dishonest at all. Likewise, the other answer choices are not supported by the paragraph.

9. **The best answer is D.** Answer choice D is correct because it clearly and concisely states the comparisons between one species and most other species. The phrase "but not," used in answer choices A and E, does not clearly convey that most species require a "blood meal." Likewise, the phrases "instead" and "not" in answer choices B and C do not clearly convey which species requires a blood meal.

10. **The best answer is A.** The sentence is best as written because it correctly uses the plural pronoun "their" to refer to the plural noun "species," and correctly uses the phrase "greater than." The phrase "more than" in answer choice B is not idiomatic. Answer choice C incorrectly uses the singular pronoun "its" to refer to the plural noun "species." The phrase "now with," used in answer choices D and E, makes the sentence awkward and unclear.

11. **The best answer is D.** The clause "and other planets such as Mars, Saturn, and Pluto" is a nonessential clause. Therefore, the subject of the sentence is the singular noun phrase "The speed at which the Earth," which requires the singular modifier "revolves." Eliminate answer choices C and E because they include the plural modifier, "revolve." Eliminate answer choices A and B because they include the plural verb "are," as opposed to the singular verb "is." It is not correct to say "the speed are."

12. **The best answer is A.** If the interstate taxes were more than 20% of the manufacturing costs in State O, it would not be cheaper to ship automobiles from State M to State O rather than produce automobiles in State O. Answer choice B is incorrect because you have no way to determine the cost of the man-hours mentioned. Answer choice E may have appeared to be correct. However, the paragraph does not give any indication why it is cheaper to produce automobiles in State M. Likewise, the other answer choices are not supported by the statement.

13. **The best answer is B.** The passage discusses how federalism can help small nations, colonized nations, and ethnic and cultural minorities. Answer choice A is beyond the scope of the passage; there is no real discussion of other governing systems. Answer choice C may have appeared to be correct because the author mentions that federalism

may help facilitate trade and increase prosperity in federalist states. However, establishing this link is not the primary purpose of this passage. Likewise, the other answer choices are not supported by the passage.

14. **The best answer is E.** The passages states, "In most federalist states, representatives or the citizens themselves vote in legislative bodies that make decisions for all of the subunits." This best supports answer choice E. According to the passage, federalism calls for small national governments to join together, so answer choice A is incorrect. Answer choice D may have appeared to be correct. However, the passage clearly states that, "In other federal societies, the powers and authority granted to the subunits and central body vary greatly." Likewise, the other answer choices are not supported by the passage.

15. **The best answer is E.** The passage states, "The Confederate States of America joined together to form a federation to protect themselves from the United States of America. It is clear that no single Southern state would have been able to ward off the Northern armies. However, all the Southern states joined together were a daunting enemy, despite the fact that the United States of America eventually prevailed." The individual states joined together to create a federalist nation that was better able to defend itself. Answer choice B may have appeared to be correct because the author does discuss how federalism can help colonized nations. However, the author does not give any indication that the Confederate States of America was a colonized nation. You may also have selected answer choice C, but the passage indicates that the Confederate States were not actually successful. Likewise, the other answer choices are not supported by the passage.

16. **The best answer is B.** According to the passage, Einstein hypothesized that bodies moving near the speed of light will get "really heavy." This best supports answer choice B. Answer choices C and E are incorrect because Einstein believed the weights of objects would increase as their speed increased. The other answer choices are not supported by details in the passage.

17. **The best answer is C.** The context of the passage indicates that Heisenberg's uncertainty principle, although controversial, was based on scientific theory. There is some evidence for this answer choice in statements such as "...Heisenberg's 'uncertainty principle' from quantum physics" and "his theory is based on observations and experiments." The passage does not suggest that the uncertainty principle should be dismissed entirely, or that it is easily proven, so answer choices A and B are incorrect. According to the passage, Heisenberg's

theory goes "beyond the healthy variety and variance that Einstein added...." Nothing in the passage suggests that Heisenberg's theory contradicts Einstein's theory, so answer choice D is incorrect. The passage indicates that Heisenberg's theory came after Newton's classical physics, not before, so answer choice E is incorrect.

18. **The best answer is A.** The passage states that "Heisenberg has his uses, but he should be taken with a grain of salt, or preferably a whole sack of salt. We can accept his idea of uncertainty, without becoming completely uncertain about everything." This best supports answer choice A. You may have selected answer choice B, but the passage does not give any indication as to the number of physicists who agree or disagree with Heisenberg's principle. Likewise, the other answer choices are not supported by the passage.

19. **The best answer is E.** The primary focus of the passage is to present a somewhat controversial theory about the study of subatomic particles. The passage is not a persuasive argument in favor of Heisenberg's theory, nor does it suggest alternatives to the theory, so answer choices A and B are incorrect. Likewise, the other answer choices are not supported by the passage.

20. **The best answer is A.** Infants are unlikely to need the services that adolescents need. Therefore, the parents of infants would be paying for insurance that they would not likely need, and the insurance company would most likely make a profit off of these families. Answer choice B may have appeared to be correct. However, the paragraph does not state that there is any correlation between being sick as an infant and being sick as an adolescent. Likewise, the other answer choices are not supported by the paragraph.

21. **The best answer is E.** It would not be logical for parents to choose the prepayment plan if they could earn more money than the high school tuition would cost by putting their money in an interest earning account. Answer choices A and C are irrelevant and answer choices B and D would be reasons why the families would want to use the prepayment option.

22. **The best answer is C.** Answer choice C maintains parallelism with the construction of the phrase "has not only captured...but also forced," and clearly refers to "these companies." Answer choice A uses the ambiguous pronoun "them" to refer to "sporting goods companies." In answer choice B, "but it also" is not parallel with "has not only" Likewise, answer choices D and E contain the phrase "but it also," which lacks parallel construction.

23. **The best answer is E.** As it is written, the plural pronoun "they" incorrectly refers to the singular noun "group." Because the singular noun "group" requires singular pronouns, answer choices A, B, C, and D are incorrect. Furthermore, the preposition "for" is the most logical because supplies are arranged "for" a hike.

24. **The best answer is E.** As it is written, the singular verb "exceeds" incorrectly refers to the plural noun "figures," and uses the unnecessary phrase "that were." Answer choice E correctly uses the plural verb "exceed" and states the intended meaning of the sentence in the most concise manner. Answer choices B and C incorrectly use the singular verb "exceeds," and answer choice D is awkward and unclear.

25. **The best answer is E.** Restricting the use of the vouchers to the original recipients and their immediate families would still reward the people who earned the vouchers and encourage patrons to return to Restaurant R. However, the people who earned these vouchers would not be able to sell them to companies that would market them to strangers, which is in the best interest of the restaurant. None of the other answer choices would solve Restaurant R's problem and still allow it to reward its customers as it chose.

26. **The best answer is D.** If high-level employees were able to earn a living working somewhere other than a rival company, the employee's argument would be seriously weakened. The high-level employee making the argument is assuming that high-level employees are able to earn a living only by getting a job at a rival company. If this were not true, the argument would not be valid. The employee's argument would not necessarily be invalidated by any of the other answer choices.

27. **The best answer is D.** The most efficient way to express the intended idea of this sentence is with the "not only...but also" construction. Answer choice D correctly uses this construction and clearly expresses the idea of the sentence. Answer choices A, B, and C modify "water," which suggests that "hydration," in addition to "water" is a source of "essential vitamins and minerals." Answer choice E uses the "not only...but also" construction, but does not maintain parallelism and is awkwardly constructed.

28. **The best answer is C.** Answer choice C uses the correct form of the expression "as quickly as" to compare the number of submitted applications, appropriately sets off the parenthetical expression, "and in some years even more quickly than," with commas, and maintains parallelism by substituting the pronoun "those" for "the number of

applications submitted." Answer choices A and B use the comparative phrase "more quick," which is not appropriate because the adverb "quickly" should be used instead. Answer choices D and E are awkward and do not maintain parallelism.

29. **The best answer is C**. Answer choice C is the clearest, most concise selection and is idiomatically correct. Answer choice A contains "should," which is unnecessary language. Answer choice B is incorrect because it uses the passive voice. Answer choices D and E, in addition to using passive voice, are awkward and unclear.

30. **The best answer is B**. Answer choice B is the clearest parallel selection. Answer choices A and C use the pronoun "it," which creates a run-on sentence that requires extra punctuation to be correct. The phrasing of "that are doing" and "do" in answer choices D and E is not parallel with "those doing business domestically." In addition, answer choices A and E suggest that there are only two corporations by placing the word "both" directly before the word "corporations."

31. **The best answer is C**. The environmentalists argue that the reason owls are feared and mistreated is because owls are timid and nocturnal. If raccoons are also timid and nocturnal, and yet not feared, there is clearly another element about owls that frighten people. Therefore, the group's argument would be weakened if raccoons are not generally feared and mistreated. The remaining answer choices contain information that is irrelevant to the argument.

32. **The best answer is D**. Answer choice D avoids possessive redundancy and uses the correct verb tense. The phrase "contemporaries of Susan B. Anthony's" is redundant; the apostrophe is not needed to show possession. Therefore, answer choices A, B, and C are incorrect. Because the sentence refers to an event that occurred in the past, the present tense verb "is" should be replaced with the past tense verb "was." Answer choice E is incorrect because it uses the present tense verb "is."

33. **The best answer is D**. To answer this question, you must understand the context of the sentence and choose an appropriate introductory word or phrase. The context of the sentence suggests contrast between the first portion of the sentence and the second portion of the sentence. Answer choices A, B, and C do not establish contrast. Answer choice D best establishes contrast and expresses the intended meaning of the sentence. "Although" in answer choice E also suggests contrast, but creates an unclear, awkward sentence.

34. **The best answer is E**. The passage examines the Wife of Bath, her story, and her possible background as a wife and woman in the 14th century. The author presents different opinions and interpretations of the Wife of Bath and discusses aspects of the 14th century that may have inspired the Wife of Bath to behave as she did. Answer choice B may have appeared to be correct because the author suggests that courtiers and women may have experienced similar situations. However, this is not the main purpose of the passage. Likewise, the other answer choices are either too narrow to be the main idea of the passage or are not supported by information in the passage.

35. **The best answer is C**. The first paragraph is mainly concerned with giving a brief introduction to Chaucer and explaining that *The Canterbury Tales* was his most famous work. Answer choice E may have appeared to be correct, however, the first paragraph gives only a few minor details about Chaucer's life. It is certainly not an in-depth examination of Chaucer's life. Likewise, the other answer choices are not supported by the passage.

36. **The best answer is D**. The passage states that "Superficially, the Wife of Bath appears to be the ideal representation of a modern feminist." The passage goes on to say that "Many feminists believe that a closer examination of the Wife of Bath shows that the character was not precisely as she seems. Despite her bravado, the Wife of Bath was greatly affected by an abusive husband." The passage also argues, "Chaucer may have disguised the Wife of Bath's vulnerability by portraying her as a lusty, bawdy, and fun-loving female." Answer choice B may have appeared to be correct because the knight in the Wife of Bath's story escapes execution and lives happily ever after. However, there is no implication that this was typical of 14th century justice. Likewise, the other answer choices are not supported by the passage.

37. **The best answer is A**. Answer choice A clearly and logically compares Jane Austen and Charles Dickens. The remaining answer choices make illogical comparisons. Answer choice B compares Jane Austen, a person, to Dickens' "influence"; answer choice C compares a person to an action; answer choice D compares an action to a noun. In addition to making an illogical comparison, answer choice E is awkward and unclear.

38. **The best answer is A**. This sentence is best as written. The subject of the sentence is the singular noun, "number," which requires the singular verb "has," not the plural verb "have." Answer choice B uses the plural verb "have" and the unnecessary phrase "who are." Answer

choice C is wordy and awkward, and answer choices D and E are unclear and ambiguous.

39. **The best answer is B**. The paragraph argues that a reduction in restrictions will lead to more physicians who are willing to advertise. Answer choice B supports this correlation and shows that if one restriction was removed, it is likely more physicians will advertise. Answer choice E may have appeared to be correct; however, the paragraph argues only that consumers will save money when more physicians advertise. The paragraph does not suggest more consumers will seek medical services. Likewise, the other answer choices are not supported by the paragraph.

40. **The best answer is B**. If answer choice B is true, all of these physicians might be among those who do not lower their fees when they begin to advertise. Therefore, the consumers would not receive a reduction on their costs even if the newspaper removed the restriction of having to provide licensing information. This weakens the argument. All the other answer choices are either irrelevant or do not weaken the argument.

41. **The best answer is B**. If answer choice B is true, motorcyclists who wear helmets are being harmed by those who do not by having to pay higher insurance rates. Answer choice A is incorrect because the storage of motorcycle helmets is irrelevant to the argument. Answer choice C is incorrect because it addresses injuries only to motorcycle riders and ignores the possibility that others could be hurt in more indirect ways. Answer choice D is incorrect because it includes irrelevant information regarding ordinary bicycle riders. Answer choice E is incorrect because the opponents' argument addresses personal choice, which might not be affected by the number of motorcycle fatalities.

GMAT Vocabulary List

Following are words that have appeared on actual GMAT tests. They are included here because they have been selected by experienced GMAT instructors as representative of the vocabulary level that is expected on the GMAT.

A

abdicate—to give up (usually a power, an obligation, or a responsibility)

abolitionist—a person who supports the end of slavery

abstinence—choosing to refrain from certain indulgences (i.e., sexual relations, alcohol, and so on)

accretion—a gradual increase in the amount or size of something

adaptation—the process of being modified or adjusted to become more appropriate for a use or situation

advent—the anticipated arrival of something important

advocate—*v.* to support. *n.* one who supports

affiliation—a formal relationship or association with one another

affluent—wealthy; prosperous

aggregate—combined as a whole

alleviate—give relief

alluvial—relating to sediment that is left behind by flowing water

altruism—unselfish concern for others

ambiguous —unclear or capable of having more than one meaning

ambivalent—characterized by uncertainty; unable to decide between opposites

amplitude—greatness in size, amount, or magnitude

analogue—something that is similar to something else

antagonism—opposition between two things; usually a mutual hatred or hostility

anthropological—relating to the study of the development of human beings

antitrust—relating to the laws that regulate unlawful trade and commerce, specifically in regard to monopolies, competition, and price-fixing

appropriate—to set something aside for a particular use

arbitrary—determined by chance or impulse (as opposed to reason or requirement)

artisan—a person who is greatly skilled in a craft

attainment—the act of achieving something

atypical—uncommon or irregular

aura—an intangible quality that radiates from or surrounds something

autonomy—independence

B

barred—kept something in or out; prohibited

bifurcation—separation into two branches; the place where something forks

brazen—bold or shameless; insolent

breadth—range or extent

bureaucracy—a complex administrative system

C

capital—financial assets

capricious—impulsive; whimsical

cartography—the art of mapmaking

caste—social position based on class

catalyst—something that causes something else to happen, usually without being directly involved in or changed by the process; a trigger for an event

catastrophe—a sudden, disastrous event

cessation—stopping or bringing to an end

charter—*v.* to grant or establish by charter. *n.* a document issued by a certain authority creating a public or private institution and defining its purpose and other details.

chauvinism—a belief that one group is superior to another

chronology—a sequence of events and dates in time

cite—to quote as an example or proof

clandestine—done secretively, sometimes because it is dishonest or inappropriate

cognitive—relating to conscious intellectual activity, such as thinking, reasoning, and learning

commensurate—corresponding in size, degree, or duration

commercialize—to do something for profit

complainant—the plaintiff, or person who makes a complaint

complement—something that completes or perfects

compulsory—required; enforced; mandatory

concurrent—occurring at the same time

conglomerate—*v.* to gather or merge to form a whole. *n.* a group of companies

consortium—a cooperative association

contraband—a material or thing that is illegal to possess or transport

convoluted—complex; intricate

correlate—to establish a relationship or connection between two things

credence—credibility; believability

culpable—deserving of blame; guilty

D

deduce—to reason or gather something; to reach a conclusion

deem—to think or believe that something is a certain way; to have an opinion

degradation—a progressive decline in quality

deprecate—to state disapproval

detriment—damage or harm

devise—to plan

discrepancy—a variation or difference

discrete—separately identifiable

disintegration—the breaking up or decaying of something

dislodge—to remove from a former position

disparity—the state of being different or unequal

diverge—to move apart or extend in different directions; to differ in opinion

diversify—to vary or spread

divulge—to announce or reveal something, sometimes a secret

dogma—a set of beliefs that are considered to be true although no proof exists

dynamics—forces that work together in a system or process

dysfunction—the impairment of a function or system

E

ecosystem—a system created by the interaction of a community and the environment

egalitarian—*adj.* favorable or equal standards for all. *n.* one who believes in equality of all people

elliptical—having a rounded oval shape, like an egg

emancipation—the act of freeing or liberating

eminent—prominent

empirical—based on, or can be proven by, observation and experience

emulate—to follow an admirable example; to imitate

encompass—to surround or enclose

endemic—common to a certain group or region

engender—to give rise to; to originate

enticed—drawn or lured in

entrepreneur—a risk taker in business (one who creates new companies or products)

enumerate—to state things in a list

eradicate—to destroy completely

essence—the important, central element of something

esteem—*v.* to appreciate or value something. *n.* admiration

ethnocentric—the belief that one's own ethnicity is superior to all others

ethnologist—a branch of anthropology that specializes in culture and race

exacerbate—to intensify bitterness or violence; to make worse

excavate—to dig

exemplify—to show or serve as an example

exhaustive—very thorough and comprehensive

exodus—an escape or departure of a large group of people

expulsion—the act of forcing or squeezing something out

extraneous—unnecessary; irrelevant

F

familial—relating to the family

feasible—practical; capable of being done

fickle—unpredictable and inconsistent

fiscal—relating to finances

fluctuation—recurring variation or characteristically unsteady

formidable—capable of arousing fear or awe

foster—to encourage or look after growth

G

genre—a type, class, or category

gimmick—an innovative device or idea, often designed to promote a product

H

herbivore—an animal that eats only plants

heterogeneous—comprised of dissimilar elements; not homogeneous

hierarchical—classified according to various criteria into successive levels

hoary—whitish or grayish in color because of age

homeostasis—a state of equilibrium in the body of an organism

homogeneous—uniform; the same throughout; unvarying

hone—to make better; to bring attention to; to sharpen

humane—compassionate or merciful

hypothesis—a tentative explanation that can be tested by further investigation and experimentation

I

idealize—to regard as ideal or perfect

illicit—not sanctioned by law; contrary to standard conventions

implement—*v.* to put into effect or carry out. *n.* a tool for doing work; an instrument or agent

implication—something that is inferred; the act of involving as a consequence

incentive—*n.* something that induces or brings about a certain action. *adj.* serving to induce

incriminating—suggestive of guilt or involvement in a crime or wrongdoing

incur—to acquire; to become subject to

indigenous—native; innate

inducement—something that helps to motivate or create action

inequity—injustice or unfairness

inertia—resistance to action or change; a disposition to remain inactive

inevitable—impossible to avoid; predictable

inextricable—intricate; difficult or impossible to solve

infer—to conclude from evidence

influx—a flowing in; a mass arrival

inherent—naturally occurring, permanent element or attribute

inhibit—to hold back; to prohibit

intangible—not able to be perceived by the senses; incapable of being defined

integral—essential or necessary

integrate—to make whole; to join together or unify

intermediary—something existing or occurring between; an agent or mediator between people or things

intervening—coming between two things; occurring between two points of time

intricate—highly involved or elaborate

irreconcilable—impossible to settle or resolve

isotope—one of two or more atoms with the same atomic number but with different numbers of neutrons

J

judicious—sensible; having good judgment

juxtapose—to place things next to each other in order to compare or contrast

K

keen—quick-witted; sharp

L

laden—weighed down; burdened or oppressed

landward—to or toward land

linguistic—relating to language

liquidate—to pay off or settle; to put an end to

locomotion—the act of moving or ability to move from place to place

M

mandatory—required by authority or rule

marginal—relating to or located at a margin or edge; of questionable quality; barely adequate

maxim—a saying or principle that is widely accepted

methodology—a set of specific practices or procedures

monopoly—exclusive control by one group; a market where there are many buyers but only one seller

moorings—elements providing stability or security (often tie-off points for a ship or balloon)

N

niche—a situation or position particularly well-suited to the person or organism holding it; a special area of demand for a product or service

nonpartisan—free from political party affiliation

novelty—*adj*. the quality of being new. *n*. a small, inexpensive mass-produced item, usually a toy

nucleus—the central part around which other parts are organized; the core

O

obsolete—no longer in use; outmoded or old-fashioned

optimum—most favorable or best

outmoded—unfashionable; no longer practical or efficient

P

pallid—abnormally pale; lacking in radiance

paltry—lacking in importance; not worth considering

pantheon—a group of highly regarded people; the group of Greek/Roman gods

par— *adj.* equal to the standard; typical. *n.* a standard; the level considered to be average

paradigm—a generally accepted perspective or way of thinking

paradox—a self-contradiction; something that appears to be self-contradictory, but is nonetheless true

particulate—*adj.* relating to distinct particles. *n.* a small discrete mass of particles

paternalism—questioning a group's ability to look out for its own best interests; often has a negative connotation

patriarchal—relating to or ruled by a patriarch, or male

per se—inherently; clearly; by operation of statute; as such

perennial—lasting throughout the year or for an indefinite period of time; continual

perpetuate—to prolong the existence or idea of; to make everlasting

perturbed—greatly disturbed; anxious

perversion—a deviant or abnormal act

phenomenon—anything very unusual

photosynthesis—the synthesis of chemical compounds by plants with the aid of light

plausible—reasonable; likely

posterity—future generations

pragmatic—practical

precedent—an example or event that is used to justify similar occurrences at a later time

predecessor—one who comes before or precedes

predicated—stated, affirmed, or predicted

predominate—to have control over; to prevail

preponderance—superiority in numbers or influence

prestige—level of respect, honor, or esteem

prevalent—widely or commonly occurring or accepted

primordial—happening first or very early

private sector—the part of the economy that is not controlled by government

privatization—to convert from government or public control to private control

propagate—to cause to multiply or spread

propitious—favorable or gracious

protocol—code, conduct, or etiquette

provenance—place of origin

proviso—a conditional stipulation or agreement

psychoactive—affecting the mind

public sector—the part of the economy concerned with providing public services

purview—the extent or scope of an interest or activity

Q

quantitative—relating to measurement or number

quantum—a specified, measurable portion

quest—*v.* to seek, pursue, or search for something. *n.* a search

R

recipient—one who receives or gets something

reconcile—to reestablish a connection; to resolve or settle

refute—to prove to be false; to deny the truth of

reluctant—unwilling; resistant

reminiscent—tending to remind; suggesting something from the past

renal—relating to the kidneys

revenue—income or yield from a particular source

rigor—strictness or severity

rudimentary—relating to basic facts; elementary

S

salinity—a concentration of salt

sedimentary—containing or derived from sediment

sentinel—one who keeps guard

simultaneous—happening at the same time

spherical—having the shape of a sphere or ball

stimulus—something that causes a response

stipulate—to guarantee in an agreement or contract; to agree with

stringent—severe; tight

subsequent—following in time or order

subsidy—financial assistance given by one person or entity to another

supposition—an assumption; a hypothesis taken for granted

symbiotic—having a close, mutually beneficial relationship

T

taboo—*n.* a ban or prohibition. *adj.* forbidden from use

tabulating—condensing and listing; sorting by category or counting

tactical—relating to a plan to accomplish a particular goal; characterized by skill

tangible—*adj.* possible to touch. *n.* something that is possible to touch or perceive

temperance—moderation and self-restraint

thesis—a hypothetical proposition put forth as a premise in an argument

turbulent—violently disturbed; chaotic

U

ubiquitous—seeming to be everywhere at the same time

V

velocity—high speed; swiftness

vertebrate—having a backbone or spinal column

voluminous—large in volume or bulk

W

warranted—authorized, justified, or sanctioned

Math Reference

It is assumed that most GMAT test-takers will have a basic understanding of certain mathematical concepts and skills.

The following reference information should serve as a review of the concepts tested on the GMAT Quantitative section.

Arithmetic

These questions might involve basic arithmetic operations, operations on radical expressions, operations involving exponents, factoring, absolute value, prime numbers, percents, ratios, and number lines.

The Properties of Integers

➤ Integers include both positive and negative whole numbers.

➤ Zero is considered an integer.

➤ Consecutive integers follow one another and differ by 1.

➤ The value of a number does not change when multiplied by 1.

➤ Multiplication by 0 always results in 0.

➤ Division by 0 cannot be defined.

➤ Multiplication or division of two integers with different signs (+ or –) yields a negative result.

➤ Multiplication or division of two negative integers yields a positive result.

Order of Operations (PEMDAS)

➤ **P**:First, do the operations within the *parentheses*, if any.

➤ **E**:Next, do the *exponents*, if any.

➤ **M**:Next, do the *multiplication*, in order from left to right.

➤ **D**:Next, do the *division*, in order from left to right.

➤ **A**:Next, do the *addition*, in order from left to right.

➤ **S**:Finally, do the *subtraction*, in order from left to right.

Real Numbers

➤ All real numbers correspond to points on the number line.

➤ All real numbers except zero are either positive or negative.

➤ On a number line, numbers that correspond to points to the right of zero are positive, and numbers that correspond to points to the left of zero are negative.

➤ For any two numbers on the number line, the number to the left is less than the number to the right.

➤ If any number n lies between 0 and 5, for example, on the number line, $0 < n > 5$; if n is any number on the number line between 0 and 5, including 0 and 5, $0 \leq n \geq 5$.

➤ Ordering is the process of arranging numbers from smallest to greatest or from greatest to smallest. The symbol > is used to represent "greater than," and the symbol < is used to represent "less than." To represent "greater than and equal to," use the symbol ≥; to represent "less than and equal to," use the symbol ≤.

➤ The Commutative Property of Multiplication can be expressed as $a \times b = b \times a$, or $ab = ba$.

➤ The Distributive Property of Multiplication can be expressed as $a(b + c) = ab + ac$.

➤ The Associative Property of Multiplication can be expressed as $(a \times b) \times c = a \times (b \times c)$.

The Number Line

➤ The set of all real numbers (including integers, fractions, square roots, and so on) has a natural order, which can be represented by a number line. Every real number corresponds to a point on the line.

Absolute Value

➤ Absolute value describes the distance of a number on the number line from 0, without considering which direction from 0 the number lies. Therefore, absolute value will always be positive.

Fractions

➤ The reciprocal of any number, n, is expressed as 1 over n, or $\frac{1}{n}$. The product (multiplication) of a number and its reciprocal is always 1.

➤ To change any fraction to a decimal, divide the numerator by the denominator. For example, $\frac{3}{4} = 3 \div 4$, or .75.

➤ Multiplying and dividing both the numerator and the denominator of a fraction by the same nonzero number will result in an equivalent fraction. So, $\frac{2}{7} \times \frac{2}{2} = \frac{4}{14}$, which can be reduced to $\frac{2}{7}$.

➤ When adding and subtracting like fractions, add or subtract the numerators and write the sum or difference over the denominator. So, $\frac{1}{8} + \frac{2}{8} = \frac{3}{8}$, and $\frac{4}{7} - \frac{2}{7} = \frac{2}{7}$.

➤ When multiplying fractions, multiply the numerators to get the numerator of the product, and multiply the denominators to get the denominator of the product. For example, $\frac{3}{5} \times \frac{7}{8} = \frac{21}{40}$.

➤ To divide fractions, multiply the first fraction by the reciprocal of the second fraction. For example, $\frac{1}{3} \div \frac{1}{4} = \frac{1}{3} \times \frac{4}{1}$, which equals $\frac{4}{3}$.

➤ A mixed fraction consists of a whole number and a fraction. For example, $3\frac{5}{6}$ means $3 + \frac{5}{6}$.

Decimals

➤ Place value refers to the value of a digit in a number relative to its position. Starting from the left of the decimal point, the values of the digits are ones, tens, hundreds, and so on. Starting to the right of the decimal point, the values of the digits are tenths, hundredths, thousandths, and so on.

➤ When adding and subtracting decimals, be sure to line up the decimal points. For example, 236.78 and 78.90

$$\begin{array}{r} 236.78 \\ +\ 113.21 \\ \hline 349.99 \end{array} \qquad \begin{array}{r} 78.90 \\ -23.42 \\ \hline 55.48 \end{array}$$

➤ When multiplying decimals, it is not necessary to line up the decimal points. Simply multiply the numbers, and then count the total number of places to the right of the decimal points in the decimals being multiplied to determine placement of the decimal point in the product. For example:

$$\begin{array}{r} 173.248 \\ \times\ \ \ \ .35 \\ \hline 60.6368 \end{array}$$

➤ When dividing decimals, first move the decimal point in the divisor to the right until the divisor becomes an integer. Then move the decimal point in the dividend the same number of places. For example, $58.345 \div 3.21 = 5834.5 \div 321$. You can then perform the long division with the decimal point in the correct place in the quotient.

Ratio and Proportion

➤ A ratio expresses a mathematical comparison between two quantities. A ratio of 1 to 5, for example, is written as either $\frac{1}{5}$ or 1:5.

➤ A proportion indicates that one ratio is equal to another ratio.

➤ When working with ratios, be sure to differentiate between part-part and part-whole ratios. If two components of a recipe are being compared to each other, for example, this is a part-part ratio (2 cups of flour:1 cup of sugar). If one group of students is being compared to the entire class, for example, this is a part-whole ratio (13 girls:27 students).

Percents

➤ The term *percent* means per 100. So, $52\% = \frac{52}{100} = .52$.

➤ To calculate the percent that one number is of another number, set up a ratio:

What percent of 40 is 5?

➤ 5 is to 40 as x is to 100

➤ $\frac{5}{40} = \frac{x}{100}$

Cross multiply and solve for x:

➤ $40x = 500$

➤ $x = \frac{500}{40} = 12.5$

5 is 12.5% of 40

➤ If a price is discounted by p percent, the discounted price is $(100 - p)$ percent of the original price.

Squares and Square Roots

➤ Squaring a negative number yields a positive result.

➤ The square root of a number, n, is written as $\sqrt{n}$, or the nonnegative value a that fulfills the expression $a^2 = n$.

➤ A number is considered a perfect square when the square root of that number is a whole number.

Arithmetic and Geometric Sequences

➤ An arithmetic sequence is one in which the difference between one term and the next is the same. To find the nth term, use the formula $a_n = a_1 + (n - 1)d$, where d is the common difference.

➤ A geometric sequence is one in which the ratio between two terms is constant. For example, $\frac{1}{2}$, 1, 2, 4, 8..., is a geometric sequence where 2 is the constant ratio. To find the nth term, use the formula $a_n = a_1(r)^{n-1}$, where r is the constant ratio.

Factors and Multiples

➤ A prime number is any number that can be divided only by itself and by 1.

➤ Factors are all of the numbers that will divide evenly into one number. For example: 1, 2, 4, and 8 are all factors of 8.

➤ Common factors include all of the factors that two or more numbers share. For example: 1, 2, 4, and 8 are all factors of 8, and 1, 2, 3, and 6 are all factors of 6. Therefore, 8 and 6 have common factors of 1 and 2.

➤ The Greatest Common Factor is the largest number that will divide evenly into any 2 or more numbers. For example: 1, 2, 4, and 8 are all factors of 8, and 1, 2, 3, and 6 are all factors of 6. Therefore, the Greatest Common Factor of 8 and 6 is 2.

➤ A number is a multiple of another number if it can be expressed as the product of that number and a second number. For example: $2 \times 3 = 6$, so 6 is a multiple of both 2 and 3.

➤ Common multiples include all of the multiples that two or more numbers share. For example: $3 \times 4 = 12$; $3 \times 8 = 24$; $3 \times 12 = 36$.

$$4 \times 3 = 12; 4 \times 6 = 24; 4 \times 9 = 36.$$

12, 24, and 36 are all common multiples of both 3 and 4.

➤ The Least Common Multiple is the smallest number that any two or more numbers will divide into evenly. For example: the smallest number that 3, 4, and 5 divide into evenly is 60 ($3 \times 4 \times 5$).

➤ The arithmetic mean is equivalent to the average of a series of numbers. Calculate the average by dividing the sum of all of the numbers in the series by the total count of numbers in the series. For example: a student received scores of 80%, 85%, and 90% on 3 math tests. The average score received by the student on those tests is 80 + 85 + 90 divided by 3, or $\frac{255}{3}$, which is 85%.

➤ The median is the middle value of a series of numbers. In the series (2, 4, 6, 8, 10) the median is 6.

➤ The mode is the number that appears most frequently in a series of numbers. In the series (2, 3, 3, 4, 5, 6, 7) the mode is 3.

Algebra and Functions

These questions may involve rules of exponents, factoring, solving equations and inequalities, solving linear and quadratic equations, setting up equations to solve word problems, coordinate geometry (slope, y-intercept, x-intercept, graphs), and functions.

Factoring

➤ The standard form of a simple quadratic expression is $ax^2 + bx + c$, where a, b, and c are whole numbers. $2x^2 + 4x + 4$ is a simple quadratic equation.

➤ To add or subtract polynomials, simply combine like terms. For example:

$$(2x^2 + 4x + 4) + (3x^2 + 5x + 16) = 5x^2 + 9x + 20$$

➤ To multiply polynomials, use the distributive property, expressed as $a(b + c) = ab + ac$. Also remember the *FOIL* Method: multiply the *F*irst terms, then the *O*utside terms, then the *I*nside terms, then the *L*ast terms. For example:

$$2x(4x + 4) = 8x^2 + 8x; \text{ and } (x + 2)(x - 2) = x^2 - 2x + 2x - 4,$$
or $x^2 - 4$

➤ You may be required to find the factors or solution sets of certain simple quadratic expressions. A factor or solution set takes the form, ($x \pm$ some number). Simple quadratic expressions will usually have 2 of these factors or solution sets. For example, the solution sets of $x^2 - 4$ are $(x + 2)$ and $(x - 2)$.

➤ To find the common factor, simply look for the element that two expressions have in common. For example:

$$x^2 + 3x = x(x + 3)$$

➤ You may have to find the difference of two squares. For example:

$$a^2 - b^2 = (a+b)(a-b)$$

Exponents

➤ $a^m \times a^n = a^{(m+n)}$

➤ $(a^m)^n = a^{mn}$

➤ $(ab)^m = a^m \times b^m$

➤ $\left[\dfrac{a}{b}\right]^m = \dfrac{a^m}{b^m}$

➤ $a^0 = 1$, when $a \neq 0$

➤ $a^{-m} = 1/a^m$, when $a \neq 0$

➤ $a/b^{-m} = ab^m$, when $b \neq 0$

Inequalities

➤ Greater than is expressed with this symbol: >

➤ Greater than or equal to is expressed with this symbol: ≥

➤ Less than is expressed with this symbol: <

➤ Less than or equal to is expressed with this symbol: ≤

➤ Inequalities can usually be worked with in the same way equations are worked with.

➤ When an inequality is multiplied by a negative number, you must switch the sign. For example, follow these steps to solve for x in the inequality $-2x + 2 < 6$:

➤ $-2x + 2 < 6$

➤ $-2x < 4$

➤ $-x < 2$

➤ $x > -2$

Word Problems

➤ When solving word problems, translate the verbal statements into algebraic expressions. For example:

➤ greater than, more than, sum of means addition (+)

➤ less than, fewer than, difference means subtraction (–)

➤ of, by means multiplication (×)

➤ per means division (/, ÷)

➤ Rate = Distance × Time.

➤ To calculate simple annual interest, multiply the principal × interest rate × time.

➤ If interest is compounded, interest must be computed on the principal as well as on interest that has already been earned.

Functions

➤ A function is a set of ordered pairs where no two of the ordered pairs has the same x-value. In a function, each input (x-value) has exactly one output (y-value). For example: $f(x) = 2x + 3$. If $x = 3$, $f(x) = 9$. For every x, there is only one $f(x)$, or y.

➤ The *domain* of a function refers to the x-values, and the *range* of a function refers to the y-values.

Geometry

These questions may involve parallel and perpendicular lines, circles, triangles, rectangles and other polygons, as well as area, perimeter, volume, and angle measure in degrees.

Coordinate Geometry

➤ The (x,y) coordinate plane is defined by two axes at right angles to each other. The horizontal axis is the x-axis, and the vertical axis is the y-axis.

➤ The origin is the point $(0,0)$, where the two axes intersect, as shown in this figure:

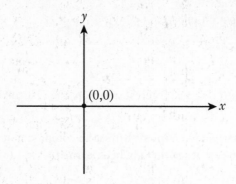

➤ The slope of a line is calculated by taking the change in y-coordinates divided by the change in x-coordinates from two given points on a line. The formula for slope is $m = (y_2 - y_1) / (x_2 - x_1)$ where (x_1, y_1) and (x_2, y_2) are the two given points. For example, the slope of a line that contains the points $(3,6)$ and $(2,5)$ is equivalent to $(6 - 5)/(3 - 2)$, or $\frac{1}{1}$, which equals 1.

➤ A positive slope will mean the graph of the line will go up and to the right. A negative slope will mean the graph of the line will go down and to the right. A horizontal line has slope 0, and a vertical line has an undefined slope.

➤ Two lines are parallel if, and only if, they have the same slope.

➤ Two lines are perpendicular if, and only if, the slope of one of the lines is the negative reciprocal of the slope of the other line. In other words, if line a has a slope of 2, and line b has a slope of $-\frac{1}{2}$, the two lines are perpendicular.

➤ The slope-intercept form of the equation of a line is $y = mx + b$, where m is the slope of the line and b is the y-intercept (that is, the point at which the graph of the line crosses the y-axis).

➤ To find the distance between two points in the (x,y) coordinate plane, use the following formula $\sqrt{([x_2-x_1]^2+[y_2-y_1]^2)}$, where (x_1, y_1) and (x_2, y_2) are the two given points.

➤ To find the midpoint of a line given two points on the line, use the following formula: $\left(\dfrac{[x_1+x_2]}{2}, \dfrac{[y_1+y_2]}{2}\right)$

➤ A translation slides an object in the coordinate plane to the left or right, or up or down. The object retains its shape and size and faces in the same direction.

➤ A reflection flips an object in the coordinate plane over either the x-axis or the y-axis. When a reflection occurs across the x-axis, the x-coordinate remains the same, but the y-coordinate is transformed into its opposite. When a reflection occurs across the y-axis, the y-coordinate remains the same, but the x-coordinate is transformed into its opposite. The object retains its shape and size.

Quadrilaterals, Lines, and Angles

➤ A line is generally understood as a straight line.

➤ A line segment is the part of line that lies between two points on the line.

➤ Two distinct lines are said to be parallel if they lie in the same plane and do not intersect.

➤ Two distinct lines are said to be perpendicular if their intersection creates right angles.

➤ In a parallelogram, the opposite sides are of equal length, and the opposite angels are equal.

➤ The area of a parallelogram is A = (base)(height).

➤ A rectangle is a polygon with four sides (two sets of congruent, or equal sides) and four right angles. All rectangles are parallelograms.

➤ The sum of the angles in a rectangle is always 360°.

➤ The perimeter of both a parallelogram and a rectangle is P = $2l$ + $2w$, where l is the length and w is the width.

➤ The area of a rectangle is A = lw.

➤ The lengths of the diagonals of a rectangle are congruent, or equal.

➤ A square is a special rectangle where all four sides are of equal length. All squares are rectangles.

➤ When two parallel lines are cut by a transversal, each parallel line has 4 angles surrounding the intersection that are matched in measure and position with a counterpart at the other parallel line. The vertical (opposite) angles are congruent, and the adjacent angles are supplementary (they total 180°).

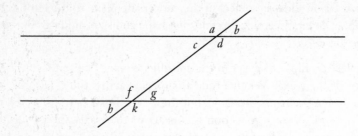

➤ $a = d = f = k$

➤ $b = c = g = h$

➤ $a + b = 180°$

➤ $c + d = 180°$

➤ $f + g = 180°$

➤ $h + k = 180°$

➤ An acute angle is any angle less than 90°.

➤ An obtuse angle is any angle that is greater than 90° and less than 180°.

➤ A right angle is an angle that measures exactly 90°.

Triangles

➤ In an equilateral triangle, all three sides have the same length.

➤ In an isosceles triangle, two sides have the same length.

➤ The sides of a 3-4-5 right triangle have the ratio 3:4:5.

➤ The sum of the interior angles in a triangle is always 180°.

➤ The perimeter of a triangle is the sum of the lengths of the sides.

➤ The area of a triangle is A = $\frac{1}{2}$ (base)(height).

➤ The Pythagorean theorem states that $c^2 = a^2 + b^2$, where c is the hypotenuse of the triangle and a and b are two sides of the triangle.

➤ The following are angle measures and side lengths for Special Right Triangles:

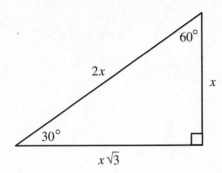 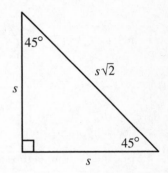

Circles

➤ The radius (r) of a circle is the distance from the center of the circle to any point on the circle.

➤ The diameter (d) of a circle is twice the radius.

➤ The area of a circle is A = πr^2.

➤ The circumference of a circle is C = $2\pi r$ or C = πd.

➤ The equation of a circle centered at the point (h,k) is $(x - h)^2 + (y - k)^2 = r^2$, where r is the radius of the circle.

➤ The complete arc of a circle has 360°.

➤ A tangent to a circle is a line that touches the circle at exactly one point.

Other Polygons

➤ A pentagon is a five-sided figure, as shown below.

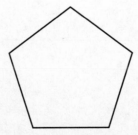

➤The sum of the interior angles of a pentagon is (5 – 2)(180°), or 540°.

➤ A hexagon is a six-sided figure, as shown below.

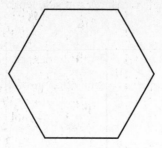

➤ The sum of the interior angles of a hexagon is (6 – 2)(180°), or 720°.

➤ An octagon is an eight-sided figure, as shown below.

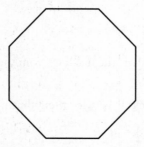

➤The sum of the interior angles of a hexagon is (8 – 2)(180°), or 1,080°.

Three-Dimensional Figures

➤ The formula for the volume of a rectangular solid is V = lwh, where l = length, w = width, and h = height.

➤ The surface area of a rectangular solid is the sum of the area of the six faces of the solid. The formula for the surface area of a rectangular solid is A = 2(wl + lh + wh) where l = length, w = width, and h = height.

Data Analysis

These questions may involve elementary probability, statistics (mean, median, mode, percentiles) and interpretation of line graphs, bar graphs, circle graphs, and tables.

➤ Carefully read the labels on the tables, charts, or graphs.

➤ Make sure that you understand the relationships between the data represented in the graphs.

➤ Average refers to the arithmetic mean. The average of n numbers is defined as the sum of n divided by n.

➤ The median is the middle value in an ordered list of n numbers. If n is odd, the median is the middle value; if n is even, the median is the average of the 2 middle values.

➤ The mode is the value that appears most frequently in an ordered list of n numbers.

➤ Standard deviation is calculated by finding the arithmetic mean of the data set, finding the difference between the mean and each of the n values of the data set, squaring each of the differences, finding the average of the squared differences, and taking the nonnegative square root of this average.

➤ Frequency distribution refers to the frequency with which a data value occurs.

Probability and Outcomes

➤ Probability refers to the likelihood that an event will occur. For example, Jeff has 3 striped and 4 solid ties in his closet; therefore, he has a total of 7 ties in his closet. He has 3 chances to grab a striped tie out of the 7 total ties because he has 3 striped ties. So, the likelihood of Jeff grabbing a striped tie is 3 out of 7, which can also be expressed as 3:7, or $\frac{3}{7}$.

➤ Two specific events are considered independent if the outcome of one event has no effect on the outcome of the other event. For example, if you toss a coin, there is a 1 in 2, or $\frac{1}{2}$ chance that it will land on either heads or tails. If you toss the coin again, the outcome will be the same.

To find the probability of two or more independent events occurring together, multiply the outcomes of the individual events. For example, the probability that both coin tosses will result in heads is $\frac{1}{2} \times \frac{1}{2}$, or $\frac{1}{4}$.

Need to Know More?

The purpose of this book is to help you prepare for the GMAT. Although this book provides you with helpful information about the test and realistic practice materials to get you ready for the real thing, the following additional resources may also be useful in your preparation:

➤ The Graduate Management Admissions Council is a nonprofit organization composed of leading business schools worldwide and serves the entire management education community. In addition to administering the GMAT, the GMAC also offers career development programs and a wealth of information for schools. Visit the Council's website at http://www.gmac.com for information about the organization, the GMAT test, and the available development programs.

➤ The GMAC also provides a wealth of up-to-date information on a website for prospective and current students. Visit http://www.mba.com for information about different careers, graduate schools, and programs; information about test centers, testing dates, registration deadlines, fees, and score reports; and information about applying to graduate schools.

➤ *The Official Guide for GMAT Review, 11th Edition*, is a great source of practice material for the GMAT. Order one as a great complement to *GMAT Exam Cram*. The Official Guide is available online at http://www.study-smart.com/gradschool.htm.

➤ Advantage Education offers many programs for students planning to go to graduate school, including programs that prepare students for the GRE and GMAT, as well as admissions counseling. To learn about individual tutoring, workshops, courses, and other programs, visit http://www.study-smart.com/.

➤ High school and college textbooks are extremely valuable resources. The content areas tested on the GMAT Quantitative Section are the same content areas that you studied in school. Hence, textbooks cover many of the relevant skills and subjects you need for success on the GMAT. If you do not have your textbooks, your school library should have copies that you can use.

➤ Don't forget to talk to professors and other students who have some experience with the GMAT. They might be able to shed some additional light on getting ready for the test. It is in your best interest to be as well prepared as possible on test day.

Index

. . . .

How can we make this index more useful? Email us at indexes@quepublishing.com

W - X - Y - Z